Market and Non-market
Hierarchies

To
Νίκος ή Αλκης

Market and Non-market Hierarchies

Theory of Institutional Failure

Christos Pitelis

BLACKWELL
Oxford UK & Cambridge USA

First published 1991

Basil Blackwell Ltd
108 Cowley Road, Oxford, OX4 1JF, UK

Basil Blackwell, Inc.
3 Cambridge Center
Cambridge, Massachusetts 02142, USA

British Library Cataloguing in Publication Data

A CIP catalogue record for this book is available from the British Library.

Library of Congress Cataloging in Publication Data

Pitelis, Christos.
    Market and non-market hierarchies: theory of institutional
failure/Christos Pitelis.
      p. cm.
    Includes bibliographical references and index.
    ISBN 0-631-15796-4
    1. Business cycles. 2. Capitalism. 3. Bankruptcy. 4. Business
enterprises. 5. State, The. I. Title.
HB3711.P58 1991
338.5′42—dc20

91-11229
CIP

Typeset in 11 on 13 pt Times
by Best-set Typesetter Ltd.
Printed in Great Britain by
Biddles Ltd, Guildford

Printed on acid-free paper

Contents

Acknowledgements

I am grateful to numerous people for comments and discussion on earlier work, on which the present monograph builds. There are too many to mention individually, and some (the referees) were anonymous anyway. Three are worthy of exception: Keith Cowling, Roger Sugden and Ioanna Pitelis, the last for academic and non-academic reasons, including a 'leave of absence' from my family duties during the writing of this book. If Sandra Mienczakowski had not typed this script, I doubt if anyone else would, or could. Dimitra Nannoussis helped me with the References list, John Taylor with the copy-editing.

1

Institutions of Capitalism and Institutional Failure

In this book I examine the reasons for the existence, evolution and failure (crisis) of capitalist institutions, in particular the firm, the market and the state. Following a long period of relative indifference in the economic analysis of capitalist institutions, there has recently been a resurgence of interest in the area. The theory of the firm has received the lion's share, following the unearthing of Coase's (1937) now influential article on the nature of the firm, in which the firm's existence is explained in terms of market failure due to excessive market transaction costs. In a number of contributions, Oliver Williamson (e.g. Williamson, 1975, 1981) has developed this insight into a full-blown theory of markets and hierarchies, or organizational failures. In this theory, market failure because of excessive transaction costs is the *raison d'être* of hierarchies, such as firms, which are thus seen as a solution to such transactional inefficiencies. Firms' evolution (e.g. vertical integration strategies and changes in firms' organiza-tional forms), is explained in a similar vein.

The existence of the capitalist state is also seen in terms of market failure by mainstream (neoclassical) economic theory. Here the market is said to fail for reasons related to the existence of 'externalities', 'public goods', oligopolistic or monopolistic market structures etc. (see Stiglitz, 1986, for a survey). More recently, however, an attempt has been made to generalize such *instances* of market failure, in terms of excessive market transac-tion costs, in a very similar vein to the explanation of the firm (see, for example, Arrow, 1970). This, with the mainstream assumption of pre-existing markets or of markets being the natural (original) means of resource allocation, allows a generalization of the mainstream analysis of capitalist institutions in terms of transaction costs. The market, the firm and the state can be seen as alternative devices for the allocation of resources, their choice (or the choice of the 'right' institutional mix) depending on their degree of transaction costs economizing. Given this, efficiency can be seen as the driving force of the emergence and evolution of capitalist institutions.

Critics of the mainstream perspective have found it hard to swallow such a sanguine view of capitalism. Concerning the firm, for example, Marglin (1974) considered it more likely that the prevalence of the factory system over its predecessor, the putting-out system, was because of capitalists' need and desire to subjugate labour in order to advance their own sectional interests, i.e. profits. The Marglinian line has been pursued by numerous people in a number of related issues, such as firms' organizational forms or the transnational corporation. Concerning the state, on the other hand, it has long been the case that authors of Marxian (but also neoliberal) persuasion regarded it as a device allowing and/or facilitating the pursuit of sectional interests, such as those of the capitalist class (the Marxist case) or the politicians and bureaucrats (the neoliberal case). Besides these alternative views on capitalist institutions, a large number of authors from various perspectives have criticized very widely the assumptions and implications of the mainstream approach. Despite this, the mainstream perspective is arguably dominant.

A reason for this dominance is that critiques and alternatives largely share with mainstream 'neo-institutionalism' a rather static, non-evolutionary and non-historical approach. This and the fact that most critiques are rather *ad hoc*, i.e. not derived from a general theoretical framework, explains in part their failure to undermine and/or replace the mainstream programme. My starting point in this monograph is that a dynamic evolutionary and historical approach is necessary and that its pursuit provides substantial new insights on the issues in hand. Such an approach is pursued in the following chapters.

Chapter 2 critically examines the mainstream approach to market failure and firms, its critics and the alternatives proposed. Observing the limitations of both the mainstream and the alternatives, it is proposed that, as far as the employment relation is concerned, market relationships themselves are hierarchical under capitalism. In this sense the choice is between market and non-market hierarchies, the title of the book. The reason for this is that, if we focus on the production process, the putting-out system in which cottage labourers were working *for* merchant-manufacturers can be seen as a hierarchical one. Accepting this removes the need to view the objectives and existence of firms separately. The two are inseparable in the sense that transition from one form of hierarchy to another, such as from putting-out to factory, can be explained in terms of the principals' objectives. In particular the objectives of a firm's controllers (principals) are the reason for the firm's existence. Efficiency may well be the means and/or the result, but it is not the sole independent objective. I suggest that the principals' objective is long-term profit through expansion, the motive being conflict with labour and rivalry with other firms. If so, new insights can be obtained on a wide range of issues concerning the evolution of firms, such as the 'managerial revolution' the 'pension funds revolution', integration and disintegration by firms, and the transnational firm.

The line of thought adopted in chapter 2 is pursued in chapter 3, where the important issues of the determinants of market structure and pricing policies, or more generally the monopoly versus competition debate, are discussed. In particular, the mainstream, Marxist, post-Keynesian and Austrian perspectives on the issue are reviewed critically. It is then suggested that to the extent that conflict with labour and rivalry with other firms motivates firms to expand in order to increase long-term profits, the growth (often achieved through efficiency improvements) gives rise to increased concentration of markets and monopolistic, first-mover advantages to incumbent firms, and the incentive to exploit these advantages. Such incentives provide a reason for international production and the transnational corporation (TNC), and drive these tendencies to a global plane, because TNCs have incentives to interpenetrate markets so as to reduce rivalry. A tendency towards global monopolization of markets and increasing concentration of power emerges. This process incorporates both efficiency and inefficiency aspects, but it is only controlled by a minority of the stakeholders.

Increasing concentration of markets has historically gone hand in hand with increasing participation of the capitalist state in market economies. Chapter 4 examines and assesses critically the major theories intended to explain the emergence, evolution and role of the capitalist state. The answers of three major theoretical perspectives, the mainstream-neoclassical, the 'new right' and the Marxist, to four major questions are examined. First, why do capitalist states exist? Second, who are their principals? Third, what are the principals' objectives and constraints? Finally, what explains the growth of the state sector in most capitalist economies? Following my account on these issues, it is suggested that existing approaches lack dynamics and history. Pursuing such an approach, I conclude that the capitalist state is an institutional device complementary to the market and the firm for the exploitation of the benefits derived from the division of labour and from team work in order to further the interests of the principals.

Historically, the capitalist state emerged from a feudal state, through an alliance between the merchants and the crown, to further their mutual interests, given their dependence on each other. Given its emergence from a feudal-repressive state, it may well be that the capitalist state has been a Pareto improvement in both an *ex ante* and *ex post* (its emergence) sense. However, it was driven by power-distributional and not efficiency considerations. Put more mildly, when efficiency was considered, it was for power-distributional motives. A multitude of factors, relating to the demands and needs of the state's principals (but also of labour and the state's functionaries) and related economic developments such as the concentration and centralization of capital, explain the growth of the public sector. They also explain the possibility of a state failure, a fiscal crisis. Other factors that have been suggested as explanations of state or government failure are also discussed in chapter 4. Moreover, I discuss the relationship between the (nation) state, the (transnational) firm and the emergence of international state apparatuses, both for developed countries and for the less developed ones. The concepts of the 'withering away of the capitalist state' and of dependent development, among others, are also critically assessed in this chapter.

The mainstream neo-institutionalist tradition has found little recognition in macroeconomic theory, where the concepts of institutions and institutional failures are largely unknown. Neoclassical general equilibrium theorists (but also neo-neoclassicals of the rational expectations school), take the market as the only available institution and treat it as failure-free. In chapter 5 I critically assess this idea, from the transaction costs perspective and that of Keynesian, monetarist and Marxist critics. It is suggested that Keynesian theory forcefully introduces the concept of macroeconomic market failure to the debate, while monetarists and the 'new right' are doing so for 'government failure'. Together they can be taken to imply the possibility of institutional failures. I provide a micro-microeconomic foundation for this possibility, in terms of transaction costs economizing, in this chapter. Following this, I examine the Marxian approaches to market economies institutional failures – the theories of economic and fiscal crisis, in particular the theory of the rising organic composition of capital-declining profit rate, the theory of underconsumption-realization crisis and the theory of rising labour strength.

In contrast to prevailing views to the opposite, I suggest in chapter 5 that the three theories are logically consistent and synthesizable. In line with mainstream views, however, they lack history and dynamics, and they treat the state as a *deus ex machina*, i.e. they do not integrate it in the analysis. Given this, I first attempt to endogenize the role of the state in the analysis, and in so doing critically assess other variants of Marxian crisis theory, such as the 'regulation school'. I then try to relate all these to the internationalization of capital and the theory of the TNC, paying particular attention to the links between crisis tendencies, internationalization, the 'new international division of labour', 'deindustrialization' and theories of 'relative decline'. Observing that all these are static and non-historical, I try to bring together all the theoretical elements of the preceding chapters in the last section of chapter 5, where a theory of capitalist institutional crisis is proposed. This synthesizes aspects of mainstream and Marxian theory, but bears close affinity to the realization crisis theory of the Marxian tradition. Some of its empirical aspects are discussed and tested in this final section.

Overall, the present volume should be seen as an attempt to bring together a large number of apparently disparate areas of economic analysis relating to capitalist institutions and institutional crisis. The firm, the market and the state are obvious choices. However, having said this it is usually the case that the markets and hierarchies programme only focuses on the choice between firms and markets. States are not discussed. Public economics does consider the state (but not the firm). Even so it gives the transaction costs perspective a low profile. Industrial organization has gradually incorporated aspects of the transaction costs framework but normally this is confined to the firms versus markets choice. No integration is attempted as to how (and whether) transaction costs analysis can be integrated with the more traditional framework. The transnational firm, notably, is normally the concern of a totally different set of theorists. Macroeconomics has ignored microeconomic developments, such as those of the transaction costs type. More impressively, neo-classicists have ignored Marxists (and others), while Marxists prefer to debate among themselves. My hope is that I have indicated in this volume that all these fields of economic enquiry *and* economic ideology can be brought together, indeed should be brought together for a comprehensive account of the issues to be given. I do not claim that I have done so successfully. For my part I am quite happy if this volume contributes towards a widening of the debates or even if its plea for a catholic approach to political economics is given some thought. When developments in this direction have been achieved, we will be ready to start thinking about the incorporation of more wide and equally interesting aspects in the analysis; sociological, psychological and, importantly, ecological spring to mind.

In conclusion this introductory chapter is intended to be a very rough guide to the concerns of, and main issues covered in, this book. It does not attempt even briefly to summarize all the points developed. For these the volume has to be read.

2

The Nature, Objectives and Evolution of Firms

1 Introduction

In the past twenty years or so economic theory has experienced a major transformation. In large part this consists of a renewal of interest by mainstream economists in the analysis of the economic institutions of capitalism, particularly the market, the firm and the state. This 'new institutional economics' (NIE) starts from the premise that the existence, form, functions and evolution of capitalist institutions need to be explained and that such explanation is a potentially very fruitful endeavour of economic analysis.[1] Neo-institutional economists have made substantial inroads in most areas of economic analysis,[2] and in fields such as politics, sociology and 'organization studies', which were traditionally regarded as lying outside the scope of economic analysis, thus renewing fears of 'economic imperialism' among other social scientists.[3]

The single most important contribution to the renewal of interest in institutions has been the classic work of Coase (1937) on the nature of the firm. Coase set out to explain the emergence of the firm in terms of market failure. After a very long gestation period, Coase's work has been taken up, particularly by Williamson (1975, 1985, 1986), who developed Coase's insight in a full-blown theory of 'transaction costs' (or of governance structures, markets and hierarchies and organizational failures). The premise of this theory is that transaction cost economizing is the most important explanatory variable underlying the emergence and evolution of hierarchies (firms) from the market. The sheer size and breadth, and the potentially revolutionary implications for mainstream economics, but also for politics, sociology and organizational studies, of Williamson's work (in itself a major credit to the man) have given rise to substantial concern and criticism from many quarters. Still, Williamson's research programme is alive, kicking and going from strength to strength, as growing interest and contributions in the area confirm.

My argument here will be that one important reason for the transaction costs success story is that existing critiques are basically *ad hoc*, i.e. they do not originate from a coherent, integrated alternative framework.[4] The task of this chapter is to make a first step in this direction. In the next section I expound the Coase–Williamson perspective and its underlying assumptions. Following this, I summarize the criticisms advanced against it and the proposed alternatives.

A criticism of the Williamson theory is that it attempts to explain the nature of capitalist institutions without explaining the nature of (or even defining) capitalism. My starting point in section 3 is that such an explanation is a necessary pre-condition for the analysis of capitalist institutions, and has dramatic implications for the markets–hierarchies perspective. In particular, I claim in this section that as far as the most important concern of transaction costs economics, the emergence of the 'employment contract' (the firm or the factory system), is concerned, by focusing on the process of capitalist production (as opposed to Williamson's focus on exchange) we can regard the market itself as a hierarchy! From this perspective the 'choice' of institutional forms is not between markets and hierarchies, but between market and non-market hierarchies. With the help of this insight we can accommodate previous criticisms of transaction costs economics in a coherent new framework.

Viewing the market as a hierarchy renders obsolete the need *first* to explain the emergence of the hierarchy (firm) and *then* to analyse its objectives. I suggest that existence and objectives are inseparable, and in particular that the objectives of those who own and/or control the firm are the very *raison d'être* of the existence of the firm. This point is raised in section 4.

Section 5 discusses the objectives of firms, within a proposed unified existence-equals-objectives framework. It is suggested that firms exist in order to realize the interests of the principals (employers), which can be seen as long-term profits through growth, motivated by conflict with labour and rivalry with other firms. This framework can help us to explain the evolution of firms, in particular the 'managerial revolution', the 'pension funds revolution', disintegration and decentralization phenomena (section 6), and the transnational corporation (TNC), to which section 7 is devoted. A summary and conclusions follow in section 8.

2   Markets and Hierarchies: Coase, Williamson & Co.

Coase's concern is to explain the existence of firms. His starting point is that resource allocation in market economies is ordinarily regarded by economic theorists as taking place through the price mechanism. Yet, he observes, economists often employ the assumption that such allocation depends on the entrepreneur–coordinator. The two assumptions however, are incompatible. In fact, in his view: 'It can . . . be assumed that the distinguishing mark of the firm is the supersession of the price mechanism' (Coase, 1937, p. 389). If this is so, one has to explain the choice of alternatives, in particular the existence of (in D. H. Robertson's vivid metaphor), 'islands of conscious power in this ocean of unconscious cooperation like lumps of butter coagulating in a pail of buttermilk' (Coase, 1937, p. 388). Coase's own answer is that 'the operation of the market costs something and by forming an organisation and allowing some "authority entrepreneur" to direct the resources, certain marketing costs are saved' (p. 392). Marketing costs are 'the costs of using the price mechanism' (p. 403).

Coase mentions a number of these 'marketing costs', such as discovering the relevant prices, negotiating and concluding separate contracts for each exchange-transaction. Contracting costs in particular, he observes, are not eliminated but are greatly reduced if the 'factor of production' owner of the firm does not have to make a series of contracts with the other factors of production with whom he or she is cooperating within the firm, but replaces them with one contract whereby the latter factor agrees to obey the directions of the former factor (the entrepreneur) within certain limits. Within these limits the entrepreneur can direct the other factors of production. In particular, 'it is the fact of direction which is the essence of the legal concept of "employer and employee"' (Coase, 1937, p. 409). To summarize, Coase's argument is that under the assumption that the market pre-exists, the existence of firms implies that the latter reduce costs associated with the price mechanism.

Coase's insight is a revolutionary one (and potentially very damaging to the neoclasscial tradition) as it provides a reason why planning may be preferable to the market. Although Coase limits himself to a comparison between the market and the firm, the 'ghost' of central planning is lurking behind his analysis. This is particularly obvious when one observes that Coase compares his views to those of Marxist economist Maurice Dobb, in the latter's analysis of 'Russian' economic development (see Coase, p. 397). However, this challenge was not to be taken up for some time. Although some insights resembling those of Coase were developed in the 1960s and early 1970s, particularly by authors in the theory of the transnational firm (especially Hymer, 1976, written in 1960; McManus, 1972), it was not until Williamson's *Markets and Hierarchies* (1975) that a serious attempt to develop Coase's insight into a full-blown new 'research programme' in economics started.[5]

Williamson's starting point was that of Coase: 'in the beginning there were markets' (Williamson, 1975, p. 20). Given this, the core methodological elements of the markets–hierarchies perspective are that:

1　The transaction is the basic unit of analysis.
2　Human agents are subject to bounded rationality and self interest.
3　The critical dimensions for describing transactions are frequency, uncertainty and transaction specific investments.
4　Economizing in transaction costs is the principal factor that explains viable modes of contracting; it is the main issue with which organizational design ought to be concerned.
5　Assessing transaction costs differences is a comparative institutional exercise. (Williamson and Ouchi, 1983, p. 33)

Williamson (1985, pp. 2–12) traces these elements back to an impressive array of contributors in the theory of economics, law and organization, such as Knight, Commons, Coase, Barnard, Hayek, Arrow, Calabresi, Simon, Chandler and Polanyi.

A transaction occurs, for Williamson, 'when a good or service is transferred across a technologically separable interface' (Williamson, 1986, p. 139). Transaction costs are taken to be the costs of running the economic system (Arrow, 1970), which Williamson considers it useful to think of in contractual terms.[6] Following Coase (1960) and Dahlman (1979) such costs include search and information costs, bargaining and decision costs, and policing and enforcement costs.

Bounded rationality refers to behaviour that is 'intendedly rational, but only limitedly so' (Williamson, 1990, p. 11, quoting Herbert Simon). Limits to rationality arise from limited knowledge, foresight, skill and time. Self-interest is of a special type, in that it makes allowance for guile: specifically, agents can be selective in information disclosure and can even distort information. They can try to 'mislead, disguise, obfuscate and confuse' (p. 12). Self-interest sought with guile is called 'opportunism' (but also moral hazard and agency). The importance of these two behavioural assumptions, Williamson claims, is profound, in that: 'Given bounded rationality, *all complex contracts are unavoidably incomplete*. Given opportunism, *contract-as-promise unsupported by credible commitments is hopelessly naive*' (Williamson, 1990, p. 12, emphasis in the original). It follows that transactions should be organized so as to economize on bounded rationality, while safeguarding transactions from the hazards of opportunism.

Transaction specific investment (or asset specificity) refers to the extent to which assets can be re-deployed to alternative uses and by different users without loss of productive value. Its forms include site specificity, human asset specificity, physical asset specificity and dedicated assets. The contracting ramifications of these are said to differ (Williamson, 1985). Of the three – asset specificity, uncertainty and frequency – the first is thought to be most important and distinctive.

In the original 'organizational failures' framework, Williamson (1975) considers the co-existence of opportunism and uncertainty/ complexity as the cause of information impactedness, i.e. asymmetric information among parties concerning the true underlying circumstances relevant to a transaction (or a set of related transactions). Information impactedness then leads to small numbers of actors, a situation of (*ex post*) bilateral dependencies. Small numbers are taken in this version as an *ex ante* situation as well as an *ex post* one. Later, the asset specificity concept, with its pervasive presence, is taken to be the important factor underlying the (asserted) commonality of *ex post*, as opposed to *ex ante*, bilateral dependency (see Williamson, 1990).

The co-existence of asset specificity, bounded rationality and opportunism creates a situation where market transaction costs are too high *vis-à-vis* those incurred by superseding the market and organizing resource allocation within the firm. Thus the 'internalization' of the market by the firm is due to the latter's ability to economize in market transaction costs, arising from the co-existence of these three factors. If any of the three factors does not exist, markets can still allocate resources economically (*vis-à-vis* firms). In the absence of bounded rationality, all potential problems can be settled from the outset, and thus the market can be relied upon to solve the problems of opportunism and asset specificity. In the absence of opportunism, the principle of stewardship (where the transactors can be relied upon to keep promises) can be used instead of a hierarchy. Finally, in the absence of asset specificity, contestable markets, i.e. markets characterized by perfectly easy entry and costless exit (Baumol, 1982), will exist.

Williamson considers the co-existence of all three factors as pervasive, however, implying the possibility of market supersession by hierarchies. In particular the advantages of internal organization are that they facilitate adaptive, sequential decision-making, in circumstances where complex, contingent claim contracts are not feasible and sequential spot markets are hazardous. Thus, bounded rationality is being economized. Internal organization also attenuates opportunism, in part because of the ability of authority to stop prolonged disputes, but also because members of a hierarchy feel part of a whole. Convergent expectations are more likely to appear, which reduces uncertainty. Bargaining costs arising from asset specificity can similarly be reduced through the use of authority. While these economizing aspects of internalization call for the supersession of the market by internal organization (hierarchies), Williamson points to the 'high powered' incentives of markets which can be blunted or lost by hierarchies. Thus there is a trade-off between 'high powered incentives and bilateral adaptability' (Williamson, 1990, p. 15). The advantages of internalization can explain the existence of firms. Similarly, the loss of high powered incentives can partly explain the boundaries of firms, and thus (given the assumption of pre-existing markets) the existence of the market. As Coase (1937) claimed, 'At the margin the costs of organizing within the firm will be equal either to the costs of organizing in another firm, or to the costs involved in *leaving the transaction to be "organized" by the price mechanism*' (Coase, 1937, p. 404, emphasis added). 'Leaving' is obviously the crucial word here.

The transaction costs/markets–hierarchies framework has been applied, mainly by Williamson, to explain a number of important issues, such as the 'employment relation', vertical integration, the evolution of the multidivisional structure of the firm (the M-form organization) and conglomerate and transnational corporations (see, for example, Williamson, 1981). Of these, the employment relation (Coase's exclusive concern) is of paramount importance and it is my main focus here. A largely unnoticed reason for this is that it is *only* this relation that can have legitimate claim in explaining the *emergence of hierarchies from pre-existing markets*. All others – vertical integration, the M-form, conglomeration and the TNC – presuppose the existence of firms, and thus refer to the functions and/or evolution of hierarchies. The 'employment relation' alone can, I suggest, claim to explain the emergence of hierarchies from markets as opposed to the growth and evolution of hierarchies (by *further* supersession of the market).[7]

To examine this idea, consider the case of vertical integration. In Williamson's analysis this is explained within his organizational failures perspective.[8] As Davies (1987) observes, this approach to vertical integration derives directly from Coase's observation that firms will tend to expand (integrate) up to the point where it is equally costly not to! It follows that vertical integration's *raison d'être*, in this view, is the same as that explaining firms' existence. The same arguments used above to explain why there are firms can also be used to explain why there is vertical integration (see, for example, Williamson, 1986). Two different possibilities arise here and are worth considering. The first is a firm that integrates vertically by setting up its own new suppliers and/or distributor.

This is a case of internal expansion. The second is a firm that takes over, or merges with, an upstream or downstream producer. Although arguments about opportunist suppliers, frequency of transactions, specific assets and *ex post* bilateral dependencies may be perfectly legitimate explanatory factors of a firm's decision here, the fact is that integration involves an ongoing existing hierarchy which internalizes (further) market transactions. Thus no explanation of *new* hierarchies from markets is offered here.

The case of the M-form organization is very similar. Chandler (1962) was the first to examine seriously the emergence of the multidivisional structure (the M-form firm), which gradually started replacing the unitary (U-form) firm in the USA soon after the Second World War. The organizational structure of the U-form involved a central office, responsible for strategic (long-run) decisions but also for the operational (day-to-day) decisions of the firm, and a number of functions: production, marketing, finance, personnel etc. The M-form, on the other hand, consists of a general office supported by elite staff responsible for the strategic decisions alone, and a number of operating divisions, each organized in the way the U-firm was. The operational decisions are left to the divisional managers in this structure.

Chandler's idea was that the adoption of the M-form was a response to firms' needs for diversification. By 1917 a number of firms were vertically integrated and realized that their know-how could be applied in new product lines (Chandler, 1977). The U-form was creating difficulties when the need arose to administer activities in different markets. The M-form was the step forward, as a firm would only have to add another division in a new product market to achieve its diversification plans. In this sense Chandler's thesis was that *strategy caused structure*.

For Williamson (1975, 1981) the story is different. He claims that the *size* of the U-form firm was becoming so great that: 'bounds on rationality were reached as the U-form structure labored under a communication overload while the pursuit of subgoals by functional parts . . . was partly a manifestation of opportunism' (Williamson, 1981, p. 1555). This was because the central office was taking both strategic and operational decisions. The M-form, by creating 'semi autonomous operating divisions (mainly profit centres), organized along product, brand or geographical lines' (Williamson, 1981, p. 1555), and with the operating affairs of each being managed separately, was able to reduce managerial opportunism, ease the confusion between strategic and operating goals and, importantly, re-establish the profit motive by reuniting ownership and control (see Pitelis, 1987a). In Williamson's view the M-form was adopted because of its inherent control (transaction cost eliminating advantages). In this sense it was size that led to the M-form, or *structure caused strategy*.

Economists became preoccupied with the efficiency (profitability enhancing aspects) of the M-form, while organizational studies theorists focused on the causality aspect of the Chandler–Williamson debate. Among the former, Cable (1989) gives an extensive survey of the existing evidence. This suggests that the M-form was profitable in the UK and the USA but not in Japan and West Germany. In Cable's view this is because of the closer link between industry and banking in the last two countries. By operating as an internal capital market, and financing preferentially growing divisions, the M-form could solve, in the US and the UK, problems associated with financing operations through the external market. In West Germany and Japan the close links between banks and industry had already established a quasi-internal market.

The evidence in the strategy–structure causality debate is summarized in Clegg (1990). Here things look worse for Williamson. In Clegg's words: 'The current state of the play . . . is that the relationship between diversification and divisionalization is consistently stronger empirically than the argument which leads from size to structure' (p. 43). Whatever the relative merits of Williamson's explanation of the M-form structure, here again we have a case of the organizational form this time, of an existing hierarchy. External capital market inefficiencies, and/or middle management opportunism, as well as 'control loss' problems due to the confluence of operation and strategic decisions along with increasing U-form firm size, may well have something to offer on the debate. But this debate is one of hierarchies versus hierarchies, or external versus internal markets (Kay, 1990).

Similar considerations to those about the M-form apply for the case of the conglomerate firm. The arguments are again in terms of internalizing the external capital market, because of failures in the latter (Williamson, 1975, 1981). Internalization increases the availability of information and the ability to control auditing. It also facilitates performance assessment of the M-form divisionalized profit centres. Furthermore, transaction costs can be economized by internalizing the production of separate goods. This is because firms may be better able to exploit quasi-rents from the ownership of specialized resources, either physical capital or human know-how. In both these cases conglomeration, as compared to leasing or selling in the open market, can help to reduce market transaction costs arising from opportunism, particularly in the case of organizational know-how, because of its tacit and fungible nature (Teece, 1980). Thus exploitation of the quasi-rents from intangible assets can offer an explanation for the conglomerate.[9] I will be discussing the intangible assets hypothesis in more detail later. For our purposes here, suffice it to note that in this case too what is being explained is the conglomerate divisionalization of existing hierarchies. There is an explanation of why market transactions are being superseded but not why hierarchies arise from markets.

Williamson's treatment of the transnational corporation is not extensive (see Williamson, 1981) and is on the same lines as his treatment of the conglomerate firm, namely the intangible assets hypothesis (see section 8). This allows me to conclude in favour of my main point, that it is only the employment relation that can provide a potentially legitimate claim to explain *new* hierarchies from markets. Coase was aware of that. In his paper the employment relation receives nearly exclusive attention. In this words, 'If a workman moves from department Y to department X, he does not go because of a change in relative prices, but because he is ordered to do so' (Coase, 1937, p. 387). It follows that 'failures' of (pre-existing) markets *for labour* can potentially explain the emergence of hierarchies. Transaction costs explanations of vertical integration, the M-form, conglomerates and TNCs, simply explain the (further) internalization of markets by *existing hierarchies*.

From a historical point of view, the firm (factory system) has succeeded the putting-out system. In the putting-out system a merchant-manufacturer 'put-out' raw materials to dispersed cottage labour, to be worked up into finished or part-finished products, in most cases by using the cottagers' own equipment (looms, forges, whatever the case might be). Material was moved from home to home in batches under the direction of the merchant-manufacturer. In the factory system, on the other hand, the employees have 'agreed' to accept the employer's authority, i.e. do as they are told, provided that the employer's behaviour falls within a 'zone of acceptance.' The 'agreement' (the employment contract) thus replaced the market-type relationship existing under the putting-out system.[10]

Why did this happen? In particular, what are the critical factors that led to the replacement of the market-type putting-out system by the authority-based factory system, the firm?

In Williamson's story the reason for this is transaction costs economizing. In brief, the main claim is that employees obtain 'idiosyncratic' experiences (job-related skills), which increase their bargaining power *vis-à-vis* employers. Combine this with employee opportunism and the transaction costs difficulties of market-based relationships become obvious; for example, protracted haggling. The employment relation cannot fully solve the problem of asymmetric information between employers and employees. Given this and opportunism, the firm (employer) will provide incentives to the employee to increase cooperation. Thus, the replacement of the external labour market by an internal labour market can be seen as a response to opportunism. In the internal labour market the wage rate attaches to the job, not the worker. This reduces individual bargaining and thus opportunism. Employees accept voluntarily the reduction in their freedom, but retain the right to cancel the authority relationship, to leave the employer. Although 'shirking' (by employees) is not prevented, 'consummate' (as opposed to 'perfunctory') cooperation is encouraged. Employers' opportunism is reduced for 'reputation' reasons. Cheating firms become known more quickly than cheating workers. Together with the existence of unions, which monitor the firm's commitments, this makes shirking by firms less likely (Malcolmson, 1982). Thus, idiosyncratic transactions and asymmetric knowledge necessitate the emergence of the firm (see Ricketts, 1987).

To what extent does the transaction costs story provide an accurate description of the relative advantages of the putting-out and factory systems? Landes (1966) describes a typical worker's behaviour in the putting-out system as follows: 'carouse the Saturday of pay, the Sabbath Sunday, the "Holy Monday" as well; dragged himself reluctantly back to work Tuesday, warmed to the task Wednesday, and laboured furiously Thursday and

Friday to finish in time for another long weekend' (Landes, 1966, p. 59, quoted in Francis, 1983, pp. 107–8). Although admittedly not in Williamson's sense of pecuniary gain maximization (Francis, 1983), there is little doubt here that from the employer's (merchant's) point of view this is opportunism indeed.

Further problems with the putting-out system are reported in Braverman (1974). In his view this system was 'plagued by problems of irregularity of production, loss of materials in transit and through embezzlement, slowness of manufacture, lack of uniformity and uncertainty of the quality of product' (Braverman, 1974, p. 63, also quoted in Williamson, 1986, p. 237). But the main problem Braverman observes was an inability to change the production processes. If unwillingness to work is 'opportunism', embezzlement and deceit are outright decadence. From the employer-merchant's point of view, that is, there are good reasons why the market-based putting-out system should be replaced by the authority relation. By making ability to work (labour power), rather than a quantity of a product, the subject of the contract, employers could increase their ability to control quality and more generally monitor the workers. The impetus for the factory system, North (1981, p. 169) observes, 'was monitoring of the production process by a supervisor'. This monitoring had obvious productivity advantages: the appropriation of the benefits of innovation and the checking of 'embezzlement and like deceits' (Williamson, 1985, p. 210, quoting Marglin, 1974, p. 51).

There is little doubt from the above that from the merchant-manufacturer's point of view superseding the putting-out system by a hierarchical organization had obvious efficiency (at least productivity-type) advantages. This appears to be in line with Williamson's claim that such 'changes are driven by efficiency' (Williamson, 1985, p. 232). To what extent this is true we will be better able to assess after having considered the critiques of and alternatives to the 'Williamsonian synthesis'.

3   Markets and Hierarchies: Critiques and Alternatives

As already suggested, the starting point of the Coase–Williamson framework is the pre-existence of markets, the idea that the market is the natural (or original) means of resource allocation, so that non-market institutions need to be explained. There are both conceptual and empirical problems with this assertion.

Conceptually, Fourie (1989) observes, market exchanges are nothing but exchanges between existing firms, or between such firms and their customers. The reason for this is that exchange presupposes production. Markets do not produce. Firms (including single-person ones) do. It follows that conceptually the firm precedes the market and not vice versa.[11] Historically, moreover, it is far from clear that markets predate hierarchies. Indeed, as the neoclassical economic historian Douglas North (1981) observes, if we focus on price-making markets (the concern of the transaction costs analysts), hierarchies predate the market. While the first known price-making market, the Athenian 'agora', dates back to the sixth century BC, hierarchies are known to have existed well before this. North goes on to suggest that a focus on price-making markets is misplaced and, in fact, 'any form of contractual exchange involves a market' (North, 1981, p. 92). This renders the question of whether markets pre-existed or not more complicated, but it certainly offers no obvious support to the Coase–Williamson idea. Given their exclusive focus on price-making markets, North's historical evidence appears to offer a blow to the very starting point of the Coase–Williamson scenario.

A second line of criticism of the Coase–Williamson scenario concerns the assumption that firms' existence presupposes market failure (of the transaction costs type), and therefore that firms' existence implies the superior efficiency properties of hierarchies over markets. There are a number of assumptions in this argument, most importantly concerning the process through which an efficient institution (here the firm) replaces an inefficient one (here the market). Rutherford (1989, p. 309), for example, observes that many institutions tend to contain a self-sustaining pattern of actions: 'Once a pattern is established, it may be maintained despite being socially suboptimal'. It is common for transaction costs theorists to employ 'evolutionary' arguments in order to explain the replacement process. North (1981, p. 7), for example, suggests that 'competition in the face of ubiquitious scarcity dictates that the more efficient institutions . . . will survive and the inefficient ones perish'. While this possibility cannot be excluded, it is also possible that competition can lead to monopoly (Marx, 1954; Rutherford, 1989) and/or wasteful use of resources (Baran and Sweezy, 1966; Rutherford, 1989). Thus, market inefficiencies (if present) need not necessarily lead to (efficient) firms.[12]

Another line of criticism concerning the efficiency argument relates to the nature of efficiency and to its beneficiaries, that is to the concept of Pareto efficiency. As I have suggested, the move from the putting-out to the factory system incorporated obvious productivity gains, through in particular the reduction of employees' opportunism. It also involved, however, the disappearance of labourers' opportunities to be opportunists! (Francis, 1983). Why should they want to lose this? From Landes's (1966) description, one would be surprised if 'independent' craftsmen and women were willing to sacrifice their 'independence' and obey employers' orders. It is at least as plausible to expect that labourers would be against such a change. If so, the firm was not efficient in the Pareto sense. Someone became better off, the merchant, while someone became worse off, the labourer (see Francis, 1983, and Sugden, 1983a, for this argument). A counter to this argument would be that from a purely pecuniary point of view both labourers and merchants became better off. Although this is a realistic possibility the question arises as to whether the focus of the mainstream theorists on pecuniary costs and benefits should be extended to incorporate 'psychic' costs and benefits (McGuinness, 1987). If so, the preference of the putting-out labourers for 'independence' (which Coase himself acknowledges) would suffice to invalidate the very claim that firms are Pareto efficient *vis-à-vis* markets.

A criticism of the transaction costs scenario related to that above is that it ignores or, more accurately, downplays the role of power considerations. Such considerations can refer to market power and/or power in its more general sense of ability of an agent (or group) to impose its will on others, through coercion or 'charisma'. This perspective is a distinct alternative to the Williamson scenario and will be covered as such below. It is primarily constituted in terms of 'strategic contingencies' or resource dependencies, and typically stresses control of valued resources such as capital, skill, networks and information (Clegg, 1990). Such considerations are at the heart of the analysis for radical economists, and the starting point for sociologists, political scientists and organizational theorists.

Focusing on market power, I have already pointed that competition itself can lead to monopoly (Marx, 1954). However, monopoly is itself one of the major aspects of (structural) market failure, according to conventional welfare economists (see, for example, the exposition of Cullis and Jones, 1987).[13] The ability of firms to give rise to (as opposed to solve) market failure has been noted extensively (Yamin and Nixson, 1984; Pitelis, 1987b). Particularly damaging from this point of view is Malcolmson's (1984) observation that market power and transaction costs considerations are inseparable, as it is often the case that firms attain monopoly power by reducing market transaction costs! Considering Williamson's examples of vertical integration moreover, Malcolmson concludes that, 'at least *prima facie*, the observed pattern of vertical integration is as consistent with the power argument as with the transaction costs argument. Without a separate measure of transaction costs efficiency or of the use of power, one cannot discriminate between the hypotheses' (Malcolmson, 1984, p. 125).

Malcolmson's last observation relates to the ability of transaction costs economics to claim that it can offer refutable hypotheses different from those of other perspectives. Methodologically this is being done by varying governance structures while holding the transaction constant (Williamson, 1975). However, Dow observes that this is illegitimate as changes in governance structures normally imply changes in the nature of the transaction costs involved: 'a "better" transaction must in some way be a *different* transaction. This undermines the premise that the transaction under discussion remains fixed, while governance structures can be varied to assess the transaction costs of each' (Dow, 1987, p. 18).

Sticking to issues of methodology, the reliance of the market–hierarchies scenario on methodological individualism (reductionism), that is the attribution of institutions or other social phenomena to individual action alone, has been noted and criticized by, for example, Hodgson (1988), Rutherford (1989) and Donaldson (1990). An alternative would be to explain individual behaviour in terms of institutions, or at least to recognize some sort of interaction between the two, that is to adopt as a unit not the individual but the social individual (see Hodgson, 1989). Williamson's concept of opportunism, Hodgson observes, does not depart from this tradition, as self-interest is a typical feature of 'economic man'.

Besides this criticism of its adherence to methodological individualism, the concept of opportunism has been attacked from many other sides. First, opportunism may be mediated through culture or differing types of economic organizations. Kay (1990) observes that countries like Japan rely more on 'obedience' than opportunism. The need to emphasize 'trust' relations within the firm is discussed by Hodgson (1988), and also in Ouchi's (1981) 'theory Z'. Picot and Wegner (1988), on the other hand, observe that the 'trust relation' between employers and employees in Japan is mythical. By raising wages with seniority, employers in Japan render the employees' 'exit' option void, thus reducing the incentive to 'shirk'. Furthermore, the Pareto efficiency of this is doubtful, given its association with 'high levels of dissatisfaction, stress, mental illness, and even suicide rates, as well as an unfair cleavage between regular and subcontract workers' (Picot and Wegner, 1988, p. 33). When the Japanese system of 'trust relations' had to pass the test of the oil shock of the mid-1970s, employers forced middle-aged employees with long service into 'voluntary' resignation! Picot and Wegner (p. 33) quote the president of a leading textile firm as saying: 'When a firm is about to be wrecked, heavier cargoes should be thrown off first to sea'.

Although this would appear to offer some support to the 'opportunism' idea,[14] it does so for *employers'* opportunism. This is in stark contrast to Williamson's emphasis on middle management opportunism (a reason for the M-form in his scenario) and employees' opportunism (a reason for the authority relation). This asymmetric treatment is also noted by Donaldson (1990) for middle level management and in particular by Dow (1987) for employees. In fact, Dow observes, the existence of authority is itself an inducement to employers' opportunism.

Other criticisms of the transaction costs perspective include the idea that firms supplement as well as replace markets (Auerbach, 1988); this is in line with Hodgson's (1988) 'impurity principle', i.e. the necessity of the co-existence of a variety of institutional forms (impurities) in market economies, as information provision devices (see also Schotter, 1981). The primarily static nature of the perspective has been noted (McGuinness, 1987; Pitelis, 1987b), as has its total disregard of the macro-economic structure as a potential explanatory factor in the existence and functions of institutions (Pitelis, 1991). Kay (1990) observed that, at least as far as TNCs are concerned, their emergence and growth involves the internalization of specific and non-specific assets (see also Galbraith and Kay, 1986). Cowling and Sugden (1987) suggested that if one focuses on control rather than ownership, TNCs' subcontractors should be viewed as part of the firm (the TNC), and transactions between TNCs and their subcontractors as intra-firm, rather than market, transactions. Brown (1984) and Imai and Itami (1984) observed that the distinction between markets and firms is not as clear-cut as the transaction costs framework implies, so firm-type behaviour in markets and interpenetrations of markets and hierarchies can often be found. Dugger (1983) raised the possibility that transaction costs economizing can be used to explain the state as well, which Williamson conveniently ignores (see also North, 1981; Pitelis, 1987c).

The above non-exhaustive coverage is indicative of the strong interest the transaction costs framework has aroused. Alternative perspectives have also been proposed, although not necessarily as a direct response to transaction costs ideas. Most notable among them is the (purist) neoclassical approach of Alchian and Demsetz (1972) and the radical perspective of Marglin (1974).

The starting point in Alchian and Demsetz (1972) is that there is no difference between the firm and the market, and that the firm *is* essentially a market: 'the firm can be considered as a privately owned market; if so, we could consider the firm and the ordinary market as competing types of markets' (p. 138). In a now famous quote, Alchian and Demsetz reject the idea that the firm has the power to settle issues by fiat, by authority, or by disciplinary action superior to that available in ordinary markets: 'Telling an employee to type this letter rather than to file that document is like my telling a grocer to sell me this brand of tuna rather than that brand of bread' (p. 120). Overall, the firm is a nexus of contracts, and involves continuous renegotiation of the contracts between employers and employees in terms acceptable to both parties. Thus, there is a perfectly symmetrical relationship here. The right to 'exit' implies that firing can be bidirectional. The employer fires the employee and similarly the employee fires the employer by leaving. Focus on the firm as a nexus of contracts characterizes the work of Klein (1983), who considers the question of the distinguishing features of firms as unimportant. In his view the fundamental advance is to think of all organizations as groups of explicit and implicit contracts.

If it is the case that firms are private markets, then how does the relationship between a grocer and a customer differ from that of an employer and his or her employee? The answer, Alchian and Demsetz suggest, 'is the *centralized contractual agent in a team production process* – not some superior authoritarian directive or disciplinary power' (Alchian and Demsetz, 1972, p. 120, emphasis in the original). Team production, however, involves metering problems, and difficulties of rewarding good performance and punishing bad. To do this a monitor is required to minimize 'shirking'. To make sure that the monitor is being monitored, he or she should have the right to claim the residual (profit). Thus the employer is regarded as a coordinator or orchestrator of a private market (firm). The right to be the residual claimant ensures efficient production *vis-à-vis* the ordinary market. Competition among potential coordinators, moreover, ensures that team members are not exploited (see Loasby, 1990).

The Alchian–Demsetz challenge has not gone uncriticized. Langlois (1987), for example, refuses to believe that the grocer example is meant literally. He observes that one thing an employee is *not* doing is continuously renegotiating contracts. If there is any efficiency value at all in the employer–employee relationship, he continues, it is that it dispenses with this need for continuous renegotiations. This criticism loses a lot of its thrust if renegotiations of contracts are seen as implicit; yet carrying the 'implicit contract' idea too far can be dangerous. As Hodgson (1988) observes, in the limit one could adopt Samuel Seabury's characterization (and justification) of slavery as an implicit contract between master and slave!

Despite shortcomings, the Alchian–Demsetz scenario is valuable in that it re-emphasizes the well known point that from the point of view of *exchange* and in the purely legalistic sense there is no essential difference between employers and employees. In the process of circulation, Marx (1954) observes, we find 'a very Eden of the innate rights of man. There alone rules Freedom,

Equality, Property and Bentham'. Following from this, a need arises to examine whether freedom and equality are being constrained through the actions of one or the other party *within* the process of exchange, as for example discussed by Picot and Wegner (1988), such as in labour market conditions (see Putterman, 1986). More importantly, why does the employer–employee relationship arise at all? First, I will focus on Marglin's (1974) radical account of the rise of the factory.

Marglin's 'What do bosses do?' first appeared as a Harvard Discussion Paper in 1970 and was published in 1974 in the *Review of Radical Political Economics*. Marglin's main claim was that, in contrast to neoclassical claims, the rise of the factory from the putting-out system had little or nothing to do with the technical superiority of large-scale machinery. The key to the success of the factory, as well as its aspiration, was the substitution of capitalists' for workers' control of the production process: 'discipline and supervision could and did reduce costs *without* being technologically superior' (1974, p. 46, emphasis in original). In this sense, Marglin suggests that the factory system resulted from the desire of capitalists to increase their control over labour. Given workers' relatively higher autonomy under the putting-out system, it cannot be presumed that they also preferred the factory system. Accordingly, the factory arose for distributional and *not* efficiency reasons. Stone's (1974) view of the transformation of the steel industry in the USA in the late nineteenth century is taken by Marglin as supporting his views. The Marglinian perspective has been developed in a number of other areas, including explanation of the M-form organization (Marginson, 1985) and the transnational corporation (Sugden, 1983a).

Williamson's response to the Marglinian challenge is a cautious one, and rather surprising. First, he accepts that there is 'merit' in Marglin's explanations. He also re-interprets Marglin's and Stone's analysis in a way consistent with his views and suggests that, 'Given . . . the large efficiency gains that Stone reports, the efficiency hypothesis (or a combined efficiency–power hypothesis) cannot be rejected' (Williamson, 1985, p. 236). This is effectively Malcolmson's (1984) critique of Williamson! Still, Williamson proceeds, the main problem with power ideas is that power is less operationalizable than (even) transaction costs are. So:

Inasmuch as power is very vague and has resisted successive efforts to make it operational, whereas efficiency is much more clearly specified and the possibility of an efficiency hypothesis is buttressed by ecological survival tests, we urge that efficiency analysis be made the centrepiece of the study of organizational design . . . power explains results when the organization sacrifices efficiency to serve special interests. We concede that this occurs. But we do not believe that major organizational changes in the commercial sector are explained in these terms. (Williamson and Ouchi, 1983, p. 30)

I have already noted problems with the Williamson programme, including those concerning operationalization. Similarly, I noted that from the capitalist's point of view (and, from a purely pecuniary perspective, even from the worker's point of view), the factory system did have efficiency advantages over putting-out. Finally, a focus on exchange alone does provide some apparent support to Alchian and Demsetz's idea of symmetry between capital and labour. Are they all right? To answer this we first need to analyse the 'nature of capitalism'.

4   The Nature of Capitalism, Markets and Hierarchies

In his *Economic Institutions of Capitalism*, Williamson (1985) fails to define either capitalism or institutions! A definition of 'institutional environment' and 'arrangements' is offered in Williamson (1990), taken from Davis and North (1971). Capitalism, however, still remains undefined. So what is capitalism?

A rather uncontroversial definition is that capitalism is a system of commodity production where labour service (or labour power), that is the ability of labour (workers, agents, employees) to produce commodities (products intended for sale and not personal use), is itself a commodity that can be transacted (purchased and sold) in the market for a compensation, the wage (rate), by owners (controllers and/or coordinators) of productive means such as physical capital (employers, capitalists, principals, entrepreneurs), who become residual claimants of any 'profit' (revenue minus cost) generated by the transaction by virtue of their coordinating, owning and/or controlling function.

The attractive feature of this definition is that by carefully avoiding attributing profits to ownership or control by employer-capitalists, it can encompass both mainstream and radical, including Marxist, perspectives. However, it still makes the points that under capitalism there are 'agents' who sell their labour power and 'principals' who buy it, and that for so long as the agents are contracted, they have to obey the directions (orders, authority) of the principal.[15] Why is this?

Coase (1937) raises a similar question. He observes that it may be that some people prefer to work under someone, but dismisses this idea, quoting Harry Dawes's observation that people tend to prefer quite the opposite, i.e. 'being one's own master' (p. 390). An alternative scenario would be that people realize the benefits from cooperation and the need for supervision during this process of cooperation. In order to achieve the benefits from cooperation, they are prepared to sacrifice part of their autonomy for the duration of the productive process. This is the idea underlying the Alchian–Demsetz argument. A third possibility is that people (agents) are coerced to do so, either legally or because of their inability to survive or to live what they perceive as a satisfactory life if they do not. This scenario is favoured by the Marxist tradition. Hymer, for example, summarizes this scenario very succinctly:

> In its early days, capital allied itself with the central power of the sovereign against the feudal classes. This system, working in complex ways, helped to drive the population off the land to become a free wage labor force in the towns and cities. People became unencumbered by property in the twofold sense: They were free of feudal claims on their time and had no property of their own, and therefore had no alternative to working for others. (Hymer, in Cohen et al., 1979, p. 30)

Thus it is the need to survive, given absence of property, that led people to work for others in the Marxist scenario.

Whatever the relative merits of these conflicting scenarios (or a synthesis?) may be, a consensus point which emerges is that when we focus on the process of production, there is an asymmetry between agents and principals in that the former have to obey the latter, i.e. sacrifice part of their autonomy. Thus, as far as the production process is concerned, any employment relationship is one of asymmetry, a hierarchical one. This last observation has interesting implications for the putting-out versus factory system debate. In particular, it implies that the relationship between the merchant-manufacturer (principal) and the cottage-labourer (agent) in the putting-out system was itself a hierarchical one. The labourer agreed, for whatever reason, to sacrifice part of his or her autonomy (as compared, for example, to being a merchant-manufacturer) and work for the merchant-manufacturer. In this sense, the market-type putting-out system was a hierarchy. The historical evidence seems to support this simple observation. Landes (1966), for example, observes that although most domestic weavers owned their looms and nailers their forges, 'They were not, however, independent entrepreneurs selling their products in the open market; rather they were hirelings, *generally tied to a particular employer*, to whom they agreed to furnish a given amount of work at a price stipulated in advance' (p. 12, emphasis added).

Given the hierarchical nature of the putting-out system, the transition from it to the factory system did not involve a transition from a market to a new hierarchy but rather (as in the case of vertical integration, conglomerates, the M-Form and the TNC) a transition from a hierarchy to a different hierarchy. Put more generally, any employment relationship involving an agent working for a principal is a hierarchical one. The transition from the one to the other involves a differential degree of supersession of market transactions, but it does not represent a supersession of *the* market by *a* hierarchy. As far as the employment relationship goes, the difference between its various forms is a quantitative and not a qualitative one. It involves differential degrees of supersession of market transactions and of sacrifices in the degree of autonomy the agents enjoy.[16]

As already suggested, the move from the putting-out to the factory system involved a further loss of autonomy of the agents to the principals, a point acknowledged by Williamson (1985). Why did cottage-labourers accept this? Unlike the case of the propertyless 'proletarian' discussed by Marxists (see the quotation of Hymer's above), in the case of the cottage-labourer there was some capital ownership. In this sense the 'ownership of capital' barrier to entry argument often employed by the Marxists cannot fully explain the cottage-labourer's 'acceptance' of the factory system, a further loss of independence. Acknowledging this, Marglin (1983) suggests that it was the 'organizational knowledge' of capitalists that allowed them to win the day, to oblige cottage-labourers to accept the factory system. Capitalists' motivation was their ability to further their profit by increasing their control over labour. Given their access (however obtained) to organizational knowledge and the conscious attempts on their part to protect it from becoming known to others, they only had to give the all or nothing choice to the cottage-labourers. Work for us or starve was the idea, which is further discussed by Francis (1983) and Sugden (1983a).

Marglin's rather instrumentalist account and rigid distinction between cottage labourers and capitalists solves fewer problems than it creates. Firstly, the knowledge equals power idea fails to address the possibility of outright coercion by the state and merchant-capitalists, as raised by the Marxists. Secondly, and more importantly, the organizational knowledge idea raises the 'ugly' head of the question: how is such knowledge obtained? The answer is not inconsequential: it has dramatic implications for the efficiency properties of capitalism.[17] As Hymer observes,

> Marshall, like Marx, stressed that internal division of labour within the factory, between those who planned and those who worked (between 'undertakers' and labourers) was the 'chief fact in the form of modern civilization, the "kernel" of the modern economic problem'. Marx however, stressed the authoritarian and unequal nature of the relationship based on the coercive power of property. . . . Marshall . . . argued for the voluntary cooperative nature of the relationship between capital and labour. He argued that . . . 'Undertakers' were not captains of industry because they had capital; they could obtain capital because they had the ability to be captains of industry. They retained their authority by merit not coercion'. (Hymer, in Cohen et al., 1979, pp. 57–8)

It follows that the question of organizational knowledge hinges more on the process of its derivation than on its existence *per se*.

Marglin's failure to answer this question is in part due to the fact that, from a historical perspective, he is focusing on the wrong comparison. The important question is not the transition from one form of hierarchy (the putting-out system) to another (the factory system) but rather the very emergence of the putting-out system from the single producer who exchanged his or her products in the market with the products of other producers or merchants. In fact this is the question that Coase addresses, that is the emergence of any form of entrepreneurial coordination of production from a non-entrepreneurial form, the price mechanism. As shown, in putting-out the 'undertaker' was already there.

Viewed in this light, the problem of the emergence of the 'capitalist' and the 'firm' becomes a relatively easy one. Merchants, like any other transactor, would buy from single producers in order to sell, and thus make a 'profit'.[18] To ensure the existence of a 'profit' they needed to ensure the existence of suppliers. Total reliance on the market simply could not do this. Single producers might choose not to produce for sale, might change merchant in looking for a bargain etc. Putting-out was the 'obvious' solution. The necessary condition for its existence was the need of the merchants for stable suppliers, particularly in the face of expanding markets for their products. The sufficient condition was a similar need for stable income on the part of the single producers, as well as their not being (willing or able to become) merchants themselves. Obviously some might have become merchants, rather than sacrificing their total autonomy for the merchants' authority under the putting-out. This is inconsequential. All that matters is that merchants, by virtue alone of their being merchants – that is, knowledge of markets, willingness and ability to sell – were able to 'persuade', or coerce through the state, some single producers to work for them (see below). The capitalist was born and so was the firm (putting-out). Organizational knowledge of production within the firm was obtained in the process. Given the difficulties associated with the appropriation of its quasi-rents, this knowledge was kept secret, through strategy, as Marglin and Marx discuss.[19] This allowed the merchant-capitalists to maintain power to organize and control production while the capital barrier was not important.[20] The move to the factory system and the growth of factories increased the relative significance of the capital ownership barrier, consolidating the victory of the merchant-capitalist and the capitalist firm. There is little doubt that the state facilitated the process (see, for example, Galbraith, 1987; Hymer and Resnick, 1979), particularly concerning the farmers (land enclosures). Still, it would appear that elements of both coercion and perceived self-interest led single producers and farmers to sacrifice part of their autonomy in the early stages. Similar considerations apply for the transition from putting-out to the factory, although evidence seems to be in line with the idea that coercion must have played a more significant role here (see Francis, 1983).[21]

The moral from this discussion is that exploitation of the fruits of the division of labour was the driving force behind the emergence and evolution of the firm. Furthermore, independently of the *ex post* Pareto efficiency, or inefficiency, properties of such evolutionary changes, their initiators and major beneficiaries were the principals to be. This is broadly in line with, and provides a basis for, a startling consensus among a widely divergent array of contributors on the definitions of institutions, markets and hierarchies. Thus the neoclassical economic historian Douglas North observes: 'Institutions are sets of rules, compliance procedures, and moral and ethical behavioural norms designed to constrain the behaviour of individuals in the interests of maximizing the wealth or utility of principals' (North, 1981, p. 202). North also observes that such institutions can be voluntary or involuntary, and that consensus ideologies can be 'a substitute for formal rules and compliance procedures' (p. 205). The Marxist economist Hymer, on the other hand, observes Marx's and Marshall's acknowledgement of the importance of the division of labour and regards the 'market' and the 'factory' as 'the two different methods of coordinating the division of labour. In the factory entrepreneurs consciously plan and organize cooperation, and the relationships are hierarchical and authoritarian, in the market coordination is achieved through a decentralized, unconscious competitive process' (Hymer, 1970, p. 57). The 'Austrian' economist and philosopher Friedrich von Hayek observes that 'the commands as well as the rules which govern an organization serve particular results aimed at by those who are in command of the organization' (quoted in Clegg, 1990, p. 33). Ludwig von Mises, the father-figure of the Austrian tradition, defines the market as 'the social system of the division of labour under private ownership of the means of production' (quoted in Hodgson, 1988, p. 173, where further discussions on the concepts and definitions are supplied).

To summarize, the transition from the market to the firm (putting-out first, factory after) was the result of the merchants' (rising capitalist class) desire to further their interests, by effecting a more efficient division of labour. The process involved consensus and coercion, including state intervention. *Ex ante* it was often undesirable. *Ex post*, often (Pareto) efficient!

5   Existence and Objectives

The observation that the employment relation (the firm) is the result of the merchants' attempts to effect a more efficient division of labour and the related idea that the transition from putting-out to the factory system was simply a choice between two hierarchies has this very important implication: it renders inseparable the notions of the existence and objectives of firms. In this scenario firms exist because of their principals' objectives: objectives lead to existence. How this is achieved is a different and very important issue. It is neither necessary nor helpful, however, to attempt to explain existence first and discuss objectives after (as Coase and Williamson do), or to assert the exogenous preferences of capitalists first and then to attempt to derive the existence of firms, as Marglin does. Existence and objectives are the two sides of the same coin.

As already suggested, the aim of the merchants in using the market (and underlying their successful attempt to replace the latter by an employment relationship) was to further their profits.[22] Similarly the transition from one type of employment relation (putting-out) to another (factory) was due to the merchant-manufacturers' desire to further their profits through a more efficient exploitation of the division of labour. From this it follows that both Williamson and Marglin are simultaneously right and wrong! The drive for profits by merchant-manufacturers would lead them to seek more efficient means of exploiting the division of labour. Through such efficiency improvements, profitability and power would also increase. Power and efficiency were linked inseparably. For transaction costs, in particular, it is exactly through their reduction that profit, and thus potentially market power, can increase, as observed by Malcolmson (1984). To further profits, principals would try to reduce all types of costs, including transaction and labour costs; the latter by increasing their control over the labour process, as indeed both Marglin and Williamson emphasize. In this sense what is involved here is not two different explanations of the existence of firms, but differences in emphasis concerning two sides of the more general objective and reason for the existence of firms, the furtherance of profits for the principals.[23]

In this light the Alchian–Demsetz argument also appears to be correct, subject to it being focused on the exchange side of the problem. From a legal point of view, the relationship between principals and agents is one of symmetry. Labour market conditions (affecting the agents' alternatives) as well as actions by principals and agents affecting the 'exit' conditions of agents in particular, can put limits (constraints) on the relative power of the two parties, but cannot change the fundamental 'equality in the face of the law' between the two. Once, however, we focus on the production side – once it is recognized that the agent's only alternative to an employment relation is another employment relation, or none at all – the relationship becomes one of asymmetry (hierarchy). During the production process, the agent has to obey the principal, or else 'choose' another principal to obey! Thus focus on exchange does provide support for the Alchian–Demsetz idea, which becomes flawed once we focus on the production side.

Was the aim to further profits maintained and pursued following the emergence and evolution of the capitalist firm? If so, why? From a Marxist perspective, the answer to the first question would be unequivocally yes. The reason is that, given the labour theory of value (that labour power is the source of economic 'surplus' and thus profits), the *conflict* between capitalists and labourers to change the part of the surplus going to each class would lead capitalists to try to increase labour productivity, by technological and/or organizational changes. Still, Putterman observes, 'even without Marx's value theory, which is not universally insisted upon by contemporary radical economists, the struggle to wrest more work out of labourers for a given wage payment remains at the heart of the study of the labour process, which in turn remains a central focus of research' (Putterman, 1986, p. 27) – see also Marglin (1984). Another equally important, and less controversial, reason for the strive for profits is competition (*rivalry*) among firms themselves, to improve their competitive position *vis-à-vis* rivals, (and thus ensure their survival), by cutting costs. The recognition of the importance of actual and potential competition in maintaining a drive for cost reductions cuts across economic ideologies, Austrian, Marxist and neoclassical (see the discussion in Scherer, 1980; Pitelis, 1990c).

The short run implication of the competition-driven strive for profit, is obviously a need by firms to exploit economies of scale, improve organization techniques and increase the intensity of labour. More important, however, are the long run implications. To keep being profitable, (or to increase long-term profits), firms will need to expand their markets and, more importantly, to remove the constraints they face in the process of this expansion (see below). Maximizing short-term profits will simply not do.[24] Hymer, for example, explains that a firm's

> position is constantly threatened by new entrants who may discover a new technology, a new product, a new form of organization, a new supply of labor. The dialectic of the product cycle gives capitalism its forward motion. An innovation is introduced; if it succeeds, the product enjoys a high rate of growth as it displaces other products and more and more consumers come to use it. As the market becomes saturated, growth tapers off while profitability is squeezed. Simultaneously other firms try to enter the market . . . production costs begin to dominate the competition of other firms . . . [and this] cuts into the original innovator's profit. (Hymer, in Cohen et al., 1979, p. 79)

The way out, Hymer suggests, involves first the development of new products and second the prolongation of the product cycle, by gaining control of marketing outlets, searching for and moving to places of cheaper labour and using secrecy. But the threat is still there, obliging the firm to reinvest profits, 'in order to improve production and expand its scale, merely as a means of self preservation and under threat of ruin' (in Cohen et al., 1979, p. 79).

The need to expand for 'self preservation' suggests that growth can and must be seen as a means of obtaining maximum possible profits in the long term. The existence of uncertainty concerning what exactly 'maximization' of long-term profit entails reinforces the idea that in order to obtain maximum possible profits, the firm needs to grow. Emphasis on growth (*per se* or as a means of maximizing long-term profits) has now received very wide recognition in the literature; see, for example, Penrose (1959), Marris and Mueller (1980), Eichner (1976) and Chandler (1986). Chandler, for example, asserts that 'the primary goal of . . . capitalist enterprises has been long term profit. The surest way to attain and maintain this goal has been to reduce unit cost' (Chandler, 1986, p. 31). Interestingly, Chandler goes on to observe that such cost reductions can be achieved by lowering costs within operating units by improving technology and organization, and by lowering transaction costs between operating units by internalizing these units within a single enterprise. Thus Chandler provides simultaneously support for my observation that transaction and other cost reductions should all be seen as part of the more general strategy of long-term profit enhancement and an explanation of growth through vertical integration in order to achieve this aim.

Similarly, Penrose (1959) observes firms' 'desire to increase total long run profits' (p. 29) and suggests that as investment by firms generates profits, firms will try to expand as fast as they can take advantage of expansion opportunities (subjectively perceived as profitable). In this sense: 'it does not matter whether we speak of "growth" or "profits" as the goal of the firm's investment activities' (Penrose, 1959, p. 30). Trying to grow implies trying to remove any obstacles to such growth. Such obstacles, I believe, fall into five major categories: (1) product market constraints; (2) labour market constraints; (3) capital market constraints; (4) technology constraints; and (5) managerial constraints.

1   Product market constraints arise from the size of the market and the product life-cycle within it. Advertising and sales promotion activities, as well as the creation of 'competing' product lines within the industry, can help firms to maintain and increase their market share. Diversification into new products is required for the solution of the product life-cycle problem, as pointed out by Hymer (Cohen et al., 1979). Vertical integration can in part at least be seen as a means of diversifying risks (Auerbach, 1988). More generally, horizontal integration (mergers) and vertical integration are important means of achieving growth within the industry.

2   Labour market constraints arise from the availability or

non-availability of an appropriate workforce and the bargaining
position of labour. The response to this is an attempt to further
the productive base and (in so doing) to reduce labour's power.
Constraints on the 'exit' option of labourers are also relevant here
(Picot and Wegner, 1988).

3 Capital market constraints arise from difficulties in raising
finance for expansion. Such finance can be found by borrowing
from financial institutions and/or by issuing shares and retaining
profits. Issuing shares is a discretionary means of socializing
corporate ownership in order to raise finance. The joint-stock
company can therefore be seen as the result of the need of firms
to remove the constraints to growth (Pitelis, 1987a). Mobilization
of further finance can take the form of compulsory occupational
pension funds. In this light the 'pension funds revolution' is also
a means of eliminating constraints to growth (Pitelis, 1987a).
Pricing policies can be used in such a way that required finance
for expansion becomes available internally, subject, of course, to
entry and other considerations, such as take-over threats and loss
of control to other principals (Eichner, 1976; Pitelis, 1987a).

4 Technological constraints to growth are removed through
the introduction of more technologically advanced products and
processes. This allows firms to reduce their costs, including
labour costs through labour-saving technology and/or better exploitation of the division of labour. Technological advancement is
therefore the *sine qua non* of growth, and thus of long-term
profits.

5 Managerial constraints have received the lion's share in the
literature (see in particular Penrose, 1959). The growth of firms
puts definite limits on the ability of management to handle information: control loss problems arise, as discussed by Williamson
(1967), and growth, through, for example, diversification, can be
halted. Organizational changes are the way to solve these problems. In particular, the M-form organization can be seen in this
light.

The above discussion does not suggest that other factors, including transaction costs considerations, are of no value in explaining the evolution of firms and their organizational structures.
Rather, they can be seen within a unified objectives equals
existence framework, where growth is the means of achieving
long-term profits and where the need to remove the constraints to

growth explains dynamically the strategies of firms, as well as their organizational structures. The major advantage of such a framework is that it endogenizes the need for changes in technology and organizational structures, which changes are often seen as the exogenous sources of profitability increases (Chandler, 1986).

6   Growth and Evolution

The focus on the need of firms to grow as a means of existing and in order to achieve maximum possible profits provides invaluable insights on three important phenomena concerning the evolution of firms: the alleged 'managerial revolution'; the so-called 'pension funds revolution' and the recently observed tendency for disintegration by large firms, in particular the growth of the subcontracting phenomenon.

'Since the beginning of the industrial revolution, there has been a steady increase in the size of manufacturing firms, so persistent that it might almost be formulated as a general law of capital accumulation' (Hymer, in Cohen et al., 1979, p. 42). In line with Chandler, Hymer observes three major phases in this development. First is the Marshallian firm of factory-level organization, single function and industry operations, and one group of owner-controllers. Second is the national corporation of continent-wide, vertically integrated production, highly elaborate administrative structures and ownership dispersion. Third is the multidivisional form of many semi-autonomous units, each specializing in one product line. The crucial difference between the second and third stages, Hymer observes, was the separation of strategic (long-term) from operational (day-to-day) decisions. This development gave these firms

the power to invest on a much larger scale and with much wider time horizon than the smaller . . . firms that preceded it. The modern multidivisional corporation is thus a far cry from the Marshallian firm in both its vision and its strength. The Marshallian capitalist ruled his factory from an office on the second floor. At the turn of the century the president of a large national corporation was lodged in a higher building . . . with higher perpectives and greater power. In

the giant corporation of today, managers rule from the tops
of skyscrapers; on a clear day, they can almost see the world.
(Hymer, in Cohen et al., 1979, p. 43)

Of the stages Hymer describes, the emergence of the 'national
corporation' has received wide attention and generated a vast
literature in economic theory. The reason for this is the ownership dispersion observed in such firms and the emergence of a
group of highly specialist managers. These two have given rise to
the debate on the 'managerial revolution'.

In summary form (see Pitelis, 1987a, for a more detailed
treatment), the debate developed as follows. Given high ownership dispersion through the issuing of shares, cohesive groups of
owner-capitalists are left without sufficient shares to warrant
control, which is now left with the managers – see Berle and
Means (1932) for the original thesis and Scott (1985) for an
extensive survey of the literature. Assuming that managers maximize a different utility function to the owners (who are assumed
to maximize short run profits), firms' objectives might have
changed. Alternative *managerial* objectives proposed have been
Baumol's (1959) sales revenue maximization, Williamson's (1963)
discretionary expenditure model and Marris's (1967) balanced
rate of growth maximization. All are subject to a minimum profit
constraint. Soon after the publication of these models, a wide
range of criticisms appeared. One concerned the empirical validity
of the phenomenon: what ownership percentage suffices to give
control to a cohesive group, how do we identify such cohesive
groups, to what extent does dispersion imply a lower share
ownership percentage for owners' control? Detailed surveys can
be found in Scott (1986). Suffice it to note here that such
considerations did raise doubts on the importance and extent of
management control.

A second line of criticism addressed the constraints managers
face in pursuing their aims. A number of such constraints have
been suggested in the literature: the market for corporate control
(Manne, 1965), the managerial compensation market (Fama,
1980) and the monitoring and bonding by shareholders and debt-
holders (Jensen and Meckling, 1976); Putterman (1986, 1988)
discusses these issues further. The crucial implication from these
neoclassical critiques is that there are sufficient constraints to

ensure that managers' interests and incentives will be closely (and even perfectly) aligned with those of shareholders.

A third line of criticism has come from Marxist authors, such as Baran and Sweezy (1966), who observed that although managers do control, they also try to maximize profits, for reasons associated with the very nature of capitalism. Namely, managers are themselves often recruited from the very wealthy and represent the highest echelon of the capitalist class. Common education, values and outlooks tend to ensure the pursuit of profits on their part too. Baran and Sweezy in fact suggest that managerialism represents an improvement in the ability of firms to pursue profits successfully, exactly because of the training and organizational knowledge and techniques of modern management. This view has been re-emphasized and supported more recently by Auerbach (1988).

A fourth line of criticism deals with the question of whether recent institutional developments put further doubt on the issue of managerial control. Williamson (1981) observes that the M-form represents a successful counter-revolution by the owners, who by virtue of their control over the general office, and the control of the latter over middle management, have re-established their control, and thus the profit maximization aim. In Williamson's view the issue of corporate control was therefore solved by internal organizational changes. A second such idea comes from observation of the dramatic concentration of share ownership in the hands of financial institutions, pension funds, merchant banks and insurance companies (Scott, 1986). Such concentration is claimed to constrain managerial objectives further since, unlike small level shareholders, institutional investors can have the knowledge, the ability and the size of ownership stakes required to push management towards policies that will ensure them a satisfactory dividend for reinvestment (Pitelis, 1987a). A counter-argument here might be that institutions themselves are management controlled. Despite the apparent appeal of this argument the obvious response is that while managers may wish to pursue their objectives in *their* firms, they are unlikely to allow other managers to do the same in the firms in which they have ownership stakes. Rather, managers with ownership stakes in other firms will tend to push the management of such firms towards profit maximization (Herman, 1979).

A further blow to the managerial revolution argument came from its other major proponent, Baumol. In his more recent work, Baumol (1982) suggests that a number of markets are contestable, that is characterized by free entry and costless exit. In such markets any inefficient (non-profit-maximizing) configurations will attract entry, which will give rise to efficient (cost-minimizing) behaviour by incumbents. In the light of this, managerial objectives cannot be pursued as they will attract new entry. Potential competition here suffices to establish the profit maximization motive.

As has been noted elsewhere (Pitelis and Sugden, 1986; Pitelis, 1987a), useful as they are, all these critiques are *ad hoc* and *ex post*, just as the very idea of the managerial revolution is. In fact, in the light of the perspective developed in the previous sections of this chapter, it is the firm's effort and need to grow which have generated the need for both ownership dispersion and a managerial stratum: the former in order to raise finance for expansion;[25] the latter in order to administer properly the resultant grown and, thus, more complex enterprise. Seen in this light the 'managerial revolution' was a response by firms to constraints to growth arising from financial and managerial-organizational considerations.

An important implication of this argument and a major blow to managerialism (especially when viewed with other *ad hoc* critiques) is that since growth for expansion led the original owners to issue shares and to recruit a new management group, owners should not be expected to relinquish control – they might, for example, retain sufficient shares or aspects of organizational knowledge. Alternatively, in this framework, owners might voluntarily relinquish control if they thought that managers were better able to satisfy their aims – by assumption maximum profits. Mistakes cannot be excluded, of course, but building a theory of managerial control on capitalists' mistakes does leave something to be desired. To be sure, my perspective here was similarly adopted by Hilferding (1981) in his *Finance Capital*, first published in 1910. At the time Hilferding was actually observing the real thing happening so it was only natural for him to observe that capitalists were issuing shares *in order to raise finance for expansion, and with an eye to keeping control* of the expanded company.

It follows from this that it was not managerialism that led firms to pursue growth-maximizing policies, as suggested by Marris (1967) and Marris and Mueller (1980), but rather that firms' *growth* led to manageralism. In this light it is hardly surprising that the growth objective has survived the fall of managerialism and been adopted by a number of influential theorists (for example, Penrose, 1959; Eichner, 1976). Another, and related, reason for this is that the long-run profit and growth-maximization objectives are formally equivalent – see Eichner (1976) and Reynolds (1989) for detailed discussion and surveys. To conclude, focusing on growth as a means of achieving long-term profits for survival in the face of uncertainty provides an endogenous evolutionary explanation for both ownership dispersion and the managerial 'revolution'. Profit through growth objectives led to managerialism rather than managerialism to growth objectives.

The discussion above is not intended to suggest that the emergence of the 'national' (joint-stock, public) corporation was of no significance. Two important effects of this emergence can be identified: first, the ability of capitalists (top management) to present as costs parts of expenditure which would otherwise show up as profits (see Eichner, 1976, and Cowling, 1982, for discussion on this point); more importantly, the raising of finance for expansion through share issues would suggest that one might regard dividends, or the part not going to controlling top management who happen to be shareholders, as costs, as an implicit interest rate for raising finance (Eichner, 1976). If this is the case then the aim of joint-stock firms is better seen as to try to obtain *maximum possible long-term retained profits subject to not losing control* to outsiders; that is, subject to paying sufficient dividends to avoid the risk of shareholders 'voting with their feet' (selling their shares) and the associated risk of a resulting low valuation ratio inviting a take-over raid, and subject to limiting or blocking new entry (Eichner, 1976; Pitelis, 1990c). The potency of the take-over mechanism has been questioned (for example, Marris and Mueller, 1980), in part because of the protection given to a firm by increased size. The fear of losing shareholders to other firms, however, has wider motivations than fear of take-overs, such as the loss of a source of internal funding for expansion. This provides a hint to an explanation of another important institutional development of modern capitalism: the pension funds 'revolution'.

The term pension funds 'revolution' comes from Drucker

(1976) who, observing the growing and substantial ownership of shares by workers through their occupational pension funds, suggested that this ownership implied an 'unseen' revolution that transformed the USA to a truly 'socialist' country. To be sure, Drucker's exclusive reliance on ownership was soon to be criticized on both empirical and theoretical grounds – see Minns (1981a), Marglin (1984) and Pitelis (1987a), where a survey of the literature is also given.

In the framework here, the pension funds revolution can be explained in terms of the firms' requirements for finance for expansion as well as the inherent unreliability of firms' reliance on 'voluntary' shareholders, who could in theory at least sell their shares exactly at the times firms might need loyalty the most, such as when they planned further expansion and so needed to reduce, or not increase, dividend payouts. By the introduction of compulsory pension funds as a condition of employment this problem is being solved: wage earners are often not even aware of their ownership claims on shares purchased through their pension funds! Moreover, the socialization of capital ownership, a source of further finance, is now extended to workers who might otherwise spend this income. Given that the introduction of the schemes is seen here as a result of firms' need to raise finance for growth, control over the funds should be expected to remain with the corporate sector,[26] an expectation in line with the evidence (Minns, 1981a). Further, the use of professional financial institutions, such as insurance companies and merchant banks, for the management of the funds, renders the firms stakeholders to each other's fortunes; by mere use of other people's money! For each particular firm, dividend pay-out decisions now have to be made following careful assessment of the potential impact of these decisions on the objectives of financial institutions; reinforcing their need to allow for a minimum dividend constraint.

My focus on long-term retained profits through expansion, subject to keeping control, can help to explain not only the tendencies of firms to integrate (vertically and horizontally), diversify and centralize their decision-making processes (the M-form), but also the opposite tendencies. Indeed, it has been widely observed in the literature (e.g. Hymer, in Cohen et al., 1979; Auerbach, 1988) that integration and centralization are far from being problem-free. Integration involves not only the loss of market 'high-powered incentives' as Williamson (1990) suggests, but also the problems associated with the ownership of human and physical capital if something goes wrong. Centralization, moreover, often implies the absence of detailed on-the-spot information, and thus the possibility of bad long-term planning decisions from the central office. Centralization may also inhibit long-term strategies of cross-subsidization when breaking into a new market (Auerbach, 1988).

If, as suggested, the aim of the firm is to obtain maximum possible long-term retained profits, subject to not losing control, one should expect firms to try to develop methods of retaining control, while removing the problems related to integration and centralization. When this happens, disintegration and decentralization should be expected to follow. Concerning the former, a remarkable foresight by Hymer was his observation of a shift of emphasis by firms away from production and towards marketing and new product development. This, he suggested, would allow small firms to own the plants (and the risks) while big firms would control the 'intangibles', and thus have control over the small firms. In recent years Hymer's prediction has actually come true in the form of an increase in the subcontracting phenomenon (Cowling and Sugden, 1987). The observation by Cowling and Sugden that by focusing on control rather than ownership, subcontractors can be viewed as part of the firm, despite the apparent use of market-type transactions, is valid when seen in my framework, but is also offered a dynamic explanation. Once firms can grow without losing control, they absolve themselves from the risks of integration and disintegrate. Integration emerged in order to expand and control. Disintegration results when expansion and control can be achieved without the problems of integration.

Such disintegration also effectively represents decentralization. Although the maintenance of control implies that the firm is a *de facto* M-form, *de jure* the subcontractor is an independent entity. This also allows the controlling 'partner' to operate as a U-form firm, exploiting the relative advantages of this form for relatively smaller entities; this is widely observed in the literature e.g. Clarke and McGuinness, (1987). Licensing and franchising phenomena could also be explained in this light.

The proposed framework also provides a starting point for the analysis and growth of the transnational corporation (TNC), probably the single most important institutional form of advanced capitalism.

7 The Transnational Corporation

Today over 50 per cent of global exchange is conducted by transnational firms (Rugman, 1987). Their sheer enormity, continuing growth and the vast literature that emerged to explain their existence and operations deserve our special focus in this section.

TNCs are firms that control production facilities outside their country of origin. As they represent previously national corporations that have 'decided' to transcend their borders, the term transnational appears a more useful one than the commonly used 'multinationals', which may convey the false impression that such firms originate in or 'belong' to many national countries. TNCs date back to the end of the nineteenth century, but it was in the aftermath of the Second World War that the TNC phenomenon started gathering the momentum it has today. Historical accounts are in Dunning (1989), among others. Unlike earlier types of foreign investment, normally of the portfolio type, the substantial expansion of US TNCs, mainly to Europe, in that period took the form of direct foreign investment (DFI), the distinguishing mark of the TNC. Why did this happen?

Hymer (1976) was the first to address this question seriously and is the undisputed father of the theory of the TNC. His PhD thesis, completed in 1960 at MIT and first published in 1976, is probably the most cited ever. Following the completion of his thesis and up to 1973, when he died, Hymer developed his views on the theory of the TNC (and the 'multinational corporate capital system') in a number of articles, some of the best of which were published in the volume by Cohen et al. (1979). Overall the result was the most complete theory of the TNC so far. I have elsewhere explained this view in detail (Pitelis, 1990a), so I will simply summarize my interpretation of Hymer's views here, compare them briefly with alternative theories and then examine whether my proposed framework in the previous sections can throw any additional light on the issue. A useful approach to

Hymer's views (and the issue of TNCs in general) is to address the questions of why national corporations were *willing and able* to expand overseas, and why they 'chose' DFI over existing market alternatives, such as exports and licensing.

Concerning the ability issue, Hymer observed that by becoming national corporations US firms had acquired a number of 'owner-ship' ('specific or oligopolistic or monopolistic') advantages, such as organizational forms (e.g. the M-form which could allow a firm to become TNC by simply establishing a new division abroad), know-how, product differentiation, access to capital etc. The existence of such advantages gave them a competitive edge over indigenous firms of prospective 'host' countries that was poten-tially sufficient to compensate for the inherent disadvantages of foreign operations – cultural, language, insufficient knowledge of local markets etc. This, along with their enhanced vision and perspective, gave them the ability to expand overseas.

Ability does not imply willingness, which Hymer explained in terms of oligopolistic rivalry and collusion, both within the USA and between the USA on the one hand and European and Japanese firms on the other. Rivalry between US firms could lead them to seek potential sources of advantage, such as cheap labour, new products and new techniques. Overseas investment was a means of obtaining such an advantage and ensuring that others would not do so first. This focus on 'defensive' investment is also emphasized with regard to potential competition by foreign firms, where Hymer regards the US DFI in Europe as a defensive step designed to restrain competition.

These arguments potentially explain international production but not the choice of DFI rather than alternatives such as export-ing and licensing. This Hymer did in terms of the problems associated with the full appropriability of 'quasi-rents' when markets are used, such as licensing; problems with con-tracting arrangements, the desire to control raw materials, and the need to defend the quasi-monopoly of knowledge! Hymer also pointed to firms' needs to expand their production base and divide labour spatially so as to increase their bargaining power and increase their power *vis-à-vis* nation states. He also regarded size and internationality *per se* as advantageous to TNCs. The long-term implication of the multinational corporate capitalist system, Hymer concluded, was a tendency towards 'uneven development' and a tendency for global collusion by TNCs, through interpenetrations of investments.

Later developments of the theory of the TNC all build upon Hymer's theory. Two main schools of thought have emerged in the mainstream literature. Kindleberger, Hymer's, supervisor, has developed in a number of books and articles Hymer's 'oligopolistic advantage' view (see in particular the collection of some of his articles in Kindleberger, 1984). Despite the observation that exploitation of such advantages by firms can help them to restrict competition, and in stark contrast to Hymer, Kindleberger emphasized the efficiency aspects of TNCs' operations, technology transmission to 'host' countries etc. The opposite line, that of monopolization of foreign markets, has been taken by Lall (1980) and Barnet and Müller (1976). In this tradition, a second line of thought emphasized the oligopolistic interaction aspects of TNCs: notably Knickerbrocker (1973) developed the idea of defensive investments, while Graham (1978) regarded cross-investments as an exchange of threats.

The second school of thought, which in part because of Williamson's influence has now gained dominance in the mainstream tradition, is the transaction costs or 'internalization' theory. Main proponents here are Buckley and Casson (1976), Williamson (1981), Teece (1981, 1986), Rugman (1986) and Hennart (1982). This theory emphasizes the transaction costs problems arising when market transactions are used across national boundaries, particularly as regards intangible assets such as know-how, management skills etc. Difficulties associated with the appropriation of quasi-rents from these intangible assets when market transactions are used (for example, because of opportunism) lead to internalization of market transactions and thus to the TNC, rather than exporting or licensing. An appropriability theory, explictly extending Hymer's views, has also been proposed by Magee (1977).

More eclectic views have been adopted by other authors, such as Caves (1971, 1982) and Dunning (1981, 1989, 1990). The former originally developed a monopolistic advantage type theory (Caves, 1971), but then moved on to emphasize the transaction costs approach (Caves, 1982). Dunning, on the other hand, developed an explicitly 'eclectic theory' combining ownership advantages (O), locational factors (L) and internalization (I) as reasons explaining the TNC. Hymer, incidentally, has referred to locational factors, building on earlier work by Dunning (1958). Non-mainstream theories have also been proposed to explain TNCs. Among them, Sugden (1983a, 1990) developed a Marglinian 'divide and rule' approach where TNCs appear in order to reduce the bargaining position of labour both domestically and overseas. The view that the TNC may be leading to a reduction in the bargaining power of nation states is discussed by Murray (1971); see the volume by Radice (1975) and also Pitelis (1991c). These theories stress the (Pareto) inefficiency aspects of the TNC.

A Marxist theory of the TNC has been proposed by Palloix (1976). Palloix's starting point is the competition-induced tendency towards the internationalization of the Marxian circuits of capital (commodity capital, money capital and productive capital). The tendency towards the self-expansion of capital leads to its internationalization, various aspects of which are linked with the capital circuits. Thus, internationalization of commodity capital is associated with world trade, of money capital with international capital movements and of productive capital with TNCs. In this sense the TNC is not seen as 'a phenomenon in its own right, but as an aspect of a broader process of internationalization of capital which tends to create a more integrated world economy' (Jenkins, 1987, p. 34). Palloix stressed the uneven development of TNCs' operations, in line with Hymer's views.

All these theories (mainstream and radical) have focused on the micro (supply-side) aspects of TNCs. A demand-side macroeconomic radical approach is that of Baran and Sweezy (1966). Building on earlier contributions, particularly by Lenin (1917), Luxemburg (1963), Hilferding (1981), Steindl (1952) and Kalecki (1971), Baran and Sweezy proposed that the monopolization of domestic markets in advanced capitalist economies was giving rise to a tendency for an increasing 'surplus'. 'Surplus' comprises all profits plus wasteful expenditures by governments (e.g. armaments) and firms (e.g. advertising, legal fees etc.). Increasing 'surplus' implies a tendency for reduced effective demand, *ceteris paribus*. This provides an incentive to firms to look for overseas markets, and thus internationalization of production.[27] TNCs represent the institutional form (are the agent) of this process.

The main limitation of the mainstream theories is their exclusive focus on the *exchange-side supply-side factors* at the expense of both production-side and macroeconomic considerations.[28] Hymer's focus on the need of TNCs to expand their productive base in their pursuit of (cheap) labour goes a step further. Similarly Palloix's theory advances the debate in arguing that capitalist expansion, internationalization and the TNC are inherent in the process of capital accumulation, and in integrating production and exchange considerations. Sugden's focus on divide and rule is in line with Hymer's focus on production-side issues and provides further insights on the benefits of such policies to TNCs. Baran and Sweezy's approach is helpful in redressing the imbalance arising from the exclusive focus of all the above theories on supply-side considerations alone. Baran and Sweezy and Palloix, however, do not provide any explanation as to why TNCs are preferred to alternative forms of international production, such as licensing arrangements. On this score Hymer's theory is undoubtedly the most complete, especially when seen in conjunction with later advancements of his ideas by mainstream theorists. My framework of conflict (with labour) and rivalry (with other firms) leading firms to look for maximum long-term profits through expansion can provide a synthesis of the theories discussed above. The main elements of this synthesis are discussed in a number of my papers (e.g. Pitelis, 1990b, 1991b), so I will only try to summarize it here.

Conflict with labour necessitates expansion of the productive base of firms. Rivalry with other firms obliges firms to look for competitive advantages in the form of new technologies, cheaper labour, new organizational forms, new products etc. The two types of competition provide an incentive for profits through strategies of cost minimization *and* expansion-growth. The removal of the constraints to growth through share issuing, organizational changes (the M-form) and compulsory socialization of capital ownership (through pension funds) allows firms to grow more and more. Within a national economy, this may lead to a tendency towards monopolization of markets – a tendency potentially facilitated by conscious strategies by firms to obtain and maintain monopoly positions, and reduce entry.[29] If so, monopolization (through shareholding) will tend to increase the proportion of aggregate income controlled by the corporate sector. This will tend to give rise to effective demand problems, providing an additional incentive (over and above the one inherent in firms' striving for expansion of their *productive* base) for internationalization of production, this time on the demand side. 'Choice' of the institutional form of the TNC in this framework can be explained in terms of global cost minimization (i.e. transaction and labour costs minimization) in line with both the transaction costs and divide and rule approaches.

My proposed integration of the existing theories (mainstream and Marxist) is in line with my general proposed framework of a competition-induced striving for long-term profits through expansion of both the production and exchange bases of TNCs, and encompasses transaction and labour costs considerations within this general framework. To be sure, in so doing, the theory emphasizes both (Pareto) efficiency and inefficiency aspects, casting doubt on both the Williamson tradition and any naive anti-TNC rhetoric. The emergence and growth of the TNC will also tend to globalize the very forces that led to its emergence, giving rise to international production, international division of labour, international rivalry between firms, international capital markets and socialization of corporate ownership; and, potentially, international collusion and monopolization, and the need for international state apparatuses, as Hymer predicted. The analysis of these tendencies is beyond the scope of my focus here.

8 Summary and Conclusions

My starting point was that any explanation of the nature of capitalist institutions requires an analysis of the nature of capitalism. Given the commodity nature of labour power under capitalism, any employment relation, seen from the production side, is a hierarchical one. In this sense the transition from the putting-out system to the factory system involved a transition from one form of hierarchy to another. It was the result of the desire of merchant-manufacturers to increase their income (profit) through improvements in the division of labour. This can also explain the very emergence of an employment relationship at all (in conjunction with factors such as the perceived interests of other parties, like the state and the labourers). In this light, organizational knowledge was obtained by merchants in the very process of them becoming manufacturers. They maintained it through secrecy.

My framework suggests that the existence and objectives of firms are inseparable. Firms exist because of the principals' objective to obtain profits. Such profits can be obtained by efficiency improvements and by changes in technology and organization that are often inimical to labour. Efficiency and power considerations are also inseparable, different sides of the same coin.

Once firms exist, conflict between employers and employees and rivalry between different firms sustain the motive to further profits. Expansion and growth by firms is the means of achieving this, particularly given uncertainty. The need by firms to overcome constraints to expansion arising from the product, labour and capital markets, as well as technology and organizational-managerial constraints, can help to explain the evolution of capitalist firms, including the 'managerial revolution', the 'pension funds revolution', the M-form organization and the transnational corporation. The socialization of corporate capital through discretionary and compulsory (pension funds) shareholding is a particularly important stage of the evolution of firms; it arises from firms' attempts to remove constraints in the capital markets, and necessitates a reformulation of the long-term motives of firms, in terms of *retained profits*, subject to maintenance of control by the principals and the avoidance of entry by rivals. The emergence and growth of transnational firms tend to globalize the aforementioned tendencies.

In conclusion, it would appear to be inadvisable to focus only on efficiency aspects of the firm's evolution, as transaction costs theorists invariably do, *or* on power considerations alone, as Marglin and the 'power school' do. Reality is far more complex than unidimensional theories would have us believe.

Notes

1   'New institutional economics' consists of work on the nature and evolution of institutions developed from neoclassical (including game theoretic), 'Chicago school', 'public choice' and Austrian perspectives. The neoclassical contribution includes work on 'property rights' (e.g. Alchian and Demsetz, 1972), and transaction costs

analysis (e.g. North, 1981 on economic history, and Williamson, 1975, 1981, 1985 on the internal organization of firms and the markets–firms juxtaposition). Game theoretic approaches include Schotter's (1981) attempt to explain both political and economic institutions. 'Chicago school' theorists, such as Friedman and Friedman (1980), are interested in the comparative properties of markets versus planning, in particular the state, as are the 'public choice' school and the Austrian school, which is mainly represented by Hayek (1978). Mueller (1989) has an extensive survey of the 'public choice' school, as does D. G. Green (1987). Green also discusses the Austrian and Chicago school approaches. 'New' institutionalism, unlike the 'old' institutionalism (such as the work of Veblen, Commons, Mitchell and Ayres) shares a lot with the mainstream neoclassical perspective; see Hodgson (1989) and Rutherford (1989) for expositions and comparisons between the two.

2   Williamson (1990) quotes R. C. O. Mathews' list, which includes industrial organization and corporate governance, labour economics, public choice, development and economic history.

3   See, for example, Donaldson (1990), and the contributions and debate in Francis et al. (1983), particularly the introduction, and in Aoki et al. (1990), particularly the chapter by Williamson.

4   Other reasons also exist: notably the prominence of 'efficiency' in the Williamson story, which allows it to be seen more as a complement to the neoclassical perspective than an alternative, as he himself acknowledges (Williamson, 1990), and the associated 'policy implications' of this view, on which there is more later.

5   This delay led Coase (1972) to observe that his 1937 paper was much cited, but little used.

6   Kay (1990) observes that these two definitions are not necessarily compatible. He claims that transactions can exist that are not due to any agreements to exchange.

7   The particularly important status of the employment relation is pointed out by, for example, Malcolmson, (1984) and Picot and Wegner (1988). The latter observe that, 'from the beginning, transaction cost analysis found its most important application in the employment relation' (p. 31). However, the main reason for this, that it is only this relation that may be able to explain hierarchies arising from markets, is not observed. Kay (1990) does observe that Williamson's (as opposed to Coase's) comparative basis is one of internal markets versus external markets, or hierarchy versus hierarchy, not market versus hierarchy. In this sense, he concludes, Williamson's analysis involves false hierarchies.

8   Davies (1987) and Williamson (1985), as well as most texts in

industrial organization, have surveys on other explanations of vertical integration.

9   Clarke (1987) has a more detailed summary of the Williamson–Teece thesis and surveys other explanations of the conglomerate.

10   In actual practice, there are many more institutional arrangements for the 'organization of work'. Williamson (1986), for example, examines six – two entrepreneurial (putting-out and federated), two involving collective ownership (communal-emhs and peer group) and two capitalist (inside contracting and the authority relation) – and compares their relative efficiency properties on the basis of transaction costs economizing. The putting-out versus authority relationship has received the lion's share in the literature and will also be employed in this section. Dow (1987) summarizes other types of transactions, such as informal reciprocity arrangements, franchising, long-term contracts, inside contracting, joint ventures and quasi-vertical integration.

11   The question of whether exchange presupposes production or not and the issue of whether single producers qualify as firms are very complex indeed and depend crucially on the definitions of exchange and/or firm one is willing to adopt. Von Mises, for example, considers the possibility of 'autisitic exchange' (e.g. an 'exchange' of leisure for hunting), where no change of property rights takes place, since no other individuals are involved (see Hodgson, 1988). Coase's definition of the firm, moreover, is based exclusively on the existence of an entrepreneur–coordinator (of other people's work), and so differs from Fourie's definition. Marx (1973) argues for the inseparability of production, exchange and distribution. In this sense Fourie's contribution is in making clear the need for unambiguous definitions of terms employed and more importantly in pointing to the importance of production, which transaction costs economists ignore. For this see below.

12   Rutherford (1989) and Kay (1990), among others, have more detailed criticisms of the neo-institutionalists' reliance on evolutionary processes and 'invisible hand' arguments, Kay with particular emphasis on the U-form versus M-form debate.

13   The distinction between structural and 'natural' (or cognitive) market failure, whereby the former is the result of market power reasons, such as structural barriers to entry (scale economies, product differentiation etc.), while the latter is the result of transaction costs, is implicit in the Coase–Williamson programme. It has been introduced and discussed explicitly by Dunning and Rugman (1985).

14   Obviously the fact that Japanese employers behave 'opportunistically' does not in itself invalidate the observation that 'opportunism'

fails to account for a number of human actions, such as charity, blood-giving etc. These issues are discussed in Hodgson (1988).

15 Note that this argument does not contradict Alchian and Demsetz's idea that the 'exit' possibility and the ability of employees to 'order' their principals to pay them wages imply a symmetrical relation between the two. It simply points out that, for the duration of the production process, obeying the principal's directions is part of the employee's contractual requirements.

16 In the limit even autistic 'exchanges' can be said to involve some loss of autonomy. However, this does not involve hierarchy, i.e. loss of autonomy to others. Similarly, the independence of the single person firm is only relative as it is constrained by the need of the person-firm to sell products. Principals (employers) are constrained by the market, customers etc. Again, however, the relationship is not hierarchical, as it does not involve direct authority by others.

17 A further issue arises from the possibility that some cottage-labourers did manage to become capitalists, a historical fact acknowledged by both Marx (1959) and Marglin (1974). In fact cottage-labourers, through their capital ownership, were already capitalists in germ.

18 For this to happen, merchants should be able to sell for more than they bought: because they can buy a product below its 'value' (the socially necessary labour time of average skill embodied in the product as the labour theory of value would have it) or because of the supply–demand and relative scarcity conditions of such products in the markets. I will not enter the 'value' debate here, as it is inconsequential for my analysis. The *existence* of a pool of merchants suffices to make the point that some 'surplus' (however derived) was present. For different theories of value see, for example, Dobb (1973). A consoling (albeit not uncontroversial) view is that of Marglin, who suggests that, 'the essence of capitalist profit does not lie in exchange – a point of view that is now common to virtually all economic theory' (Marglin, 1984, p. 462).

19 Commonly referred to examples are the use of semi-idiotic persons and the specialization of tasks for both workers and low-level supervisors.

20 This is not to say that no capitalist could fail or that no labourer could become a capitalist; rather, from a systemic point of view, organization of production was such that at any particular time the vast majority had to work for a small minority, with little mobility between the two groups. This is still the case (see Edwards, 1979).

21 A reason for this might be that while, in the pre-putting-out era, the choice was between the uncertainty of producing for exchange

versus the certainty of a stable buyer in a relatively autonomous setting, in the transition from putting-out to the factory an existing relatively stable income derived in a relatively autonomous setting would need to be exchanged for a non-appreciable increase in the expected stability of income, with a substantial reduction in the degree of autonomy.

22 This is not to deny the importance of other motives, such as control over others, power, prestige etc. In a capitalist economy, however, these can plausibly be suggested to be positively and strongly related to profits. For discussions see Schumpeter (1942) and Eichner (1976).

23 The similarity between the two models is also observed by Putterman (1986), who, however, attributes their apparent differences to their different assumptions concerning the conditions of the labour market. 'Once market conditions are made explicit . . . the radical theory . . . translates sensibly into the "mainstream" terminology' (Putterman, 1986, p. 27).

24 Unless of course, the long run is seen as a sequence of short runs, as in Kalecki (1971). In this case it could be argued that firms try to maximize long run profits, by trying to maximize profits at any point in time (the short run).

25 Reasons for this can be the non-availability of sufficient finance through the capital market or a preference for internal over external finance (an internalization of the capital market). Reasons for the latter can be that the availability of internal finance helps firms raise more external finance (as argued by Kalecki, 1971), and that firms may prefer internal to external finance because of uncertainties or inefficiencies in the external capital markets, *à la* Williamson. There is substantial evidence to suggest that firms do prefer internal to external funding: see, for example, the discussion in Auerbach (1988).

26 Other hypotheses on the emergence and growth of occupational pensions in the UK are discussed in Green (1982) and Pitelis (1985b). Further issues are also covered there, such as labour's attitude towards such funds.

27 A more detailed discussion of Baran and Sweezy's 'theory of crisis' and other related theories is in chapter 5.

28 A number of 'macroeconomic' mainstream theories have been proposed in the literature; see Cantwell (1990) for a survey. However they do not consider aggregate demand side-issues as here.

29 These issues are discussed in detail in chapter 3.

3

Competition, Monopoly and Prices

1 Introduction

Does the emergence and evolution of capitalist firms lead to increasingly monopolized markets, nationally and internationally, or is it the case that firms' objectives and actions render capitalist economies increasingly more competitive? How does an answer to this question affect our views on the performance of capitalist economies?

Since the emergence of economics as a discipline the above questions have been at the heart of the debate from economists of all ideological spectra. The first, the 'competition versus monopoly' debate, was a major preoccupation of classical economists of the standing of Adam Smith and Karl Marx, as well as many others. Along with the issue of 'performance', it has been elevated to a new field of study more recently: industrial organization (IO).

Despite the immense theoretical input in this area, views are as divided as ever. An important reason for this is that the terms competition and monopoly can often mean different things to different people and in different theories. In this sense, there is a very real need to examine what these concepts entail, so that a clearer understanding can be obtained. A second reason is the rather restrictive focus of IO theorists on a limited aspect of the problem, namely that of competition and monopoly as different types of *market structure*. This is in stark contrast to virtually all other ideological perspectives, which tend to regard competition as a *dynamic process*. The two views can lead to diametrically opposed conclusions concerning firm pricing behaviour and the performance of industry and the economy. However, ideas that differences are to be found only *between* perspectives could not be further from the truth. Differences *within* perspectives are as great. The monopoly – competition debate genuinely cuts across economic ideologies with Marxists 'agreeing' with Austrians, Austrians with neoclassicals and the latter with (some) Marxists. Paradoxically this ability of the mainstream perspective to incorporate, in part, alternative ideas can explain, to a degree, its predominance.

In the next section I discuss the concepts of competition and monopoly in the various ideological perspectives and traditions. In section 3 I briefly expound the main tenets of the neoclassical tradition and discuss three models of IO developed within it, in order to explain the structure, conduct and performance of industry. Following this, in section 4 I explore some links between the neoclassical models and Austrian, post-Keynesian and Marxist views. In section 5 I discuss the impact of market structure on the emergence of the transnational corporation (TNC) and the impact of TNCs on domestic and international market structure. Some empirical evidence is discussed in section 6 to throw some light on the issues in hand. Implications and conclusions are in section 7.

2   Competition and Monopoly in Economic Theory

For John Stuart Mill the 'principle of competition' is political economy's only pretension to being a science: 'So far as rents, profits, wages, prices, are determined by competition, laws may be assigned for them. Assume competition to be their exclusive regulator, and principles of broad generality and scientific precision may be laid down according to which they will be regulated' (quoted in Eatwell, 1982, p. 242). Competition here is between capitalists (firms) and can be restricted through natural monopolies, legal restraints, and the unwillingness of people free to compete to do so, for 'custom and usage' reasons (Loasby, 1990).

Mill's ideas were influenced by Adam Smith (1776), one of the 'two most celebrated figures in the history of the subject'

(Galbraith, 1987, p. 58). – the other being Karl Marx – and arguably the father of modern mainstream views on the subject. Smith derives his tendency for the 'natural price' (associated with the average rates of wages, rents and profits) from the ubiquitous force of competition, for he considers the 'natural' price as that of 'free competition' (Eatwell, 1982, p. 205). The effectiveness of competition, for Smith, depends both on the absence of monopolistic restrictions and 'on individual attitudes and initiatives' (Loasby, 1990, p. 213). All merchants and manufacturers welcome profit, but some are more assiduous in seeking it. Smith's mistrust of monopoly and more generally of any restrictions on trade (domestic and international) is neatly summarized in the following passage: 'People of the same trade seldom meet together, even for merriment and diversion, but the conversation ends in a conspiracy against the public or in some contrivance to raise prices' (Smith, 1776, book 1, chapter 10, part 2).

Smith's conception of competition ('perfect liberty'), Eatwell (1982) explains, consists of the mobility of labour stock between different uses. All, capitalists, workers and landlords, are active agents of this mobility. In Ricardo (1817), on the other hand, the emphasis shifts decidedly towards the distinctive role of capital. For Marx (1959), emphasis on capital is retained. Indeed, 'competition becomes synonymous with the generalization of capitalist relations of production' (Eatwell, 1982, p. 208). Free competition represents the real development of capital and it tends to increase as capitalism develops. Competition is the force behind the establishment of a general rate of profit, through a removal of restrictions on the mobility of capital. In this sense, competition refers to accumulation as a whole (production, exchange, distribution) and not to exchange alone. Mobility of resources becomes the crucial determinant of the degree of competition (Jenkins, 1987).

In the Marxian sense of competition, increases in it need not imply the absence of monopoly. Instead, competition is viewed as the very driving force behind the tendency towards concentration and centralization of capital. Monopoly and competition, however, are not polar opposites, but a real-life example of dialectics: 'In practial life we find not only competition, monopoly and the antagonism between them, but also the synthesis of the two, which is not a formula but a movement. Monopoly produces competition, competition produces monopoly . . . monopoly can only maintain itself by continually entering the struggle of competition' (Marx, quoted in Jenkins, 1987, pp. 45–6). The two major forms that competition assumes in the Marxist scheme are between capital and labour (for the extraction of surplus value) and between different capitals (for the appropriation of surplus value realized as profit).

In the Austrian tradition, competition is viewed as a process of discovery. Hayek (1978), one of the most prominent contributors, considers competition as a method of discovering particular facts relevant to the achievement of specific temporary purposes, and considers the benefits arising from such a discovery as generally transient. Littlechild (1988) considers two types of market process within this tradition: broadly, the Austrian-type (e.g. Kirzner, 1973), which focuses on market participants discovering and reacting to new opportunities on the basis of known or unknown data; and the radical subjectivist type (e.g. Shackle, 1969), which focuses on action taken 'in the light of *imagined* future conditions, and hence emphasizes creativity and uncertainty' (Littlechild, 1988, p. 58). In both of these, expected profit is the motive behind successful entrepreneurship. Any such profit, however, is bound to be short-lived because of the competitive process.

The concept of competition as a process is shared by Schumpeter. Drawing on Marx, Schumpeter considers capitalism as a system that is not and cannot be stationary. 'The opening up of new markets, foreign or domestic, and the organizational development from the craft shop and factory to such concerns as US Steel illustrate the same process of industrial mutation . . . that incessantly revolutionizes the economic structure *from within*, incessantly destroying the old one, incessantly creating a new one. This process of Creative Destruction is the essential fact about capitalism' (Schumpeter, 1942, p. 83, emphasis in original). What counts more for Schumpeter is not existing price competition but competition from 'the new commodity, the new technology, the new source of supply, the new type of organization . . . competition which commands a decisive cost or quality advantage' (p. 84). This competition 'acts not only when in being, but also when it is merely an ever-present threat. It disciplines before it attacks. . . . In many cases, though not in all, this will in the long run enforce behaviour very similar to the perfectly competitive pattern' (p. 85). Monopolistic situations, as a result, are rare and in general 'no cushion to sleep on' (p. 102). Although *in the short run* genuine monopoly positions are not rare, in the longer term they can only be retained by alertness and energy. In this light any genuine monopoly gains are the 'prizes offered by capitalist society to the successful innovator' (p. 102).

Common to all the above theories is the idea of competition as a dynamic process. In all cases the motive is profit, however derived (production or exchange). This is in stark contrast to the neoclassical view, which regards competition as a state, or a type of market structure. In its purest form, *perfect competition* is taken to be characterized by the absence of rivalry. No entry barriers in an industry, large numbers of buyers and sellers and homogenous products lead to price-taking behaviour by firms. In a less restrictive version, *imperfect competition* (Robinson, 1933; Chamberlin, 1933) allows firms some power over pricing through the effects of their advertising and selling activities on demand. At the other end of the spectrum lies monopoly, a situation with one firm, no entry and thus downward sloping firm (equals industry) demand curves.

An element of dynamics (a type of implicit process) enters the neoclassical tradition from the kind of imperfect competition called duopoly or oligopoly (two and few sellers respectively). Oligopoly is a type of market structure characterized by interdependence. Oligopolists' decisions are influenced by (their expectations concerning) the behaviour of competitors. Such behaviour therefore needs to be analysed. From this analysis hints concerning an implicit process from competition to monopoly can be obtained. In this sense imperfect competition and oligopoly are the forerunners of IO theory, which tries to analyse the structure, conduct and performance of industries on neoclassical lines. A focus on conduct, as well as structure, also underlies Clark's (1940) idea of '*workable competition*', under which some positive 'degree of monopoly' is allowed to exist in most industries, with action on structure and conduct by, for example, the state helping to make it workable (as opposed to the unworkability of the perfect competition model) (Reid, 1987). Despite its manifest difference to the views of such a diverse and prominent set of economists, as Marx, Hayek and Schumpeter, the neoclassical 'quantity theory of competition', as Weeks (1981) calls it, has remained the dominant approach in economics in general and IO in particular. In part this is because of its simplicity and the related property of analytical rigour. A second reason, however, is that IO models have gradually succeeded in incorporating parts of alternative ideas, adding a degree of realism to the basic structure, as shown in the next section.

The alternative views on competition and monopoly can often lead to different conclusions concerning the issue of increasing or declining competition in capitalism, simply for semantic reasons. This is rarely appreciated, with the associated result of different answers to the same question depending on different underlying implicit definitions of competition. An example from the Marxist tradition is that of Baran and Sweezy (1966) and Clifton (1977). The former focus on the oligopolistic nature of modern capitalist industries and, stressing their collusive behaviour, can claim that monopoly replaces competition as a *type of market structure*. Clifton, on the other hand, focuses on the Marxist definition of the degree of capital mobility and concludes that from this point of view competition under capitalism is increasing, as the modern corporation involves much greater capital mobility than the small atomistic firms of earlier capitalism (see Jenkins, 1987). It would seem here that the two sides simply answer a different question, and therefore it is not legitimate to criticize one in terms of the other, as, for example, Auerbach (1988) does. As already noted, for Marx increasing concentration and centralization (thus potentially oligopolistic market structures) and increasing competition in the sense of capital mobility can go hand in hand. More to the point, the latter leads to the former. It is possible to claim that focus on market structures alone runs the important risk of under-emphasizing the production process and leads to a restrictive view of monopoly power as *market power* (Jenkins, 1987). However, this is not in itself a reason for not analysing market structures as long as it is recognized that market power is only one aspect of monopoly power, and that the underlying conditions in the process of production should not be forgotten.

A related source of confusion in the Marxist tradition arises from the use of the term competition in its 'rivalry between firms' sense. If such rivalry is observed to decline (lead to collusion), as, for example, Hymer (in Cohen et al., 1979) claims, it need not be the case that competition in its broader sense, which incorporates 'conflict' with labour, also declines. Indeed collusion (reduction of competition in the rivalry sense) almost by definition leads to increasing competition in its conflict sense. It also recreates the conditions for increased rivalry when firms attempt to appropriate the potentially increased realized surplus due to collusion.

In light of the above, my focus here will initially be on competition as a type of market structure. Increasing centralization and concentration of capital will thus be viewed as *ceteris paribus* reductions in competition (in the sense of increasing collusion, but not reduction in capital mobility). I will then analyse the effects of departures from the competitive structures on pricing behaviour, and industry profitability, in neoclassical, Austrian, post-Keynesian and Marxist models of industry organization. Broader considerations will be discussed in the final section.

3 Neoclassical Models of Industrial Organization

Departures from the neoclassical perfectly competitive norm are the result of increasing concentration: the number and size distribution of firms in an industry. Concentration increases are normally viewed as a result of three main factors: the size of the market, scale economies, and barriers to entry (anything that prevents new entrants from entering an industry). The relationship between concentration and market size is expected to be negative and that between concentration and scale economies or barriers to entry positive. Concentration can refer to a market or the economy as a whole (or a sector of it, like manufacturing). The latter is called aggregate concentration. The explanation for aggregate concentration in the neoclassical tradition is on much the same lines as that for market concentration. A major difference is that aggregate concentration can increase even when market concentration does not, for example by conglomerate mergers.

Historically, both market and aggregate concentration tended to increase in advanced capitalist countries – see for example Clarke (1985) and Geroski and Jacquemin (1989) for some evidence. This tendency slowed down in the USA after the late 1940s. Between 1947 and 1972, Scherer (1980) observes, the share of the four largest firms (four firm concentration ratio) in a sample of 154 four-digit manufacturing industries increased from 39.7 per cent to only 41.5 per cent. However, aggregate concentration in US manufacturing (measured by the largest 200 manufacturing firms in terms of assets) increased from 48.2 to 60.0 per cent. Given the data on market concentration, the increase can be attributed to diversification (Clarke, 1987).

In the UK, on the other hand, market concentration *and* aggregate concentration were on the increase during that period: average three firm employment concentration in UK manufacturing net output went up from 22 per cent in 1951 to 41 per cent in 1968; and the share of the 100 largest firms in manufacturing output increased from 29 per cent in 1951 to 41 per cent in 1968. Ninety per cent of the 1963–8 increase has been attributed to increases in market concentration, suggesting that diversification and conglomeration were less prominent in the UK than in the USA (Clarke, 1987). Still, observed increases in concentration raise a number of important questions concerning pricing by concentrated (oligopolistic) industries, and thus industry and economy performance, and the impact of these on consumers' welfare. The branch of economics developed to answer these questions is that of industrial economics or industrial organization (IO).

Neoclassical industrial organization is based on versions of the so-called structure–conduct–performance (SCP) 'paradigm'. According to it there is a largely unidirectional causal link between the structure of the industry (concentration, barriers to entry, product differentiation etc.), the conduct of the industry (pricing policies, advertising, strategic behaviour etc.) and the performance of the industry (profitability, efficiency etc.), the causality going from S to C to P. Given the obvious interconnections – for example, advertising being a potential barrier to entry, or profitability attracting entry or instead helping incumbents to raise entry barriers – feedback relationships have gradually been allowed in the model; Scherer (1980) provides detailed discussions.

The theoretical link between market structure and performance goes back to the oligopoly model of Cournot. Under the assumption that oligopolistic firms take the quantity of rivals as given, Cournot predicted a continuous monotonic relationship between concentration and departures from perfect competition, the latter arising in the case of large numbers, and monopoly emerging with one firm. The Cournot model's major rival was the model by Bertrand, which, assuming price-setting behaviour, derived competitive behaviour with the presence of only two firms (see Cubbin, 1988, for further discussion). Both models have the useful property of 'Nash-equilibrium', a situation where each firm optimizes given the strategy pursued by its rival. Despite their 'naive' assumptions, and other problems,[1] the Cournot–Bertrand models have formed the basis of recent theoretical developments in the SCP tradition. The first such model, that of limit pricing, was developed by Bain (1956), Sylos-Labini (1962) and Modigliani (1958). Its main innovative feature is that it allows barriers to entry of the structural type (e.g. economies of scale) to affect pricing by incumbent firms in the industry. Interestingly, however, the threat of potential entry by rival firms in the industry is also allowed to affect the pricing decisions of incumbents. As a result, incumbents can be said to pursue a policy of constrained profit maximization (Sawyer, 1982b), that is to maximize profits subject to no entry taking place. To achieve this, incumbents use price as their policy variable, as in Bertrand.

More specifically, following Modigliani's (1958) classic synthesis, I assume the existence of economies of scale, giving rise to a minimum efficient scale – that is, an output level below which entrants will suffer a cost disadvantage, and thus are assumed not to enter. Given this, and under the Sylos postulate that incumbents do not change post-entry output and entrants know this to be the case, entry is effectively impeded when the incumbents charge a limit price, consistent with the rule, $Q_L = Q_C - \bar{Q}$, where Q_L is the limit output, Q_C the perfectly competitive output and $\bar{Q}$ the minimum efficient scale of the industry-entrant.[2] Modigliani has shown that the limit price P_L will be positively related to $\bar{Q}$ and negatively to Q_C (the size of the market) and the industry elasticity of demand, η. On the other hand, the limit pricing model can be expressed in terms of price-cost margins (the ratio of the variation of price from marginal costs to the price), $P - MC/P$, where MC is marginal costs; in the model, this will be related positively to $\bar{Q}$ and to $Q_C - \bar{Q}$) and negatively to η (Clarke, 1985). A dynamic version of the limit pricing model is that of Gaskins (1971), who argued that incumbents will try to regulate the rate of entry rather than blockade it, sacrificing gradually their market share in order to maximize their wealth.

In more recent years limit pricing has experienced a revival following the re-interpretation by Milgrom and Roberts (1982). In this model a limit price can be used to signal the existence of a cost advantage by incumbents, provided the entrant has incomplete information concerning the incumbents' costs. The problem here is that a rational entrant may perceive this, which may induce the incumbent to change strategy, and so on. As Fudenberg and Tirole (1986) observe, we are led to an infinite regress situation and the possibility of multiple equilibria. This allows very few general conclusions, but has been used to suggest that limit pricing may not be detrimental to welfare (i.e. higher prices than with perfect competition) (Tirole, 1988). In fact it is doubtful whether limit pricing ever did have any strong implications of this sort, given that its overall implication is that, in general, prices will be below the joint profit maximum (Cowling, 1982). In the limit, if entry below $\bar{Q}$ is allowed, the perfectly competitive outcome obtains even in the conventional version of the static model.

The model by Cowling and Waterson (1976)[3] starts from the assumption that entry need not be a problem for the incumbents, who can therefore maximize short-run profits, unconstrained by the fear of entry. The model is based on Cournot-type behaviour, but takes the *reactions* of rivals, rather than the output of rivals, as given (Cubbin, 1988). Under the assumption of a constant conjectural variation (expected response by firm j to output change by firm i (see Clarke and Davies, 1982), it is shown that the price cost margin in the industry (or the profit share, assuming fixed MC), is positively related to the degree of concentration (measured by the Herfindahl index of concentration, H, i.e. the sum of squared firm sizes) and the degree of collusion by incumbents (α), and negatively related to the industry elasticity of demand, η.[4] In the limiting cases where $\alpha = 0$ and $\alpha = 1$ respectively (the Cournot and joint-profit maximizing assumptions), the price cost margin will equal $H/2$ and $1/\eta$ respectively.

The Cowling–Waterson model is the structure, performance specification *par excellence*, as it links theoretically concentration and profitability, the almost exclusive concern of early industrial economics (see Curry and George, 1983, and Cubbin, 1988, for surveys). It has led to a number of extensions and criticisms; most notable, perhaps, among the latter is the observation that the relationship need not imply a causal link from conduct and structure to performance, as Cowling and Waterson assumed. Clarke and Davies (1982), for example, show that profits and H are jointly determined. Fine and Murfin (1984b) criticize the restrictiveness of the 'competition' concept adopted by Cowling and Waterson.[5]

The third theoretical model of IO is that of contestable markets, as proposed by Baumol et al. (1982) and Baumol (1982). The model is a more sophisticated version of the Bertrand oligopoly model (Cubbin, 1988), but focuses on the role of *potential entry*. The main starting point is the very opposite of the Cowling–Waterson one: that entry is all that matters. For a perfectly contestable market four assumptions need to be satisfied. First, all producers should have access to the same technology. Second, scale economies such as fixed costs are allowed but not sunk costs (costs arising from the existence of specific assets of limited redeployment use and/or resale value). Third, incumbents cannot change prices instantly. Fourth, consumers respond to market differences instantaneously. Under these assumptions entry will be free and exit costless. Given this, contestability implies price-taking behaviour, as in perfect competition. The reason is that the absence of cost minimization and/or the presence of 'excess' profits or cross-subsidization will attract (profitable) entry. Exit will follow costlessly when and if retaliation occurs. Overall this will establish efficient industry configurations. This generalizes the perfectly competitive norm even in the absence of large numbers and also in the presence of economies of scale and scope (Dixit, 1982; Spence, 1983). This endogenizes market structure. Put differently, it breaks the link between structure and performance.

The contestable markets model has been criticized extensively, particularly for its patently unrealistic assumptions. An irony worth noting is that contestability gained interest and enjoyed wide discussion at the very same time that Williamson's (1975, 1981) markets and hierarchies programme was enjoying similar recognition. In contrast to contestability, markets and hierarchies are based on the explicit observation of pervasive asset specificity, which is assumed to lead to market failure because of high market transaction costs. Also notable is that contestability flies in the face of all earlier IO theory, which Dixit (1982), among others, observes to be based on the presumption that prices can be changed more quickly than sunk capacity (see also Gilbert, 1988). Despite these and other criticisms (disregard of externalities, strategic behaviour, irreversibilities, consistency of assumptions etc. – summarized in, among others, Shepherd, 1984, 1985; C. Green, 1987; Gilbert, 1988), contestability appears to have achieved substantial recognition as a benchmark, more realistic than perfect competition, against which real-life situations should be compared.[6] Spence (1983) suggests that the model may also have wider applicability in real life, if it is the case that barriers to entry are not durable in the long run.

From this last statement, and the overall discussion, it becomes clear that the relative strengths of the three models considered here depend heavily on their assumptions concerning entry and, more specifically, the importance of barriers to entry in the short and long run, as well as the importance of potential competition. The limit pricing model lies between its two rivals in allowing the simultaneous existence of barriers to entry and potential entry.[7] Its potential limitation is that it focuses on economies of scale alone – although it can be extended to other such barriers, such as product differentiation and advertising (Gilbert 1988) – that is, it ignores the possibility of strategic barriers by incumbents.[8] Obviously this is also true for contestability.

Strategic barriers is Cowling's (1982) starting point in his attempt to provide a justification of the no entry assumption, asserted in the original Cowling and Waterson (1976) model. This is done on the basis of the idea that incumbents may undertake strategic investment in excess capacity. This idea has a very long history. Schumpeter (1942) was the first to notice the possibility of investment in excess capacity. According to Schumpeter this is in order to 'build ahead of demand' or to provide capacity for cyclical peaks. This he calls 'strategic', although he does not take it to imply an attempt to prevent entry.

The possibility of non-strategic excess capacity being a barrier to entry is first discussed by Steindl (1952). More recently Eichner (1976) has specifically criticized the limit pricing model for ignoring capacity expansions ahead of demand that are intended to forestall the possibility of barriers to entry being overcome by growing industry demand. Eichner traces the argument back to Dewey (1959): 'For Dewey, the probability of entry depends on whether there is excess capacity in the industry, this probability being close to zero when the established firms have sufficient excess capacity to supply whatever share of the market the potential entrant might hope to capture' (Eichner, 1976, p. 106). In more recent years the literature on strategic entry deterrence (mainly of the excess capacity type) has proliferated, following the influential article by Spence (1977). Gilbert (1988), Lieberman (1987) and Paraskevopoulos and Pitelis (1990) have detailed discussions. Briefly, the argument is that capacity expansions of the strategic type can deter entry, if the commitment is credible. For such commitments to be credible they should be optimal for the incumbent to carry out post-entry (Dixit, 1982). When this is the case, strategic capacity pre-entry alters the conditions of any post-entry game in a way favourable to incumbents.

There are other types of deterrence strategies. One is investment in a reputation for toughness. Entry challenges here are fought even when it is not optimal for the incumbent to do so, so that future entries are deterred (see Waterson, 1984, for discussion). Predatory behaviour towards existing rivals can also help to establish reputation, and thus deter entry. Using product proliferation, an incumbent crowds the product market with a variety of brands so as to leave little space to entrants. This strategy combines product differentiation with fixed set-up costs (Geroski and Jacquemin, 1989). As Geroski and Jacquemin observe, incumbency is associated with 'first mover advantages' such as the above, which 'may allow dominant market position to be maintained for long periods which are relatively free from entry challenges' (p. 313). Thus a relative separability is established between incumbents' price output decisions and the decision on what to do about entry.[9] The possibility of successful strategic entry deterrence raises doubts on the limit pricing and contestable markets models, provided, of course, that it is observed in real life. To be sure, the very possibility of its adoption depends on a number of factors, most notably the field and nature of the potential entrants. It has been observed for sometime (see Eichner, 1976, for example) that it makes a difference whether potential entrants are new firms or established firms in other industries. In the latter case entry may take place even in the presence of credible commitments, as entrants may believe that they can win the day in a prospective price war.

A deterrent to such entry may arise from the possibility of inter-industry collusion (Pitelis, 1990c). This is the case where incumbents whose positions are threatened by potential entry from other industries are themselves threatening to enter these latter industries. This could provide a rivalry-induced incentive for inter-industry collusion. In general such collusion would be more likely to exist where there was a relative parity in the abilities of firms to inflict mutual damage. This allows the following useful classification. Incumbents in one industry may enter another, if the incumbents of the latter are smaller firms with limited ability to retaliate through cross-entry. This possibility implies that in industries where the pool of potential entrants includes big established firms in different industries, the incentive to pursue excess capacity type strategies will be reduced, given the futility of such strategies. Similarly, when the pool of potential entrants only includes small firms, relative to the incumbents, the incentive to build excess capacity will be limited. Non-strategic barriers or the fear of predatory pricing post-entry may suffice to put the entrants off in this case. It follows that excess capacity investments may only be useful where incumbents and elsewhere-established potential entrants are relatively equal. In this case, however, the possibility of inter-industry collusion can still provide some support to the Spence-justified Cowling–Waterson ideas.

The above discussion does not aim to suggest that in industries where potential entry and exit are easy, limit pricing or contestability are likely. A reason for this may be uncertainty concerning whether and when entry will take place. Such uncertainty may lead incumbents to joint-profit maximizing pricing, so as to enjoy excess profits for as long as they are available and then to accommodate or fight an entrant post-entry. Furthermore, even when potential entry is very real it may pay incumbents to behave as joint-profit maximizers pre-entry and perfect competitors post-entry rather than as perfect competitors throughout. In the former case an additional profit would have been earned (Pitelis, 1990c).

The last mentioned possibility relates to an argument going back to Schumpeter (1942). In an ironic anticipation of attempts to apply in the short run his ideas concerning the long-run disciplining power of potential competition (which contestability theory does), Schumpeter observes that 'perfectly free entry into a new field makes it impossible to enter it at all' (p. 105). The reason, he explains, is that the introduction of new commodities or production methods is inconceivable with perfect competition from the start, in that the latter defeats the very motive for operating at all in such a field. In a similar vein, Dasgupta and Stiglitz (1988, p. 573) suggest that 'a firm's incentive to undertake the risk of entering a market . . . will be diminished, if it believes that if it is initially successful in doing so other firms will simply enter the market to take its profits away'. They conclude that potential competition is far less able to achieve and maintain efficiency than usually thought. In fact, they continue, the presence of many firms in the market is itself a less than adequate means of discipline, as collusion can be chosen over price competition.

The above discussion suffices, I believe, to make the point that it will normally take no less than *actual rivalry* (entry and exit) for incumbents to resort to competitive pricing. Moreover, even when such rivalry is present, one should not disregard the possibility that rivalry will lead to collusion. The existence of such rivalry, in all cases moreover, is an empirical question and has to be shown to be true before any credibility can be attached to the contestable markets story. The discussion here would appear instead to lend some support to the Cowling–Waterson model, albeit for reasons often different from those proposed by Cowling (1982), in particular inter-industry collusion and the 'unprofitability' of entry in industries approximating the contestability ideal.

To the extent that this is true, the neoclassical perspective derives some *static* social welfare losses from high concentration (monopoly or oligopoly power). Such static losses are reinforced if one accepts Arrow's (1962) analysis, according to which monopolies have a lower incentive to *invent* than perfectly competitive firms. Arrow bases his prediction on the observation that monopolists earn a positive profit (Π') pre-invention while competitive firms do not. Given this and assuming that post-invention both monopolists and competitors can charge the monopoly price (for a patent) and thus earn the same profit (Π), the monopolists' incentive to invent will be ($\Pi - \Pi'$), which is less than Π, the profit of the perfect competitor.[10] On the other hand, on the positive side Williamson (1968) has suggested that monopolists should be expected to have lower unit costs than perfect competitors. If this is true, then there is an efficiency gain due to monopoly, which should be 'traded-off' against any welfare losses due to market power.[11] Another argument in favour of monopoly is based on the Coase (1937) and Williamson (1975, 1981) markets and hierarchies framework. According to this, monopoly can be the result of market transaction costs reductions. To the extent this is true, one should not be comparing monopolistic market structures to perfectly competitive market structures but rather efficient hierarchies (monopolies) to inefficient markets.

The Coase–Williamson perspective introduces an element of dynamic analysis to the static neoclassical model. Additional such elements relate to the concept of *international competitiveness* and the so-called Schumpeterian hypothesis that monopolies have a higher rate of innovations than perfectly competitive firms. International competitiveness relates to the idea that big concerns can be more competitive in international markets because of their exploitation of scale economies and research and development capabilities. This implies that any short-run welfare losses of domestic consumers might be offset by positive dynamic gains arising from increased export surpluses. This expectation underlies much of the European Community's stance towards big size and mergers in the late 1960s and early 1970s (see Geroski and Jacquemin, 1989, and Pitelis, 1991d, for detailed discussions).

The Schumpeterian hypothesis has been interpreted by neo-classicists to imply that monopoly power provides ability to big firms to *innovate*. A wide range of reasons is offered: the existence of finance, in the form of retained profits; the ability to secure patents; the ability to pay and thus attract good scientists; the possible existence of a minimum efficient scale of research laboratories; and the uncertainty of the research and development (R & D) outcome, which implies that multi-product diversified firms have a better chance of making use of unexpected inventions (Utton, 1982). To the extent that this is true, dynamic gains from monopoly may suffice to offset any static losses to consumers; see also Scherer (1980) for a discussion of cases, such as the benefits from Xeroxing.

4 Alternative Perspectives

Depressing as it may sound, the neoclassical perspective is but one of many; to be sure, the dominant one. Alternative perspectives include the Marxist, the post-Keynesian/Kaleckian and the Chicago school/Austrian.[12]

As already noted, Marx (1959) was the first well known economist to propose a 'law' of increasing concentration and centralization of capital. The underlying reason for this is the conflict with labour and rivalry with other capitalists. These lead to the need to expand the productive base and the market, and thus to technological change, in Marx of the labour-saving type. Such change results in an increasing importance of large-scale production, which generates cost advantages to big firms, thus reducing the scope for smaller firms in markets. Joint-stock companies allow further expansion of giant firms, through the use of other people's money. The fear of potential competition leads to integration, diversification and conglomeration, so that monopoly positions can be maintained. Crises further facilitate the process, by eliminating weak firms.

Extending the Marxian insight, as developed particularly by Hilferding (1981), Baran and Sweezy (1966) proposed that the extent of concentration in most markets of advanced capitalist economies is such that one could legitimately take the giant firm as the unit of analysis and assume that most industries behave in a way very similar to that of the simple monopoly model of neoclassical theory! Developing Sweezy's (1942) earlier 'kinked demand curve' model of oligopoly, Baran and Sweezy observe that price reductions will tend to be matched by rival firms in an industry and thus to give rise to potentially reduced market shares through price wars. This provides an incentive to oligopolists to collude so as to obtain the joint-profit maximum and to try to keep potential rivals out of the markets by raising barriers to entry. Competition in this scenario can take forms other than price, such as advertising and sales promotions expenditures.

Non-price competition, joint-profit maximization and barriers to entry together imply the monopoly price. In this the Baran–Sweezy Marxian account is perfectly in line with the Cowling–Waterson model, if we assume a degree of collusion equal to unity in the latter. This apparently paradoxic 'coincidence' disappears when it is observed that both Baran and Sweezy and Cowling and Waterson build upon earlier work by, particularly, Kalecki (1971) and Steindl (1952). Kalecki, who is generally recognized to have had a two- or three-year lead over Keynes in proposing the main tenets of the General Theory (within an imperfectly competitive framework in contrast to Keynes's reliance on perfectly competitive markets), had proposed the price-cost margin as a measure of monopoly power in an industry, his 'degree of monopoly'.[13] Kalecki suggested a number of factors that influence the degree of monopoly – industrial concentration, sales promotion activities, trade unions, and the relation of overheads to prime costs – but provided no theoretical link between these factors based on a model of oligopoly behaviour.[14] A reason for this, I believe, is Kalecki's conviction that given uncertainties in the process of price fixing, it was illegitimate to assume that firms could maximize profits 'in any precise sort of manner' (1971, p. 44). Yet this was exactly the assumption required to produce such a link. As already seen, Cowling and Waterson did exactly this, thus providing a formalization of the Kaleckian theory and simultaneously of the Baran and Sweezy theory. Given this the model has more recently gained a prominent position in the post-Keynesian/Kaleckian perspective (see Sawyer, 1985; Reynolds, 1987).

The other major model explicitly developed within the post-Keynesian/Kaleckian tradition is that of Eichner (1976; see also Eichner and Kregel, 1976). Eichner assumes growth of profits maximization, which he considers as consistent with the growth of other variables, as well as with long-run profit maximization. Given this aim, pricing policies take place with an eye to raising internal funds sufficient to finance expected investment expenditure. Average variable costs are assumed to be constant up to the full capacity level of output. A certain degree of excess capacity is assumed, in the form of firms typically operating at a level less than full capacity, defined as the 'standard operating ratio' (SOR). A price-leader is assumed to exist, who estimates SOR and then adds to it a mark-up sufficient to cover fixed costs (which include dividends as the price of internal finance, but exclude expenditures designed to maintain or enhance the giant firm's – megacorp's – long run position in the market) and the 'corporate levy', which is the amount of internally available funds for investment.

Despite the presence of a certain degree of excess capacity, and explicit recognition on his part of the entry-preventing role of building ahead of demand, Eichner takes into account potential entry in the form of an implicit interest rate for internal funds. Other factors affecting this rate are 'substitution effects' and 'government intervention'. The former accounts for the influence exerted by the industry elasticity of demand, as in conventional pricing models. Government intervention 'in all its possible forms' (Eichner and Kregel, 1976, p. 1307) is considered to incorporate 'an exogenous political factor'. All three factors constrain the megacorp's pricing discretion. The higher the mark-up, the greater will be the cost (implicit interest rate) to the firm of an internal investment fund, leading firms to external borrowing when the implicit interest rate exceeds that available in the financial markets. The corporate levy is determined by incorporating a marginal efficiency of investment schedule (demand for additional investment funds). For as long as the marginal efficiency of investment schedule lies at, or on the right of, the intersection point between the implicit interest rate and the market interest rate, the megacorp will be able to increase the mark-up to its maximum rate, which is determined by the equality point between the internal (implicit) and external interest rates.

The Eichner model's novel features (focus on long-run profit maximization, which, however, collapses to a mark-up type behaviour,[15] pricing with an eye to investment, allowance for inter-industry rivalry through the substitution factor[16] and government policies through the government factor, as well as its definition of fixed costs) do not permit easy comparisons with other models. What can be said is that the allowance for an 'entry factor' implies that in general megacorps will not charge the joint-profit maximum, and thus adopt a form of limit pricing (see also Reynolds, 1989). Given the very complex nature of the factors involved it is also impossible to say where in the competition–monopoly range the 'limit price' will lie. Given the long run nature of the model and the Kaleckian observation that, in view of uncertainties, the short-run profit maximum may be infeasible or unknown, it could be suggested that Eichner's model is nearer to the Kaleckian spirit than Cowling and Waterson's (Reynolds, 1989). A cautionary note is in order. As far as the 'entry factor' is concerned, it is not obvious why megacorps cannot prevent such entry through, for example, credible commitment in excess capacity. To the extent that this is allowed, 'entry factors' would not enter the calculation of the implicit interest rate, allowing a higher mark-up, in the limit equal to the joint-profit maximum price.

In stark contrast to the Marxist and post-Keynesian/Kaleckian models discussed here, Austrian and Chicago school theorists stress the competitive nature of markets, often quite independently of any observed highly concentrated market structures. There is a multitude of reasons for this, but three normally stand out. First is Demsetz's (1973) differential efficiency hypothesis. Second, and related, is an emphasis on a dynamic version (nearer to Schumpeter's own) of the Schumpeterian hypothesis to suggest that high innovation itself leads to monopoly (rather than monopoly producing higher innovation rates). Third is the importance of potential competition, in a framework of a search for the discovery of new information by alert profit-seeking entrepreneurs.

Demsetz's differential efficiency hypothesis effectively suggests that an observed relationship between size and profitability should not necessarily be interpreted as evidence of market power by large firms. Rather, an 'intervening variable' (efficiency) could explain both higher concentration and higher profitability within industries. In this sense, more efficient firms grow larger and also yield high profits, because of their efficiency. The apparent existence of market power is a simple reflection of differential efficiency. Demsetz's argument is very much in line with Schumpeter's views that the search by firms (existing and new) for new techniques, products, etc. implies that those firms more successful in finding and adopting such 'innovations' will tend to be more successful in the short term; always subject to fear of entry by new innovators. Seen in this light it could be suggested that a dynamic interpretation of the Schumpeterian hypothesis is that successful innovation leads to temporary monopoly situations, and transient excess profits. A similar interpretation was put forward by Almarin Phillips. In this view,

It is not so much that large firms lead to innovation as that innovation leads to large firms. In the shake out that invariably occurs in an innovative regime, the successful innovator will become larger and the unsuccessful will contract or disappear. . . . In other words industry structure is an endogenous result of a competitive learning process. (In Langlois, 1987, pp. 12–13)

Schumpeter's 'differential innovation' hypothesis lends support to Demsetz's views. Both attribute large size and high concentration levels to efficiency aspects of firms' behaviour. However, given that the underlying reason for this very efficiency is to obtain higher profits, one is left wondering why firms should *not* try to exploit the 'first mover advantages' conferred on them by efficiency to exercise some sort of market power. From the purely theoretical point of view, it is simply impossible to separate efficiency from market power as it is often through the former (in all its forms, including transaction costs economizing and labour cost reductions) that the latter is obtained. For the Demsetz–Schumpeter argument to follow one also needs some restraints on the exercise of efficiency derived market power. This is an observation that leads us naturally to the concept of potential competition.

Potential competition is prominent in both Schumpeter and the Austrian theorists, such as Reekie (1979) and Littlechild (1981). The market process is one of discovery of new profitable opportunities by entrepreneurs.[17] This continuously undermines the position of other previously successful entrepreneurs, in that any profit derived by them simultaneously represents an incentive to new entrepreneurs to enter the market. This competitive process erodes in the long run any profits resulting from the exercise of monopoly power. In this sense apparent monopoly profits are transient rewards to successful entrepreneurs and under constant threat of erosion. Profits can only persist through successful innovations or diversification in new areas. In the long term any observed profit is due to successful entrepreneurship, including alertness, luck, insight, chance factors, efficiency and innovation.

Strategic barriers to entry are ignored by the Austrians and the Chicago school. Structural barriers are also not considered important. In Stigler's famous definition, entry barriers only exist if a production cost is borne by the potential entrants but not by the incumbents. This, as Cubbin (1988) observes, includes both positive and normative aspects, and would exclude in some cases a number of traditionally viewed barriers, such as advertising.

More restrictively, Austrian authors focus on barriers, and monopolies, as arising only when firms have exclusive control over a resource and they (not the government) exclude others from using it (see Utton, 1982, for a discussion). Overall, Langlois observes, structural barriers (which he terms *ad hoc*) 'to the extent that they exist, are far less important for economic analysis and policy than the legal barriers that come from investing competitors with the legal right to prevent entry' (Langlois, 1987, p. 15). It follows that concentration (to the extent it has risen at all) does not matter. Reekie (1979), for example, suggests that it matters little whether one firm or one hundred firms are in an industry. All that matters is potential competition.

Given their rejection of the long run equilibrium concept embodied in the conventional diagrammatic expositions of competition–monopoly and IO models, as well as their emphasis on uncertainty, Austrians have not produced a formal model of IO. Still, it is evident from the above discussion that the Austrian (and Schumpeterian) ideas of the endogenous nature of market structure predate the idea of contestable markets. In fact the latter could be viewed as an attempt to formalize and apply in the short run the long-run dynamic arguments of the Austrians. If a general observation is allowed, it is that in the long run, for the Austrians prices will tend to oscillate around the minimum of the long-run average cost curve.

I have already discussed the theoretical case for and against potential competition. For the purposes of this section it is possible to summarize the (primarily static) aspects of most of the models discussed so far in diagrammatic form. Thus, in figure 3.1, I assume L-shaped long-run average costs (equal marginal costs post $\bar{Q}$). LAC_1 is the average cost of the monopolist, assumed to be equal to that of a competitor. Then with minimum efficient scale output $(\bar{Q})$, the limit price will be P_1, the monopoly price P_m and the competitive price P_c. P_m will also reflect pricing under the Marxist Baran – Sweezy model and the Cowling–Waterson model, assuming the degree of collusion is equal to unity. P_c will also be consistent with contestability and the Austrian perspective. Losses in consumer surplus can be easily identified in each case as the (remaining) area lying above the respective prices and within the demand curve.

Viewing LAC_1 as the result of a dramatic reduction in costs

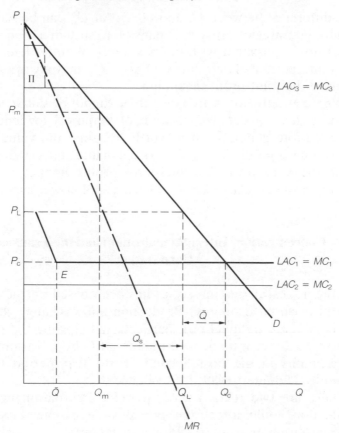

Figure 3.1 *A common expository diagrammatic framework for neoclassical Austrian and Marxist approaches to industrial organization*

$\bar{Q}$, minimum efficient scale; Q_s, strategic capacity output; Π, monopolist's disincentive to invent; E, efficiency gains; P_m, monopoly price; P_l, limit price; P_c, perfect competition price

(originally assumed to be LAC_3) resulting from an invention, Π will be the monopolist's disincentive to invent, according to Arrow, under his assumptions, which have been discussed. Allowing the monopolist to have a lower cost curve (LAC_2) we obtain the Williamson productive (efficiency) gain, to be traded off against any consumer surplus losses. Eichnerian prices can be found anywhere between P_c and P_m depending on the factors discussed.

The difference between Q_c and Q_l and/or Q_m can be seen as the required (strategic) capacity expansion to sustain a monopoly (or limit) price consistent with the possibility of entry deterence. In the limit, (strategic) investment of $Q_c - Q_m$ may always suffice to produce the joint-profit maximum.

Where exactly prices are going to be cannot be said *a priori*. At the very least a detailed account of empirical evidence is required. More generally, it is worth stressing, the value of such expositions is purely instructive. In a dynamic, uncertain environment the very need for long-term profits implies almost by definition the co-existence of efficiency and power aspects.

5   Concentration, Internationalization and the Transnational Corporation

My theoretical discussion so far has been based on the assumption of a closed economy. Production and exchange, however, are highly internationalized, particularly following the domestic growth of direct foreign investment (DFI) by US transnational corporations in the post Second World War period (see, for example, Dunning, 1989, for evidence).

There are two related ways in which internationalization of production could affect the previous discussion. First, internationalization may necessitate a redefinition of markets[18] in terms of a group of countries (e.g. the European Community) or the world as a whole (global markets). Such a redefinition may cast doubt on the very notion of increasing concentration. If imports are taken into account in the conventional calculations of concentration ratios, the latter may be reduced, often very dramatically.[19] If so, observed domestic increases in concentration may be a simple artefact, reflecting instead increased internationalization of production and exchange. Reekie (1979) has argued just that. The second major way in which internationalization affects the discussion so far is in the concept of *international competition*. The reduction in trade barriers (e.g. in the European Community), and more importantly the emergence and growth of TNCs, can provide a very powerful threat indeed to incumbents of one nation state. As TNCs are already established firms in their domestic countries and normally the 'domestic champions', they would not be deterred to the same extent as smaller new entrants by the existence of conventional and even strategic entry barriers. Part of the reason for this is that building capacity sufficient to supply, say, the British market still allows possible excess profits to TNCs intending to supply the European market (even if capacity is used post-entry).

International competition (and its threat) can in fact provide some apparent support to the contestable markets and Austrian ideas. Even a critic of contestable markets like Green observes that 'one might justifiably question the relevance of the contestable markets paradigm for competition policy on the grounds of non-generality, if it were not for the growing influence of foreign competition' (C. Green, 1987, p. 485). Other critics, such as Shepherd (1984), make similar points. Authors in the Marxist tradition suggest that increasing international competition makes capitalism increasingly more competitive (See Jenkins, 1987, for a survey). In a version of Marxian crisis theory, moreover, Glyn and Sutcliffe (1972) use international competition as one of the two major factors (the other being trade union militancy) that are said to have led to a decline in the British rate of profits in the post-war era, and thus to the 'relative decline' of the UK.

As I explain in section 2, increased competition in terms of capital mobility should not be confused with increased rivalry between firms. The former is, according at least to Marx, inherent in the process of capitalist development. The latter may or may not lead to collusion and thus reduce rivalry. All the above-mentioned views on international competition, in fact, tend to see internationalization in an *ex post* non-historical manner. When viewed from a dynamic historical perspective, TNCs can both be explained by (partly at least) *and* explain increasing global concentration.

From a methodological point of view, one can approach the issue of internationalization by taking the whole world (the global economy) as the unit of analysis. This obviously endogenizes *international* competition, which becomes just *competition*. In this light the discussion so far would apply for the global economy, as would the theoretical models and perspectives discussed. The only amendment required is to view the typical industry-market as a global one and the typical firm (megacorp) as a global firm (TNC). In this framework, concentration changes should be measured for global markets and global concentration ratios can be used to test whether concentration has been increasing or not. In such a framework, reductions in concentration due to opening of markets would simply be an artefact. As far as global markets are concerned concentration might be on the increase all the time, the only reason for apparent reductions being the *ad hoc* change in definition from 'domestic' to 'global' markets.

Focus on global markets is useful, I believe, to put arguments about internationalization and concentration in perspective. However, it fails to provide a historical account of the process of internationalization and its possible links with concentration and monopolization. Historically, firms emerged and grew in national markets and expanded from that base to foreign territories. It is this process that needs explaining. The conventional explanations of the TNC, normally based on Hymer's (1976) concept of 'monopolistic advantages' and the Hymer, Coase (1973), Williamson (1975, 1981) and Buckley and Casson (1976) transaction costs framework, as well as Dunning's (1989) eclectic synthesis of ownership locational and internalization (OLI) factors, are primarily concerned with the *static choice of institutional forms*, such as DFI versus licensing, and so provide only limited insights to the process of internationalization (Pitelis, 1991b).

Hymer's (1976) concept of 'monopolistic advantages' in his PhD thesis incorporates an element of a dynamic theory, which has been lost by subsequent neoclassical theorists. This pertains to the way in which such advantages have been derived, which Hymer explains in a historical account of the growth of US firms, particularly in his subsequent extensions to his thesis, as summarized in his papers in Cohen et al. (1979). The central elements of Hymer's scenario are that historically American firms operating in a framework of rivalry and collusion have grown from being small (single owner, manager) to being joint-stock companies, then multidivisional (with separate strategic and operational decisions) and then TNCs. Their power, perspective and advantages in technology, organizational forms, know-how, access to capital etc. grew hand in hand with their increased size. Such advantages obtained by their domestic operations over foreign firms provided them with the ability to undertake international production (DFI). Along with the threat from the growing European and Japanese firms, US DFI took off as a means of defensive pre-emption, with an eye to reducing conflict inter-nationally (see chapter 2).

Put slightly differently, Hymer's view is that rivalry in domestic markets leads to collusion, which allows firms to exploit better the 'monopolistic advantages' resulting from their increasing size. The threat of potential entry by foreign rivals leads to defensive attacks, in order to reduce rivalry internationally and thus to increase global collusion. In this sense concentration (and col-lusion) in domestic markets is seen as an important factor leading to TNCs, which themselves can be seen as an important factor leading to global collusion and global monopolization.[20] All incentives, Hymer suggests, are for potential rivals from other nations, particularly the Europeans and the Japanese, to choose collusion over conflict through interpenetration of investments. He goes on to observe that while the Europeans had an oppor-tunity to compete with the USA, they had chosen interpenetra-tion and that all the signs suggested that the Japanese would do the same. Concerning future trends, Hymer predicted that following European and Japanese investment in the USA, partly in reaction to US penetration to their markets and partly because of their own growth, US retaliation in the form of further DFI would follow: 'A period of rivalry will prevail until a new equi-librium between giant US firms and giant European and Japanese firms is reached, based on a strategy of multinational operations and cross penetration' (Hymer, 1970, p. 60).

Hymer's views are invaluable. Not only is the link between concentration, TNCs and global concentration made in a rivalry leading to collusion framework (thus justifying the viewing of figure 3.1 as if in the context of global economy), but the whole process of internationalization is put in a historical dynamic con-text. His views help to clear the confusion that TNCs are necess-arily rivalistic, which arose from confusion of rivalry with the Marxian concept of competition in terms of capital mobility. More recently, some of Hymer's views have been extended and formalized in the work of Cowling and Sugden (1987), who focus on both the role of TNCs in monopolizing product markets and their role in the international division of labour, another of Hymer's major concerns (Pitelis, 1990a).[21] Further support has also been provided by Chandler, who views the organization created by firms to exploit the costs advantages of scale and scope of certain technologies as the source of transferable capital and skills that provided market power and offered competitive advantages to TNCs. Such 'first movers advantages were so powerful that the pioneers continued to dominate the resulting global oligopolies for decades' (Chandler, 1986, p. 53). But the proof of the pudding is always in the eating and it is eating to which we now turn: to the existing empirical evidence.

6   Existing Evidence

Given the observed tendency for increasing concentration in domestic markets of advanced capitalist countries, do such increases lead to collusive behaviour and excess profits? Do structural and strategic barriers to entry deter entry or are they not durable in the long run? Do 'excess' profits (if existent) persist in the long run? Can (persistent) 'excess' profits be explained in terms of differential efficiencies? Do the 'dynamic gains' from size (innovation, international competitiveness, reduced transaction costs) lead to dynamic welfare gains sufficient to offset any static welfare losses? Do TNCs lead to increasing competitiveness globally or they are a factor leading to the globalization of the tendency towards monopolization? Empirical studies attempting to answer these questions could easily number many hundreds if not thousands, in part reflecting growing interest in IO and the theory of the TNC. Fortunately, a number of authorative surveys have been produced in recent years, which greatly facilitate my purposes here. I focus on them.

The conventional approach to testing monopoly power is by examining the empirical relationship between concentration (and barriers to entry) and profitability. The presence of a positive relationship is then interpreted as evidence in favour of the 'market power' hypothesis, that concentration and entry barriers lead to excess profits through collusion. The substantial evidence on this issue has recently been summarized by, among others, Curry and George (1983), Schmalensee (1988), C. Green (1987) and Cubbin (1988). It is in line with the idea that concentration, and structural barriers to entry, have a positive and significant influence on industry profitability. Moreover, the entry barriers effects are seen to be independent from those of concentration, scale economies appearing to be the most important of them (Cubbin, 1988). Evidence summarized by Cubbin also suggests that such profits are persistent for long periods. Although over the longer term (fifty to sixty years), he argues, technical progress and structural change may reduce the relative importance of major monopolies, persistence beyond fifteen to twenty years can still imply very long perods of resource misallocation. Gilbert (1988) also observes the long decay rate of excess profits.

There are relatively few attempts to test empirically for strategic entry deterrence. These are summarized in, for example, Geroski and Jacquemin (1989), Lieberman (1987), Gilbert (1988) and Paraskevopoulos and Pitelis (1990). Usually they are associated with (excess) capacity expansion, but product proliferation arguments have also been tested. The balance of the evidence seems to suggest that such strategies have been pursued on a number of occasions, although they have not always been successful. In the Paraskevopoulos and Pitelis (1990) paper the focus is on plant announcements in the Western European chemical industry (as well as actual expansions), and the evidence is in line with the view that such announcements could be interpreted as a strategic signalling game aimed at pre-empting existing rivals expansions and establishing industry coordination. More work is certainly needed in this area.

Collusion is inherently difficult to measure, given especially that it is illegal in most industrialized countries. In the work discussed so far, collusion is only inferred. This has to counter the possibility of 'differential efficiency'. The test of this hypothesis is based on the assumption that collusion is a 'public good' (see Geroski, 1988) and therefore if collusion leads to high profits both large and small firms in an industry should enjoy high profits. If differential efficiency exists only large firms should enjoy high profits. The tests in the area are summarized in Geroski (1988) and Schmalensee (1988) and have produced mixed results, suggesting to Schmalensee 'that both mechanisms may be at work in the economy' (1988, p. 667).

Whether for 'market power' or efficiency, 'excess profits' can be associated with static welfare losses. Here again a substantial number of studies have tried to provide estimates of such 'static

losses' (summarized in Sawyer, 1986; Ferguson, 1988). Estimates
here vary very widely (depending on assumptions employed,
methodology pursued etc.) from 0.1 per cent of US gross domestic
product in Harberger (1954) to 13.1 per cent in Cowling and
Mueller (1978). In a Marxist study, Baran and Sweezy (1966) go
as far as a 50 per cent measure, by including such 'wasteful
expenditures' as advertising expenditures, legal fees of corporations and military expenditures. Even conservative estimates
(e.g. Scherer, 1980) seem to suggest a 6–7 per cent static welfare
loss owing to monopoly power in the USA. Evidence of positive
welfare losses of this type also exist for other countries, such as
the UK, Canada, Finland, France, Italy, Japan and Korea (see
Ferguson, 1988).

What of dynamic gains? Starting with innovation, Schmalensee
provides a succinct summary of the state of the art:

> Many authors have attempted to test Joseph Schumpeter's
> assertions that large firms and concentrated industries are
> disproportionally important sources of technical progress.
> But . . . R&D spending as a percentage of sales does not
> seem to rise with firm size in most industries. . . . Moreover
> the largest firms are not disproportionally important pro-
> ducers of major innovations, nor are they quickest in all
> cases to adopt innovations originating elsewhere. And, ad-
> justing for differences in technological opportunity, increases
> in seller concentration do not appear to spur R&D effort.
> (Schmalensee, 1988, p. 675)

Similar conclusions are drawn by Geroski and Jacquemin (1989).

With regard to international competitiveness, Geroski and
Jacquemin (1989) observe that the European Community policy
in support of mergers, as a means of combating the so-called
'American challenge' in the 1960s, was somewhat misconceived.
The evidence, they observe, suggests that scale economies are not
as ubiquitous or large as originally believed. In fact productivity
differences can be explained less by size than by differences
in labour relations, training and availability of skilled labour.
Combine this with problems in industrial relations resulting from
large size, and the substantial evidence on the unprofitability of
mergers (recently summarized in Cowling and Sawyer, 1989),
and one can legitimately conclude that European

industrial policy of the 1960s may have been ill-conceived. The new super firms did not give rise to a new competitive efficiency in Europe. Indeed by creating a group of firms with sufficient market power to be sheltered from the forces of market selection, the policy may have left Europe with a population of sleepy industrial giants who were ill-equipped to meet the challenge of the 1970s and 1980s. (Geroski and Jacquemin, 1989, p. 303)

Similar conclusions are drawn by Pitelis (1991d) in the context of TNC operations.

Evidence on monopolization being the result of transaction costs reductions is difficult to obtain and interpret, given in particular the difficulty in separating transaction costs reductions from market power objectives, as the former normally lead to the latter (Malcolmson, 1984). What evidence there is, moreover, appears not to offer support to the transactions costs arguments, *vis-à-vis* alternative hypotheses, including that of 'power' (Clegg, 1990). These observations also apply to TNCs. Concerning such firms, all recent evidence seems to be in line with the idea that their role has been increasing in individual countries, the European Community and globally: see Cantwell (1988) for the USA, UK, Germany, Italy, France and Japan, Cowling and Sugden (1987) for the UK and Geroski and Jacquemin (1989) for Europe. The last-mentioned authors observe that, for Europe as a whole, the percentage of the sales of the fifty largest European firms as a percentage of gross industrial output increased from 15 per cent in 1965 to 25 per cent in 1976. Rugman (1987) provides an estimate of over 50 per cent of global exchange taking place today via TNCs.

Evidence in Cantwell (1988) shows that general international-ization (measured as the proportional change in the foreign production ratio for the firms of the six major industrialized countries, combined) rose by about 8 per cent from 1974 to 1982. Overseas production by TNCs also increased very dramatically, for the USA by 50 and 68 per cent for the 1974–8 and 1977–81 periods, for Western Europe by 89 and 99 per cent and for Japan by 122 and 103 per cent, respectively. Interpenetration has also taken place, particularly from Europe and Japan to the USA: the ratio of the flow of DFI into the USA to US investment abroad increased from 19 per cent in 1970 to 58 per cent in 1980. The stock of DFI in the USA increased four-fold between 1967 and 1977; see Jenkins (1987) for a survey of the evidence and references.

The existing evidence on the impact of TNCs on domestic concentration and barriers to entry in 'host' countries is summarized in Lall (1980), Dunning (1981) and Jenkins (1987). The evidence indicates that TNCs do operate in highly concentrated industries and that their subsidiaries often enjoy dominant positions. Furthermore, predatory pricing, 'deep pocket' effects and 'defensive mergers' by local firms can often lead to increased concentration (Dunning, 1981; Jenkins, 1987). Formal collusion, interlocking directorships, market allocation and 'mutual forbearance' also appear to exist in some sectors. On the other hand, TNCs do seem to enjoy some cost advantages and experience higher productivity levels; see Jenkins (1987) for a survey.

All in all, the evidence seems to be in line with the proposition that efficiency and market power considerations are very difficult to disentangle, but whatever evidence there is supports on balance the proposition that TNCs' (like domestic firms') impact on 'host' countries has both efficiency *and* market power aspects. This, as I have already suggested, is in line with expectations, as market power itself is often derived from efficiency increases, such as transaction costs reductions (Malcolmson, 1984).

Focus on *market* power alone for particular firms, especially TNCs, may be an insufficient indicator of *monopoly* power, in its more general sense of the ability to extract high profits, through growth, extension of productive base and markets. Jenkins outlines the historical record of the 'seven sisters', the seven 'famous' oil TNCs. He observes that 'while the *market* power of the oil companies as indicated by their shares of crude oil or petroleum products may have declined, their corporate *monopoly* power in terms of ability to earn surplus profits has increased since the late 1960s' (Jenkins, 1987, p. 55). Diversification in other fields has been one way of achieving this, for example through acquisitions.

That TNCs' shares in particular markets may decline in some cases need not obviously imply that the overall degree of monopoly in such markets also goes down, or that collusion does not take place. That *monopoly* power, broadly defined, increases is perfectly consistent with the possibility that *market* power is also on the increase. In fact the existence of market power in domestic markets is often the prerequisite for the derivation of first mover advantages, which in turn facilitate expansion, transnationalization and (thus) the derivation of *monopoly* power.

7 Concluding Remarks and Implications

The competition versus monopoly debate has been one of the longer lasting and most prominent ones in economic theory. It has gradually generated a whole field of enquiry: industrial organization. It is one of the most exciting and fastest growing fields too. This is not surprising. The answer to the competition versus monopoly question has very important implications for almost every aspect of capitalist economies, including the possibility and viability of political democracy (see Cowling and Sugden, 1987). For example, the concept of (Pareto) optimality of the market underlying neoclassical welfare economics is based on the assumption of perfectly competitive market structures.

Viewing competition and monopoly as types of market structure is only one way of approaching the question in hand, and not the most interesting way. Alternative approaches, like the Austrian and the Marxist, have taken different lines, viewing competition as a process of discovery or of increasing capital mobility, respectively. More generally the neoclassical approach has taken a *static* and *non-historical* approach. The issue of market structure and performance is largely approached in an *ex post* and *ad hoc* way under very restrictive assumptions. Based on methodological individualism, the methodology adopted is that of situational determinism (Latsis, 1976; Blaug, 1976), where structural conditions can uniquely specify a course of action, under rationality assumptions. Both the determination of the 'structure' and its evolution through time are left unexplained. Any macroeconomic considerations and their potential influence on the micro-structure are simply ignored. By focusing essentially on *market power* only, neoclassical IO also fails to examine what for some is the very *raison d'être* of firms, including TNCs: the derivation of profits through expansion of their productive base (Hymer, in Cohen et al., 1979) – this despite assuming profit maximization! The possibility of *monopoly power* in the sense of increasing control over labour markets and nation states is not entertained; see Pitelis (1991c) for more on this. Issues of real uncertainty (as opposed to risk, to which probabilities can be assigned) and imperfect knowledge receive a low priority in this tradition. However, Fudenberg and Tirole (1986) survey attempts to incorporate uncertainties and informational asymmetries in the analysis.

Alternative perspectives, such as the Austrian, are helpful in emphasizing the very restrictive nature of the neoclassical research programme. Competition here is viewed as a dynamic process of discovery by alert entrepreneurs looking for profits. Synchronization of previously uncoordinated activities results through their actions, and transient profits are their reward; transient, as it is their very presence that attracts others into the field. Given this, market economies are competitive, but not in a (market) structural sense; rather as a dynamic process. Schumpeterian and Chicago school theorists add to the thrust of the Austrian critique by emphasizing the non-importance, or non-existence, of structural and strategic private (as opposed to state-imposed) barriers, emphasizing the role of potential competition and 'creative destruction' through innovations, and more generally the efficiency aspects of large firms. Marxists also view competition as a dynamic process involving an increasing mobility of capital. Capitalist development goes hand in hand with increasing competition in this sense. Whether rivalry between firms will also increase or there will be collusion and monopolization of markets is an area of dispute. Some Marxists stress the rivalistic aspects of firms' behaviour, others their tendency to collude. All agree that a wider definition of monopoly power than market power is warranted, to include power over labour, ability to extract profits etc. Such power is said to be on the increase.

Despite its severe limitations the neoclassical tradition has been successful in incorporating gradually but steadily a number of important insights from different perspectives. Issues of potential competition and strategic interactions between firms have recently received wide interest, in an attempt to solve the structure–conduct–performance 'problem'. On this basis the models of limit pricing, generalized oligopoly (unconstrained profit maximization) and contestability have been employed to give answers to the question in hand. The result often has a striking resemblance to the implications (albeit not the spirit) of alternative perspectives. This and the substantial empirical evidence accumulated over the years, with an eye to testing the issues involved, provides us with a very useful starting point. The usefulness of the neoclassical research programme lies primarily in its provision of elegant and rigorous benchmarks. Richness of analysis is admittedly sacrificed for this, but they are still benchmarks, and starting points from which other (often more interesting) issues can be approached and discussed. In the particular issue at hand this primarily involves a need to add history to the neoclassical 'snapshot' view of reality, and to make realistic assumptions. To be sure, neoclassical economists have made progress in this area too; particularly in the work of Chandler (1986) and of neo-institutional economists, such as Coase (1937), Williamson (1975, 1981) and North (1981).

My scenario here, based on the existing theoretical perspectives and empirical work, is that capitalist competition (in the form of conflict with labour and rivalry with other firms), is the driving force of the capitalist search for profits, through the expansion of markets and the productive base of capital. Growth is the prerequisite for long-term profits, especially in the face of real uncertainty. Expansion of firms in domestic markets (often achieved through efficiency improvements) has given rise to increased concentration and first mover and monopolistic advantages, and thus increased both the incentive and the ability to exploit them. This has provided incentives for internationalization and defensive DFI, which have driven the above tendencies to a global plane. All incentives are for TNCs, from whatever country, to collude through interpenetration of markets. Their ability to enter markets of host countries creates the illusion of increased rivalry. But this is only temporary. The tendency is for global monopolization of markets. Once a few TNCs dominate every single global market (and we are not far from this), collusion and market sharing will tend to be the norm. Strategic entry deterrence and the sheer scale of entry and financial resources required will tend to make impossible the entry of any firm other than those that are state-backed in these markets. The result will tend to be a dynamic version of the Baran–Sweezy–Cowling–Waterson–Spence scenario, on a global scale, but worse, since *market power* will be only part of the wider *monopoly power* of

TNCs. A handful of giants will tend to replace and supplement markets and states.

This is not to suggest that capitalism and TNCs are 'bad'. So far, they certainly do not seem worse than known alternatives! The point is simply that the logic of the system leads to an ever-increasing concentration of power, and thus potentially an eventual undermining of the economic basis of democracy. The process incorporates both efficiency and inefficiency aspects, but this is not the issue. The issue is who controls the process, and to what extent and how such control can be shared by all stake-holders. Should it be shared? Answers to this are beyond the scope of my discussion here. Suffice it to note this implication: that efficiency aspects of firms and industries, however important or even dominant, do not constitute a claim for 'free market forces'. The issues of control and distribution also need to be considered.

Notes

1　See, for example, Cubbin (1988) for a discussion, including obser-vation of inconsistent conjectures in Cournot, and the less than satisfactory outcomes of the 'consistent conjectures' models. Fudenberg and Tirole (1986) and Schmalensee (1988) have further discussion.

2　The focus on homogeneous oligopoly with all firms facing the same cost and demand conditions allows limit pricing theories to examine the industry in terms of a typical firm (Latsis, 1976).

3　See also Cowling (1976, 1981, 1982) and Waterson (1984).

4　For the historical antecedents of the Cowling/Waterson model, in particular Kalecki (1971), and Stigler (1963) see Cowling (1982).

5　See, for example, Lyons (1979) and Sugden (1983b) for extensions to incorporate international and intra-firm trade; Cowling (1982) for its macroeconomic implications and a justification of the no entry assumption; and Cowling and Sugden (1987) for an attempt to extend the model in an international framework, and some replies to critics.

6　Given the neoclassical methodological focus on predictability, as opposed to the realism of assumptions, the need for a more realistic 'benchmark' is not very clear to me.

7　This is not too surprising, given that limit pricing was originally proposed as an improvement upon the then prevalent models of perfect competition and monopoly, and the close affinity of the unconstrained profit maximization and contestability ideas to these models (see below).

8 In the model, the limit price is effectively determined by the potential entrants, Q, thus implying a defensive attitude by the incumbents (see, for example, Latsis, 1976).

9 This separability does not imply that incumbents are totally uncon-strained profit maximizers, as it is often claimed (for example, Sawyer, 1982b). In the Spence model the investment in excess capacity itself and its associated costs can be considered as *ex ante* constraints.

10 For a discussion of critiques of the Arrow model see Clarke (1985).

11 On the negative side, however, it has been suggested that mon-opolies will tend to be more X-inefficient, i.e. higher discretionary managerial expenditures, higher costs and/or lack of incentives to innovate because of reduced competition (Liebenstein, 1966).

12 Labels always irritate; particularly they irritate those who do not think they belong to a 'labelled group'. Professor Friedman, for example, the leader of the Chicago school, is reported to dislike (and dispute) his inclusion in the Austrian tradition. Marx himself declared, 'Je ne suis pas Marxiste!' Still, labels often help with exposition. Post-Keynesian/Kaleckian here is defined as in Sawyer (1985). The only reason I put the Chicago school and the Austrians together is that, unlike in other areas, for example the theory of the state, where differences are at least as great as similarities, in IO their views can be presented, I think, as a more or less unified framework.

13 A similar definition has been proposed by Lerner, so reference is normally made to on the Lerner–Kalecki degree of monopoly.

14 This led to the critique of his theory of distribution based on the degree of monopoly as tautological. However, this critique does not hold water in view of the explicit recognition on his part of structural determinants such as concentration (see Sawyer, 1985, for discussions).

15 Mark-up type models are discussed in Reynolds (1989).

16 This allows for criticism, by Fine and Murfin (1986), of the Cowling (1982) model, that it fails to consider rivalry between industries intended to attract demand from each other.

17 For alternative theories of the entrepreneur see Ricketts (1987).

18 For a detailed discussion of the problems associated with the definition and delineation of the concept of industry, see Auerbach (1988).

19 Such an exercise in the 1978 Mergers and Monopolies Commission

Green Paper included imports in the denominator of conventional concentration ratios and obtained substantial reductions in such ratios, in one case from a near monopoly situation to a perfectly competitive one! These measures have been questioned by Cowling (1982), who observed that imports controlled by domestic TNCs should be included in the measures (added to the numerator). If this is done observed domestic concentration ratios need not go down, and depending on the exact circumstances they may increase.

20 These IO-type views of Hymer's have been developed by a number of authors, most notably Knickerbrocker (1973) and Graham (1978) and more recently Cowling and Sugden (1987). For a detailed discussion of theories of the TNC by some of their main proponents see Pitelis and Sugden (1990).

21 Another interesting recent contribution on IO lines is made by Lyons (1987), who claims that TNCs can in part result from strategic behaviour *vis-à-vis* other firms, labour unions and governments and that 'local production makes a firm's commitment to a market much stronger than merely exporting because more costs have to be sunk in productive capacity' (1987, p. 78), which allows the use of credible commitments for entry deterrence.

4

The Capitalist State

1 Introduction

In Coase's (1937) classic paper on the theory of the firm, the emergence of the firm from assumed pre-existing markets (price mechanism) is explained in terms of 'excessive' market transaction costs. Use of the market can be costly. Replacing it by a private hierarchy – the firm – can often reduce market transaction costs. The reason is said to be that authority (the feature distinguishing the firm from the price mechanism) can often have economizing, or efficiency, properties. But if so, why do states exist? Could the private sector (market and firms) not achieve what the state does? Why? More generally, what can explain the nature, objectives and evolution of the state in capitalist economies?

The state is one of the three major institutions of capitalism, the others being the price mechanism and the private hierarchy. All three, I claim, are alternative, but complementary, institutional devices designed to exploit the benefits from the division of labour, in order to derive maximum *possible* benefits for their 'principals'.[1] The specific difference of the institutional form of the state from the market and the firm is that the state has a 'legitimate' monopoly of force. Market transactions, firm transactions and firm–market transactions are normally expected to take place within the rules of the game set up by the state. Firm–market transactions in capitalism are based on equality before the law. Whether there is authority (as, for example, Coase believes there is in the firm) or not (as Coase thinks for the market) there is still equality before the law. However, the law lies above the private sector as a whole. In this sense the 'public' hierarchy, the state, is the hierarchy *par excellence*, determining the broad constraints within which both markets and private hierarchies are expected to operate.

Since its emergence, the capitalist state has experienced continued growth. In every single one of the OECD countries, state receipts and outlays as a percentage of gross domestic product (GDP) have increased quite dramatically between 1960 and 1985. In the USA, for example, outlays have increased from 27 per cent of GDP in 1960 to 36.7 per cent in 1985, in the Netherlands from 33.7 to 60.2 per cent, in Japan from 18.3 to 32.7 per cent, in the UK from 32.3 to 47.8 per cent (in 1984) and in Sweden from 31.0 to 64.5 per cent, the highest in OECD countries (Mueller, 1989).

The unique position of the state in being a law-provider as opposed to law-taker and its associated (definitionally) legal monopoly in enforcing the law, as well as its phenomenal growth, have unsurprisingly generated an immense output of attempts to explain the nature, objectives and evolution of the capitalist state. In brief (based on my proposed definition of the state here), discussions have centred around four major questions: first, why capitalist states; second, who are the states' principals; third, what are the principals' objectives (and their constraints); fourth, how can we explain the evolution of the capitalist state? Three major theoretical approaches can be distinguished in the literature that have attempted to provide answers to these questions: the mainstream neoclassical theory, the Marxist theory and the 'new right' school, broadly defined to include the 'public choice' school, anarcho-capitalist theories, Professor Friedman and the Chicago school, and the Austrian school.[2] Although variations exist within the schools, there is also sufficient common ground to warrant an early answer to my questions here.

In brief, neoclassical theory views the state's existence in terms of 'market failure'. The theory views the consumers (the public) as the principals and the government (state) as the agent. The aim of the agent (the state) is to maximize the utility of the principals, which is seen as the exploitation of the benefits from trade. States grow because the demand for their services by principals does. The line of Marxist theory is different. Here the state exists in order to ensure the maintenance of the capitalist mode of production. The dominant class in this system (capitalists) are the principals. Their objective is to derive maximum *possible* profits. States grow because the needs of the principals (broadly defined) for state functions do. Finally, the 'new right' views the state's existence as the result of individuals' preference for some sort of restraint to the anarchy of the market. They view the principals as the state's functionaries *per se* – politicians, bureaucrats etc. The objectives of the principals are seen as the maximization of their personal utility functions. This maximization is considered as the main reason for the growth of the state.

My aim here is critically to assess existing theories of the state: the neoclassical theory (section 2), the new right (section 3) and the Marxist (section 4). My main claim is that with the partial exception of aspects of Marxist theory, all theories are primarily static and non-historical. In section 5 I introduce some historical and dynamic aspects to explain the emergence of the capitalist state. A number of interesting insights emerge from this concerning the nature, objectives and evolution of capitalist states. In Section 6 I examine the relationship between the (nation) state and the (transnational) firm, in particular to what extent transnationalization erodes the power of nation states or even creates the conditions for the 'withering away' of the capitalist state. Concluding remarks follow in section 7.

2   The Mainstream Approach to the Theory of the State

Concern with the economic role of the state in market economics goes at least as far back as Adam Smith's (1776) *Wealth of Nations*. In Smith's view, the duties of the 'sovereign' were:

> first, the duty of protecting the society from the violence and invasion of other independent societies. Secondly, the duty of protecting, as far as possible, every member of the society from the injustice or oppression of every other member of it, or the duty of establishing an exact administration of justice; and thirdly, the duty of erecting and maintaining certain public works and certain public institutions which it can never be for the interest of any individual or small number of

individuals, to erect and maintain; because the profit could never repay the expense . . . though it may frequently do much more than repay it to a great society. (Smith, 1776, volume 2, pp. 180–1)

The mainstream approach to the theory of the state can be traced back to this quote from Smith, in particular to Smith's reference to public works and the system of justice.

In its purest version the neoclassical theory is one of 'market failure'. It starts from the observation that a perfectly competitive market economy can lead to Pareto efficient allocation of resources (the first fundamental theorem of welfare economics). Arrow (1963, 1970) provides an excellent account and proof of this statement. If this is accepted, then one has to look for reasons why markets can fail. Such market failure could then be taken as a justification for government intervention (the state), aimed at solving for market failures.

The existence of public works and institutions (public goods) is viewed by the neoclassical theory as one reason for failure by the market. Public goods are goods characterized by jointness in supply and non-excludability. The former implies that these goods are equally available to all members of the society. The latter that it is technically impossible to charge a price for services of such goods. This is the case of 'pure' public goods, but quasi-public goods also exist. These are goods with social benefits that exceed the price that can be technically charged from the market to those benefiting, because of 'free riding' resulting from jointness of supply and non-excludability. Free riding can take the form of individual beneficiaries underplaying their preferences. As a result public goods can be underprovided (quasi-public goods) or not provided at all (pure public goods).[3]

Quasi-public goods include the transport system, education, research and development and more generally expenditures on infrastructure, which are often too expensive for any individual or firm to produce and make a profit with arm's length market transactions. Pure public goods include, among others, the legal system, national defense (Karageorgas, 1977; Stiglitz, 1986), organizational knowledge (Marglin, 1983) and efficient government (Dasgupta, 1986). Obvious from the above is what Dasgupta calls the pervasiveness of market failure. Its presence provides a rationale for the state's emergence (provision of public goods, such as Smith's 'defense' and 'justice') and functions (such as the provision of Smith's public works). In this sense the presence of 'public goods' suffices to provide a theory of the *raison d'être* of the state in market economies, particularly given that the very existence and smooth functioning of the market is predicated upon the existence of such 'public goods' (Karageorgas, 1977).

Additional important reasons for market failure are said to be the existence of externalities, the presence of oligopolistic or monopolistic market structures and the often associated existence of major distributional inequities.[4] Externalities are interdependencies not conveyed through the price mechanism, thus giving rise to a divergence between social and private benefits. External economies are when social benefit exceeds private benefits (price), and external diseconomies when the opposite is true. As private (market) prices do not reflect social costs or benefits, Pareto efficiency cannot be achieved even in the presence of perfectly competitive markets (Arrow, 1963). This necessitates state intervention to correct for such externalities.

The case of oligopoly and monopoly is also straightforward, as they imply the absence of perfect competition and thus the possibility of prices exceeding competitive prices.[5] Such pricing is normally taken to represent a redistribution from consumers to producers (loss in consumer surplus, increase in monopolists' profits), and thus the possibility of unsatisfactory ('excessive') inequities.[6] Once again this provides a rationale for state intervention aimed at controlling for monopoly power and the associated redistributional consequences.[7] In the presence of distortion in other markets too, states will be faced with second best situations and a first best optimum will not be attainable. Despite the problems associated with second best situations (Lipsey and Lancaster, 1956), there seems to be some consensus that a piecemeal policy accounting for such distortions can be applied – see Cullis and Jones (1987) and Reid (1987) for discussions.

'Market failure' need not give rise to state intervention, if individuals can internalize such imperfections. That this will tend to happen is exactly what Coase's (1960) theorem suggests. Coase focuses on externalities, and suggests that they will tend to be internalized by individuals concerned (Cooter, 1989). All the state needs to do, therefore, is to establish clear property rights.

If one accepts that public goods and monopoly are themselves forms of externalities (Kay, 1984), then Coase's theorem can be taken to imply no need for state intervention, other than the delineation of clear property rights. This, however, depends heavily on whether individuals can internalize externalities cost-lessly. In fact, Cooter (1989) suggests, this is unlikely because of the presence of transaction costs. This is particularly true when public good-type externalities are concerned (Cullis and Jones, 1987). This generalization and limitation of Coase's theorem allows us to look at a more general neoclassical theory of the state, based on transaction costs.

Building on his own classic 1937 paper on the nature of the firm, Coase approaches 'market failure' in terms of transaction costs:

> In order to carry out a market transaction it is necessary to discover who it is that one wishes to deal with, to inform people that one wishes to deal and on what terms, to conduct negotiations leading up to a bargain, to draw up the contract, to undertake the inspection needed to make sure that the terms of the contract are being observed and so on. These operations are often extremely costly, sufficiently costly at any rate, to prevent many transactions that would be carried out in a world in which the pricing system worked without cost. (Coase, 1960, p. 15)

Coase goes on to observe that the firm could be one obvious solution to this problem, but it is not the only possible one. 'An alternative solution is direct Government regulation. . . . The government is, in a sense, a super firm but of a very special kind since it is able to influence the use of factors of production by administrative decisions' (p. 16). Coase also observes that while firms are subject to the forces of competition by other firms,

> The government is able, if it wishes, to avoid the market altogether which a firm can never do. . . . Furthermore, the government has at its disposal the police and the other law enforcement agencies to make sure that its regulations are carried out. It is clear that the government has powers which might enable it to get some things done at a lower cost than could a private organisation. (p. 18)

Arrow (1970) also considers market failure from the point of view of transaction costs. A more general formulation to the question of market failure, he observes, is that of 'transaction costs, which are attached to any market and indeed to any mode of resource allocation. *Market failure is the particular case where transaction costs are so high that the existence of the market is no longer worthwhile'* (Arrow, 1970, p. 68, emphasis added). Arrow's definition of transaction costs is generally 'costs of running the economic system' (p. 60). He does, however, distinguish them from production costs in terms of the extent to which they can be varied by a change in the mode of resource allocation. The claim is that transaction costs do vary with such a change while production costs do not; they depend only on tastes and technology, and will be the same in all economic systems. Two main sources of transaction costs are then identified: exclusion costs and costs of communication and information. A third source is said to be costs of 'disequilibrium'; that is, costs arising even under perfect information, 'for it takes time to complete the optimal allocation, and either transactions take place which are inconsistent with the final equilibrium, or they are delayed until the computation is completed' (Arrow, 1970, p. 68). In similar vein to Coase, Arrow concludes that 'The state may frequently have a special role to play in resource allocation because, by its nature, it has a monopoly of coercive power and coercive power can be used to economize on transaction costs' (p. 69). The similarities between Arrow's arguments and those of Coase (1937) and Williamson (1975, 1981, 1986) concerning markets and private hierarchies (firms) are straightforward enough not to require any elaboration here. Suffice it to note that in the Williamsonian jargon, bounded rationality, opportunism and asset specificity would be the sources of high market transaction costs and that the monopoly of coercion (the state) could help to economize in such transaction costs.

My discussion so far suffices to make this important point (indeed an elaboration of Arrow's own): that transaction costs can be considered as the *general cause* of market failure, and therefore economizing in market transactions costs is the *raison d'être* of the state, according to the neoclassical theory. Unfortunately, this generalization solves fewer problems than it creates. To start with, Coase's (1937) insight was to see the firm *replacing* (or superseding) the market because of its superior transaction efficiency properties. This view is qualified in his 1960 paper, where he observes that firms cannot fully avoid the market. States can, though. Given this, and given the potential superior efficiency properties of the state, why do states not fully replace the market *and* the firm? In fact the observation that firms can reduce market transaction costs implies that states generally need not exist, unless firms also fail. Accordingly, to explain states in the neoclassical tradition what we need is *private sector failure*: failure of both markets and firms. Given this it could be suggested that private sector transaction costs are being reduced when a third party exists, which provides a general legal framework within which private sector transactions can take place. The ability of such a party (the state) to set these rules once (a constitution) and change them gradually and when the circumstances require it, and its ability to guard and enforce agreements (often through the presence alone of threat of punishment), might help substantially to reduce the private sector's transaction costs. This would be in line with the neoclassical theory. The private sector failure theory of the state would suggest that states exist in order to reduce private sector transaction costs.

The private sector failure theory still fails to explain why states do not supersede (rather than supplement) the private sector. An answer, once again from Coase (1960) is in terms of costs due to government intervention. 'All solutions have costs and there is no reason to suppose that government regulation is called for simply because the problem is not well handled by the market or the firm' (Coase, 1960, p. 18). This Coasian insight has been developed more recently into a theory of 'government failure' (see below). Although again within the neoclassical framework of no-intervention because of the costs of such intervention (rather than no-supersession), one could suggest that transaction costs associated with using the state as an *alternative* means of resource allocation can often be high enough to explain the existence of markets and firms, that is their non-supersession by the state.

The informational problems associated with the use of central planning *alone* as a means of allocating resources, even in the presence of today's high-powered computers (Hodgson, 1988), and the loss of what Williamson (1990) calls the high-powered incentives of market prices, would lend some support to this idea.

Given this, I would be tempted to propose a neoclassical theory of capitalist institutions including the state in terms of each institutional form's relative transactional properties. In this theory the choice of the institutional form-mix would be on the basis of transaction costs economizing. Given the failure of all institutional forms to perform certain transactions economically, the right mix would be chosen on the basis of overall transaction costs minimization.

The 'principals' of the state in the neoclassical theory are thought to be the consumers, the general public, in line with the neoclassicals' more general focus on consumers' sovereignty. In particular, the state is taken to be the reflection of the general will (Arrow, 1963). Given this, the state emerges (from the market) in order to satisfy this general will, which in this framework is to achieve a more efficient allocation of resources, by reducing market transaction costs. The principals' objectives are to maximize their utility. It is with the demands associated with this, that Wagner's (1958) 'law' of increasing state activity (first published in 1883) can primarily be explained; see Hadjimatheou (1976), Cullis and Jones (1987) and Mueller (1989) for detailed expositions. In Mueller (1989), for example, four main factors are used to explain government size: provision of public goods and elimination of externalities, redistribution of income and wealth, interest groups demands, bureaucratic power and 'fiscal illusion'. The first three, he observes, 'are essentially drawn from a classical theory of the democratic state. . . . Ultimate authority lies with the citizens. The state exists to carry out the "will of the people". State policies are reflections of the preferences of individual voters' (p. 344).

To summarize, the state in the neoclassical tradition is the result of private sector failure because of excessive transaction costs. The state's principals are the 'general public' (the sovereign consumers), whose objectives are to increase this utility (consumption, profit) by reducing inefficiencies in the form of private sector transaction costs. Increasing demand for state services explains the growth of the government sector in market economies.

There are a number of problems associated with (my generalized version of) the neoclassical theory: first, the assumption of pre-existing markets; second, the assumption that the underlying aim of individuals is to achieve (Pareto) efficiency; third, and related, that the state reflects the 'general will', which means it is 'neutral' towards all individuals or groups of individuals. I have explained the first two problems in chapter 2, so I simply repeat the main arguments here. The issue of pre-existing markets is an assertion which deprives neoclassical economics from any analysis of institutions at all. The assumption that markets pre-exist and have to fail for alternatives to emerge does not explain how markets emerge. In this sense the question of whether (and how) other institutions can emerge in the absence of markets (failure) is not addressed at all. What is more, the very pre-existence of markets, historically, is by no means a foregone conclusion. That states predated markets is probably a more plausible assumption to start with (North, 1981).

The assumption that individuals aim at (Pareto) efficiency is also problematical. The main reason is that this assumes that there is an agreement between agents that existing distributional disparities – e.g. in terms of income, power and positive freedoms[8] – are *not* sufficiently important (in the minds of individuals) to preclude them from focusing on *efficiency* given *distribution*. If this is not true, and if, for example, some individuals believe that their situation *ex ante* is unsatisfactory, they may choose to seek a state for redistribution purposes, or even 'exit' or 'revolt'; that is, not participate in the efficiency seeking game. If the state is pursued for distributional reasons, it can no longer be claimed that it represents the 'general interest'; the emergence of the state could represent an imposition by one group of individuals on another. This line of thought is taken in the Marxist theory, which I examine in section 4. More important, however, for my purposes here is the observation that even when the state is *ex post* (Pareto) efficient, it may still be the case that it is the result of distributional rather than efficiency considerations. This is true when existing distributional disparities are such that the 'unprivileged' would prefer an improvement in their relative position vis-a-vis the privileged, but realize that they have no power to enforce such a situation. Given fears on their part that their relative status could be worsened by the actions of the 'privileged group', they 'agree' to setting up a state that guarantees the status quo. The desire of the privileged to retain their privileges, to avoid 'exit' or 'revolt' by the unprivileged, leads them to 'agree' in setting up such a state.

The above possibility was first raised by Machiavelli (1958). He suggested that both the privileged and unprivileged wanted 'the Prince': the former to maintain their privileges and the latter to prevent their situation from worsening. This case is particularly interesting because it highlights the possibility that even when (Pareto) efficiency is the *ex post* outcome of the emergence of the state, and even when such (Pareto) efficiency appears to be the driving force of agents' actions, distributional considerations may well lurk behind such apparent motives. In this sense efficiency and distribution cannot be safely, or usefully, separated. In the Machiavellian case the unprivileged would, by assumption, prefer a distributional state to their favour, or no state at all, if they could otherwise achieve their aims. The 'choice' of focus on efficiency *given* distribution is therefore a 'second best' outcome, conditioned by the actors' entry qualifications to the game (Lively, 1978). In fact the extent to which actors will agree to focus on efficiency *given* distribution may well depend at least partly on the extent of distributional disparities (Lively, 1978). In extreme cases 'revolt' may be the preferred alternative, in which case any emergent state (if at all) will be of the imposition type.

It is worth noting that my concern here with distribution is not the usual criticism addressed to the Pareto criterion – that is, that the latter disregards distributional issues and that Pareto efficient configurations can be compatible with a multitude of distributional situations, even very extremely inequitable ones (e.g. Dasgupta, 1986). These considerations normally refer to the functions of the state, given its existence, and *not* the issue of existence *per se*. In this sense, my critique goes further into the heart of the efficiency argument.

The neoclassical response to the issues raised above is in terms of the *assumption* of pre-existing *competitive* markets. In such markets, by assumption, there are large numbers of buyers and sellers, all facing parametric prices. Accordingly no individual or group has any *market* power. This implies that with pre-existing competitive markets, large distributional inequities should not be expected to exist, to start with. If oligopolistic or monopolistic distortions arise *ex post*, it is the aim of the state to control them. In this sense, distribution should not be expected to give rise to the state to start with. Moreover, state actions should be viewed as 'neutral', in the sense that, by trying to ensure the maintenance of the original competitive equilibrium (where no major distributional disparities exist) no particular individual or group is favoured.

The focus on *pre-existing perfectly competitive* markets stretches the imagination to its limit. Even accepting pre-existing markets, the concept of them being perfectly competitive is based on sufficiently unrealistic assumptions (perfect knowledge, for example) to have generated a consensus that it is mythical among all but the true devotees; see, for example, critiques by Schumpeter (1942), Hayek (1978) and Weeks (1981), for Schumpeterian, Austrian and Marxist perspectives, respectively. More recent attempts to revive competitive behaviour in the face of oligopolistic market structures, in the form of Baumol's (1982) theory of contestable markets, do not adequately address these critiques; see Pitelis (1990c) for a discussion and also chapter 3. Even if one is prepared to accept the concept of pre-existing perfectly competitive (or contestable) markets, this will only imply the absence of *market* power, the absence of inequities in exchange. This still allows the possibility of inequalities in production, that is the existence of individuals or groups of individuals who have to work for others, because if they chose to enjoy the negative freedom of being unemployed, they would have insufficient income to live on. If such inequities exist in production, the arguments I raised above about efficiency versus distribution still hold, and provide a simultaneous attack on the concept of state neutrality. The reason is that, given that the aim of the state is seen by neoclassicals to be the maintenance of the original perfectly competitive equilibrium, the *status quo* (Mueller, 1976), the existence of distributional inequities (in production) in this original equilibrium by definition implies a partisan state favouring those better off in the original equilibrium.

This neutrality towards the status quo has been called 'weak neutrality' elsewhere (Pitelis and Pitelis, 1991). Two other possible types of neutrality examined there are 'consensual neutrality' and 'structurally induced neutrality'. The former is when state actions are *thought* to be neutral by all actors; the latter when the overall structure of market economies is such that neutrality is imposed on the state. Both are very problematical.

'Consensual neutrality' presupposes a pre-existing consensus about what neutrality is, which itself could be related to existing distributional disparties. Inferring 'consensual neutrality' by observing the lack of demands for redistribution (Arrow, 1970; Dasgupta, 1986) does not allow for the possibility of administered consensus, through, for example, investment by the state on legitimization. Such investments have been viewed as the *sine qua non* of the capitalist state by Marxist authors (see section 4) but more recently by neoclassicals too (e.g. North, 1981). Structurally induced neutrality is the socio-political analogue (and extension) of the perfect competition assumption. It has been forcefully proposed in the so-called 'pluralist theory'; see, for example, Dahl (1956). Connolly (1969), Miliband (1969), Lively (1978) and Vincent (1987) provide detailed critical assessments. For Lively (1978), the main strands of pluralist thought are summarized as follows: 'the necessary diversity of interests, the right of groups to self protection, men's attachment to group rather than general interests, the necessity of the state to intervene in a conciliatory or accommodating role and the need for power to be diffused amongst social groups' (p. 190).

Following Connolly (1969), Lively distinguishes between two main versions of the pluralist approach, the arena and arbiter theories. The former views the state as 'standing above the group battle' (p. 191); the latter views politicians as 'co-equal participants in the group battle' (p. 191). In both cases, Lively argues, a rough distributional parity is required to sustain the pluralist outcome, as well as a consensus on what represents an acceptable distribution. He concludes that, 'Despite the pluralist emphasis on conflict, competition and division of power, contemporary pluralism in both its formulations must fall back on an appeal to consensus . . . the fall back on consensus is necessary to maintaining the coherence of the theory of the state' (p. 201). If this is so my considerations concerning 'consensual neutrality' apply equally to the concept of 'structurally induced' neutrality. Since the latter is the public sector analogue of the neoclassical assumption of perfect competition, it is effectively equivalent to 'weak neutrality'. Given inequities in exchange or production, this implies partisanship in favour of the better off.

To conclude, the theoretical case of neoclassical theory concerning the *raison d'être*, principals and objectives of the state is a weak one. It effectively boils down to asserting that pre-existing and perfectly competitive markets fail because of high transaction

costs, giving rise to firms (which also 'fail') and states that intend
to solve such 'private sector failures'. It asserts that the state's
principals are the general public, who are only interested in
(Pareto) efficiency, and finally that the state is neutral towards individuals and groups. All these, I have argued, are problematic.[9]

3 'New Right' Perspectives

The neoclassical assertion of pre-existing and competitive markets, the alleged expression through the state of consumer sovereignty, the state's emergence from, and striving for, (Pareto)
efficiency and its associated 'neutrality' represent the starting
point (and reason for common treatment of an otherwise disparate group of people) of the 'new right', which can be broadly
defined to include neo-liberal, anarcho-capitalist, public choice,
Chicago school and Austrian theories (D. G. Green, 1987). In
stark contrast to the neoclassicals, 'new right' theorists regard the
state as resulting 'spontaneously' from a 'state of nature', regard
state functionaries (politicians, bureaucrats etc.) as the principals
of the state and suggest that the objective of these principals is to
maximize their own utility, something which often leads to state
partiality in favour of powerful groups, as well as inefficiently
high levels of outputs and supply-side driven growth of the state
sector.

Although all new right theories are broadly in agreement with
these views, it is the public choice school which has recently
acquired wide influence among mainstream economists, partly
because of its rigorous treatment of the issues at hand. More
recently some support for the public choice analysis of the derivation of the state has been provided by the game theoretic treatment of Schotter (1981), albeit from the different perspective of
an immanent critique of neoclassical theory.

Mueller (1976, 1989) gives the classic and most comprehensive
analysis of the public choice school. He attempts to explain the
emergence of the state by considering the familiar issue of the
'benefits of trade' within a 'prisoner's dilemma' framework, as
follows. Two individuals are being considered, X and Y, who
specialize in the production of goods A and B respectively. The
game is such that the best strategy for each individual is to steal

from the other and not to be stolen from. The worst outcome is when both steal. The second best strategy is to cooperate. In an 'anarchy' both A and B will be inclined to choose the dominant strategy: steal. This is a Hobbesian state of nature, so defined from Hobbes's (1651) classic *Leviathan*, where life in the absence of a state is portrayed as a jungle. Starting

> From this 'natural' state, both individuals become better off by tacitly or formally agreeing not to steal. . . . The movement is a Pareto move that lifts the individual out of a Hobbesian state of nature. . . . An agreement to make such a move is a form of 'constitutional contract' establishing the property rights and behavioural constraints of each individual. The existence of these rights is . . . a necessary precondition for the creation of 'postconstitutional contracts' which make up a system of voluntary exchange. (Mueller, 1989, p. 10).

Public goods can be analysed in a similar framework (see Pitelis, 1987d; Mueller, 1989).

Realization of the benefits from trade may be expected to lead eventually to the adoption of the cooperative outcome provided that the game is played an infinite (or indefinite) number of times; this is a supergame (Rutherford, 1989; Mueller, 1989). Even in the absence of direct communication, the cooperative outcome can be the result of a 'tit-for-tat' strategy (Axelrod, 1984). Here the player in each game plays the same strategy as the other player's in the previous game. If all players adopt this strategy and all begin by playing cooperatively, the cooperative outcome will emerge in every play. Axelrod's (1984) famous finding was that this strategy beat all others proposed by a number of game theory experts in a computer tournament.[10]

The remarkable contribution of the public choice school is the demonstration that *even* in cases of prisoner's dilemma games, cooperation can ensue. This is also demonstrated in Schotter's (1981) game theoretic approach to the emergence of capitalist institutions where none exists to start with. Schotter examines a number of games giving rise to institutions, starting from a 'state of nature' as the public choice school does and also Robert Nozick's (1974) theory of the minimal state – see D. G. Green (1987) for a detailed discussion. In Schotter, the possibility of

players punishing non-cooperative behaviour by themselves de-
fecting, and rewarding cooperation by cooperation, also establishes co-operative behaviour in prisoner's dilemma supergames.

Important for our purposes here is that Schotter examines a
number of other games besides the prisoner's dilemma, in particular coordination problems, cooperative game problems and
inequality preserving problems.[11] He views the state as derived
organically (non-deliberately) in the context of a cooperative
game: 'The existence of the state . . . merely represents the equilibrium solution . . . of a cooperative game and emerges from
individual attempts at self-maximization. It is a result no agent
intended, but one that no agent or group of agents would rather
do without. Its existence is unanimously accepted' (Schotter,
1981, p. 46). Schotter thus lends further support to the proposition that institutions can emerge from a state of nature. The
importance of the public choice and game theoretic approach lies
in that it solves two problems relating to the pure neoclassical
tradition. First a mechanism for the derivation of the 'general
will' is found. Second, and perhaps more importantly, this mechanism generates institutions, such as the state, apparently without
simultaneously requiring the pre-existence (and failure) of other
institutions, such as the market.[12]

The other point of departure of the public choice school is the
rejection of the neoclassical assumption that states have no
interests other than those of their citizens, whose collective will
they reflect. Here, state functionaries (politicians, bureaucrats)
are assumed to try to maximize their *own* personal interests, as
does every other rational (economic) 'man'.[13] A classic in this
tradition is Downs's (1957) *Economic Theory of Democracy*, in
which political parties are seen to behave just like entrepreneurs,
formulating policies that try to maximize their votes. Similarly,
bureaucracies are taken to maximize the utility of the bureaucrats, which in Niskanen (1973) is taken to be income, power,
prestige, promotion, perks, pleasant working conditions, the
public good and an easy life, all broadly correlated to increases in
the size of their bureaus. Budget maximization is therefore seen
as the bureaucrat's analogue of the private sector profit motive.[14]
Although they are constrained by the need to satisfy their spon-
sors, Niskanen observes, the end product of bureaucrats' policies
is bureaus that are too large and too inefficient. 'All bureaus are

too large. For given demand and cost conditions, both the budget and the output, of a monopoly bureau may be up to twice that of a competitive industry facing the came conditions' (Niskanen, 1973, p. 33). The conclusion from this is that normally the government alternative is inferior to the competitive market.

The maximization of politicians' own welfare raises the possibility that the state will not be neutral *vis-à-vis* its constituents. Legislation benefiting powerful groups may be passed in order to secure financial and voting support for politicians, thus fostering sectional interests. Reaction by the majority might not be forthcoming, in part because of 'optimal ignorance', a situation where the marginal costs of obtaining information concerning state actions is equal to or higher than the cost of remaining 'ignorant' (Cullis and Jones, 1987). Accordingly the state could, far from reflecting the 'general will', be fostering the sectional interests of powerful groups.

Much of the criticism of the public choice school has been produced by Hayek (1976) and the Austrian school, of which he is a major representative. Hayek considers institutions to be the result of human action, but not human design ('spontaneous orders'), a view closely related to Adam Smith's motion of the 'invisible hand' (D. G. Green, 1987). Given limitations to knowledge, Hayek observes, any government interference with the spontaneous order can be counterproductive. Although a spontaneous order can be improved through revision of the general rules on which it rests, and organization can supplement its results, it is not possible to improve the results by commands that deprive the members of using their knowledge for their purposes. Hayek regards the market as a mechanism that, if not impeded by special interests which abuse the powers of government, encourages (through the free play of dispersed ingenuity and initiative) the discovery of the most economic ways of meeting individuals' needs. As D. G. Green (1987, p. 144) observes, moreover, 'vital to Hayek's view, is that the most economic ways of meeting needs remain to be discovered and are always changing in ways we cannot foresee'.

Friedman and the Chicago school are in line with such critiques of government intervention. Friedman (1962) regards concentration of power as a great menace to freedom. Government power is included: 'the greatest threat to human freedom is the concentration of power, whether in the hands of government or anyone else' (Friedman and Friedman, 1980, p. 309). In direct contrast to Adam Smith's invisible hand of the market, which promotes the general interest through no intention of individuals, in politics there is an invisible hand working in exactly the opposite way. Politicians intending to promote the *general interest* are led by an invisible hand to promote *special, sectional interests*, normally the interests of producers and trades unions. Concerning redistribution, George Stigler (1988, p. 9) observes that 'most redistribution programs are not simple transfers from rich to poor. Rather they are transfers from large numbers of unorganized consumers and taxpayers to smaller more cohesive and politically more powerful industrial, geographical or occupational groups'. Deadweight losses also result from every redistributive programme. Yet government intervention persists, for 'The intellectuals – people who dislike both poverty and manual labor – produce tides of opinion so powerful that, in Keynes' famous closing remark in the *General Theory* "The world is ruled by little else"'. (Stigler, 1988, p. 11).

The concept of government failure favoured by new right theorists has more recently received wider acclaim (e.g. Lindbeck, 1988).[15] Today few people would be prepared to argue for automatic government intervention when markets fail, calling attention to the possibility of government failure.[16] Such failure, moreover, can be taken to provide a supply-side explanation of the growth of government. In Mueller's (1989) typology of reasons for government growth, bureaucratic power and fiscal illusion (the presumption that the legislature can deceive citizens about the exact size of government) can both be seen within a framework where the state is placed above the citizens. 'It is the preferences of the state, or of the individuals in the government, that are decisive. Citizens and political institutions constitute at most (loose) constraints against which political leaders and bureaucrats pursue their own personal interests' (Mueller, 1989, p. 344).

Despite its apparent assault on neoclassical theory the new right shares more with neoclassicals than meets the eye. Besides the common basis on methodological individualism (reductionism), and the reliance on invisible hand, spontaneous order type theorems (Hodgson 1989; Rutherford 1989), the new right also retains the neoclassical focus on ubiquitous markets and 'efficiency seeking agents'. In this sense, it is subject to the same criticisms I raised in the previous section.

Starting from the emergence of the state, the state of nature, spontaneous order and game theoretic approaches focus on exchange, ignore the possibility of an absence of consensus on cooperating (rather than exiting, abstaining or revolting), and disallow the possibility that the state can *arise* for distributional reasons. Such reasons (non-neutrality) are only allowed *ex post* and primarily as a means of 'proving' the inefficiency of state *actions vis-à-vis* the market. What is more they downplay the 'pervasiveness of market failure', in particular the observation that the public goods nature of 'efficient government' precludes the market from providing it (Dasgupta, 1986).

The common ground between the neoclassical and new right theories allows a more powerful mainstream theory to be derived by bringing the two together – again based on transaction costs theorizing. In particular, starting from the prisoner's dilemma (or other games) examined by Mueller (1989), it can be suggested that transaction costs, in obtaining information, negotiating, contracting and enforcing agreements, could prevent individuals from realizing the benefits from trade of cooperating. Efficiency seeking agents could realize that setting up a state (a mechanism to provide the 'rules of the game') could save in transaction costs. The rules of the game would be set once (a constitution) and adjusted only gradually as new circumstances arise, while the existence of an enforcement mechanism would help to reduce opportunism, and thus bargaining costs etc.

State functionaries having special interests could also be a transaction costs based explanation of government failure. Indeed, much of the government failure argument relates to limits of knowledge and self-interested politicians, bureaucrats etc. Government failure could be seen as the result of the combined presence of bounded rationality and opportunism on the part of state functionaries, giving rise to often excessive transaction costs of government actions, *à la* Williamson (1975, 1981, 1986) in the case of markets. The generalized mainstream theory would view the state as the result of efficiency seeking agents' actions; the choice of institutional form (the markets–firms–state–mix) would then be explained in terms of the transactional properties of these institutions. The merit of this theory over the pure neoclassical version is that it dispenses with the unrealistic (and inconsistent with neoclassicalism) notion of a neutral state. Furthermore, it provides the interesting possibility of *institutional failure*, in which transaction costs are such that private sector failure *and* goverment failure coincide.

The utility-maximizing state perspective of the public choice school and transaction costs are brought together by North (1981) in an attempt to develop 'a neoclassical theory of the state' (p. 20). In this model, a wealth or utility-maximizing ruler is assumed, who trades a group of services, such as protection and justice, for revenue, acting as a discriminating monopolist (that is, devising property rights for each so as to maximize state revenue) subject to the constraint of potential entry by rivals providing the same services (other states or individuals within the existing politico-economic unit, who are potential rulers). The objectives of state services (the rules of the game) are taken to be, first to maximize the rents accruing to the ruler and (within this framework), second, 'to reduce transaction costs in order to foster maximum output [and] therefore increase tax revenues accruing to the state' (North, 1981, p. 24). The constraints on the state – competition by potential rivals and transaction costs – are said typically to produce inefficient property rights. Under the first, states normally have to favour powerful constituents, even if this results in inefficiency, while transaction costs associated with metering, policing and collecting taxes often provide incentives to states to grant a monopoly. North concludes that 'These two constraints together account for the wide spread of inefficient property rights. In effect the property rights structure that will maximize rents to the ruler (or ruling class) is in conflict with that that would produce economic growth' (North, 1981, p. 28). He regards this idea as the neoclassical variant of the 'Marxian notion of the contradictions in the mode of production in which the ownership structure is incompatible with realizing the potential gain from an evolving set of technological changes'.

North's ambitious design provides support for my argument that neoclassical and new right ideas can be put together to produce a unified theory. Interpreting North's state actions in terms of opportunism leading to high transaction costs makes his theory consistent with my proposed generalization of the mainstream theory. Moreover, as the state can be seen as trying to reduce market transaction costs on the one hand, but increasing them on the other, the possibility of institutional failure also emerges.

Despite dramatic developments, the mainstream perspective regards *ex ante* efficiency as ubiquitous, and only allows inefficiencies and non-neutrality *ex post*. Its focus on methodological individualism makes it ignore any systemic considerations. Such concerns are taken up by Marxists.

4   Marxian Perspectives on the Capitalist State

The state has a very special status in Marxian economic, and political, theory. Being interested in explaining the world in order *to change it*, in line with Marx's famous dictum, early Marxists had to confront the issue of the state's nature and objectives, often as a matter of life and death. Can the capitalist state be conquered by the 'proletariat' or does it need to be smashed? This is the question.

The early classics, Marx and Engels themselves, did not provide us with anything like a well formulated, coherent, theoretical analysis of the state or even an apparently consistent one (Jessop, 1977). In his critical account of 'recent' Marxist theories of the state, Jessop is able to identify six different approaches within Marxism: the state as parasite (where it is seen as the private property of officials in their attempt to further their sectional interests); the state as *epiphenomenon* (part of the superstructure – law, religion, politics, etc. – with the economic structure being determinant in the last instance); the state as an instrument of class rule; the state as a factor of cohesion (functioning as a regulator of class struggle through repression and concession); the state as a set of institutions emerging at a certain stage in the division of labour usually identified by class-based production modes; and finally the state as a system of political domination concerned with forms of representation and state intervention, thought to be establishing a balance of class forces favourable to the long-run interests of a class (or class fraction).

The above approaches need not be viewed as mutually exclusive but the task of putting things together and developing aspects of these approaches has gradually generated an industry of writings on the Marxist theory of the state. Most prominent among these are the so-called instrumentalist theory, particularly associated with the writings of Ralph Miliband (1969), the structural-functional theory of, in particular, Nicos Poulantzas (1969), and the capital logic school (or German state derivation debate), which has a number of contributors, such as Altvater (1973) and Hirch (1978), collected in Holloway and Picciotto (1978).

The instrumentalist theory's origin is to be found in the *Communist Manifesto* (Marx and Engels, 1968) and Lenin's (1917) *State and Revolution*. In the former the executive of the state is seen as nothing 'but a committee for managing the common affairs of the whole bourgeoisie' (p. 5). Lenin regarded the state (any state) as an instrument of domination by one class of another. With this backing Miliband (1969) attempts to refute the pluralist conceptions of a neutral state. There are three strands in his argument: first, the class origin of state personnel, where the community of such class origin is stressed; second, the power of the capitalist class over the state, a result of ownership and control over resources, and the associated strength and influence; third, structural constraints on the state resulting from its operations within a capitalist mode of production.

Domhoff (1986) takes a similar viewpoint, also in an attempt to refute pluralist theories. He proposes that the concepts of 'ruling class' and 'power elite' be used to deal with the observation that not all in the upper class rule, or not all who rule are upper class. Thus, the ruling class are the wealthy, who fare better than others overall on well-being statistics, control the major institutions of the government and dominate the governmental process. The power elite, on the other hand, are 'the operating arm', the 'leadership group' or the 'establishment' of the ruling class; that is, the active working members of the upper class and high-level employees of institutions controlled by members of the upper class.[17] Domhoff claims that the power elite involve themselves in government through four general processes: the special interest process, the policy planning process, the candidate selection process and the ideology process. He concludes that 'even though there is more to American politics than the fat cats and their political friends, the "more" cannot win other than headlines, delays and an occasional battle' (Domhoff, 1986, p. 199).

The structuralist-functionalist approach of Poulantzas (1969) builds on, in particular, Engels's (1968) and Gramsci's (1971) writings. Gramsci regarded the state as a factor of class cohesion. In his view the capitalist class is not a unity outside the state. It is through the state that its cohesion and form as a class are obtained (see Buci-Clucksmann, 1978). This and the idea that class struggle is reproduced within the state apparatus itself (Poulantzas, 1975; Fine and Harris, 1979) are the main elements of the structuralist perspective. In this framework, the state is not and cannot be an instrument of one class. Rather it operates as a collective capitalist, to represent the long-term interest of the capitalist class as a whole, under the hegemony of one of its fractions. This fraction is today monopoly capital (Poulantzas, 1978). It is therefore the structural characteristics of capitalism, and not the class origins or power of individuals, that determine the class nature of the state.

For a time, the Miliband–Poulantzas debate was viewed as expressing a clash between two diametrically opposed views of the state, but it was soon felt that, in fact, the two had more in common than meets the eye. Most notable is their conception of the political as autonomous from the economic, and thus the perceived ability (and need) to analyse the state without a direct simultaneous analysis of the economic 'structure' (see, for example, Holloway and Picciotto, 1977). Related to this is the assertion (as opposed to the derivation) of a relatively autonomous form of the state in capitalist economies. Miliband (1969) traces this autonomy back to Marx and Engels's quote from the *Manifesto*. That the state serves the *common* interests of the *whole* bourgeoisie implies that sectional and potentially conflicting interests *also* exist (Gouph, 1979).

Gouph's (1979) analysis of the welfare state also starts from the assertion of a 'relative autonomy' of the state, but emphasizes the structural constraints of the state. In his view 'the autonomy and independence of the state . . . is only apparent. What distinguishes the Marxist theory is not the view that a particular class dominates the institutions of the state . . . but that whoever occupies these positions is constrained by the imperatives of the capital accumulation process' (p. 177). The economic functions of the state are then analysed in relation to such constraints, which are taken to include the concentration and centralization of capital, the growth of the proletariat, the law of combined and uneven development and the rate of profit – see also Gouph

(1975) and critiques by Jessop (1977), Fine and Harris (1976), Harrison (1980) and Schott (1982).

Despite references to autonomy, there is an implicit instrumentalism lurking behind Gouph's analysis, as noted by Jessop (1977) and Fine and Harris (1978), which is even more evident in the analysis of other 'neo-Ricardians', such as Glyn and Sutcliffe (1972); see below.[18] A similar criticism applies to the so-called 'fundamentalist' analyses of, for example, Yaffe (1973) and Gamble and Walton (1976). In Yaffe a commitment by the state to full employment, combined with the tendency of the rate of profit to fall, leads to crisis and unemployment and gives rise to increased state expenditures. However, these are financed by taxation of surplus value, since most state expenditure does not produce surplus value. The result is a reduction in the proportion of surplus value available for accumulation, which intensifies the tendency for a reduction in the rate of profit. For Gamble and Walton (1976), the end product of state actions to secure full employment is an increase in inflation, and thus social instability (see also Fine and Harris, 1979; Rowthorn, 1980).

Despite evident differences, the theories examined so far have in common a failure to *derive the form* of the capitalist state. The state's existence and relative autonomy (or otherwise) are simply asserted. Put simply, why does the state take the form of a third party, rather than assuming the form of direct domination of one class by another? This question, which is the Marxist analogue of Coase's (1937) classic question 'Why do firms exist?', is the starting point of the German debate, or the capital theoretic school (as opposed to Poulantzas et al.'s class theoretic analysis) – see Gouph (1979). Their explanation is in terms of the category of capital, or the 'capital relation'.[19]

The capital theoretic approach has been traced back to a 1938 essay by E. Pashukanis (see Holloway and Picciotto, 1978). The question is posed by Pashukanis as follows:

> Why does the dominance of a class not continue to be that which it is – that is to say, the subordination in fact of one part of the population to another part? Why does it take the form of state domination? Or which is the same thing, why is not the mechanism of state constraint created as a *private* mechanism of the dominant class? Why is it dissociated from

the dominant class – taking the form of an impersonal mechanism of *public* authority isolated from society? (Quoted in
Holloway and Picciotto, 1978, p. 79, emphasis added)

The answer follows three different strands: first, the idea that
competition between capitals implies their inability to reproduce
the conditions of their own existence; second, the idea that the
possibility of the state form is based on the apparent community
of interests between classes; third, the idea that the very nature
of the capital relation, that is the form of capital exploitation,
necessitates the abstraction of the relations of force from the
process of production (Holloway and Picciotto, 1978).

The first line is particularly associated with Altvater (1973).
The existence of capital in the form of many capitals in competition with each other is seen as the reason for the need of capital to
have a separate entity, the state, in order to ensure its existence
as such. The functions of the state follow from this inability
of capital, and are: infrastructure, legal framework, regulation
of conflict, and safeguarding the existence and expansion of a
'national' capital in world markets. The second line is associated
with Flatow and Huinsken (1978). They suggest that not only the
necessity for an 'autonomous' state, but also the *possibility* of it
needs to be derived. This can be done by focusing on exchange,
where an apparent community of interests exists between classes
in their roles as owners of a source of revenue. Given this
derivation of the possibility, the necessity comes from capitalist
competition, *à la* Altvater. The third line is associated with, in
particular, Hirch (1978). His idea is to focus on exploitation
of labour under *capitalism*. It is specifically in capitalism, he
observes, that appropriation of surplus value does not require
force in the immediate production process. The continuation of
this process guarantees the existence and continuation of exploitation. This is not to deny the need for force in general, which is
now located in an 'instance standing apart from direct producers
. . . constituting discrete "political" and "economic" spheres'
(Holloway and Picciotto, 1978, p. 24).

Building on the form derivation idea, the German school are
also able to provide a historical account of the development of
the form and functions of the state, by 'periodizing capitalism'.
Thus Holloway and Picciotto (1978) (and Fine and Harris, 1979)

identify 'moments' or stages of capitalism. The former consider, first, the establishment of preconditions for accumulation, then a liberal moment where the separation of politics and economics takes place, and finally a contemporary moment, where the tendency of the rate of profit to fall manifests itself. For Fine and Harris (1979) *laissez-faire*, monopoly capitalism and state monopoly capitalism stages are identified. Corresponding political relations are seen to change in each of these periods: from ensuring the minimization of the economic freedom of workers under *laissez-faire*, to the state's predominance in economic reproduction under state monopoly capitalism. Unlike in earlier stages, surplus value appropriation through taxation (legal compulsion) assumes significance in the last.

The focus of the German school on antagonistic intercapitalist relations and the need for the state to abstain itself from exercising force in the production process raises the possibility, for once in the Marxist tradition, that the state may be unable to represent even the long-term interests of capital. In part this is because of the reproduction of competition between capitals within the state apparatus itself (Gouph, 1979). At the opposite end, the periodization of capitalism and the emergence of state monopoly capitalism have led to a revival of instrumentalist ideas. State monopoly capitalism (StaMoCap) theories (see Jessop, 1977, and Gerstenberger, 1985, for surveys) suggest that increasing state intervention at this stage of capitalist development is possible because the state has become an instrument of dominant monopolies. As Jessop (1977, p. 360) puts it, 'theorists of this school argue that the state and the monopolies have "fused" into a single mechanism which acts only on behalf of monopoly capital'. The apparent erosion of the 'relative autonomy' of the state under monopoly capital's hegemony is also noted by Poulantzas (1978). Barker (1978), in a critique of Holloway and Picciotto, observes the tendency towards concentration and centralization of capital in different *nation* states and suggests the possibility of capitals developing into 'state capitals' within nation states. This and the inability of any nation state to manage the world economy are seen as putting further constraints on the concept of an apparently neutral state: 'The erosion of the apparent neutrality of the state . . . is a real erosion: crucial to it are all those processes, including capital concentration, which press in the direction of fusion of state and capital' (Barker, 1978, p. 124).

The growth of state expenditure is viewed in terms of capitalism's 'laws of motion' in the Marxian tradition, although differences in perspective are obviously maintained. Underconsumptionist theories (e.g. Baran and Sweezy, 1966) are employed to explain crises in terms of increasing monopolization, with government expenditure being an attempt to absorb the resulting increasing 'surplus'; see Pitelis (1987a) for a discussion. Prominent here are expenditures on armaments. Fundamentalists like Yaffe (1973) focus on the declining rate of profit necessitating a growing state activity in order to precipitate it. Instrumentalists such as Glyn and Sutcliffe (1972) take the same line, although they attribute decreases in UK profitability to rising labour power and increasing international competition. Functionalists like Poulantzas (1975) explain state expenditures in terms of 'regulation' of crises rather than prevention, given the crises' alleged role in re-establishing the conditions for accumulation (see Hadjimatheou, 1984).

The two major contributors on the issue, O'Connor and Gouph, come from the functionalist tradition. James O'Connor's position is that 'The fiscal crisis of the state is the inevitable consequence of the structural gap between state expenditures and revenues' (O'Connor, 1973, p. 221). In his model, he distinguishes a private sector, consisting of a competitive and a monopoly sector, and a state sector. The monopoly sector is the engine of capital accumulation and growth, but the growth of its production capacity is taken to exceed that of demand for its output. The state is interested in *accumulation* and *legitimization*, which together ensure successful reproduction of the system. It is claimed that the growth of the monopoly sector indirectly leads to expansion of the state sector, in particular of social expenses for production (e.g. military and welfare expenditures). Revenues do not match expenditures, in part because of low productivity growth in the public sector and wages linked to those of the monopoly sector, in part because of the monopoly sector's ability to resist taxation. The end product is an erosion of the legitimizing powers of the state resulting from the fiscal crisis.[20]

The other major contributor in this tradition, Gouph (1979), attributes the growth of the government sector (in particular the welfare state) to the growth of working class pressure and to the increasing centralization of the state apparatus, tendencies directly linked to the concentration and centralization of capital and the growth of the proletariat. All these are aspects of the socialization of production, which itself leads to a growing socialization of the cost of production. The state's need to avoid crises and demands from the working class lead to increasing growth of the state sector. 'Productive' expenditures by the state (e.g. infrastructure expenditure) are seen here to contribute to the production of surplus value and, thus, to capitalist profits. The welfare state is also viewed as a gain by the working class.[21]

Using more conventional terminology, the Marxian contribution to the debate could be synthesized as follows: the autonomous form of the state under capitalism is a more *efficient* means of 'exploiting' the workforce. This is because, given the freedom of workers (from both slavery and control of capital) under capitalism, state compulsion is not necessary in the production process, and may also be 'unproductive' if it leads to workers' discontent (compare Lenin's claim that democracy is the best shell for capitalism). It follows that it is best for capitalist production to take its course without direct state intervention, which should be limited to providing the rules of the game, which allow (re-) production to take place, that is to providing legal protection of private property. Given this (efficiency) property of the autonomous state, its *necessity* is due to competition between capitals, its *possibility* to the *apparent* community of interest *in exchange* between classes, capital and labour. For primarily structural (control of the production process by capital), but also instrumental, reasons the state's *principals* are capitalists. Their objectives are to derive maximum possible profits; the state's objectives are to provide the required framework for this to happen. This primarily entails state 'investment' in accumulation and legitimization. Accumulation *cum* legitimization also explains the growth of government and government failures (the fiscal crisis of the state).

Despite apparent differences in perspective, focus, terminology etc., the Marxian story bears often striking similarities to mainstream perspectives. First, the idea that capitalist competition disallows capitalist control without the state is the Marxian analogue of the private sector failure mainstream idea, developed in earlier sections. The *possibility* of the state because of the community of interests in exchange between classes is the analogue of the benefits from trade concept of the mainstream. The principals are asserted to be capital(ists) in exactly the same way that neoclassicals assert that all citizens are principals. Constraints on state functions (class struggle, 'laws of motion of capitalism' etc.) are introduced mechanically and *ex post*, as in the mainstream. Thus the Marxist instrumentalist theory of the state is the exact counterpart of Friedman's and Stigler's instrumentalism (Pitelis and Pitelis, 1991). The fiscal crisis idea also bears a close resemblance to the government failure thesis.

What gives Marxist theory its distinct flavour and a notable advantage over the mainstream is a focus on the *production* process (as well as the exchange process). The focus on inequality in production under capitalism provides the Marxist assertions with an intuitive appeal. Given unequal distribution of control over production, it seems plausible that the state may emerge as an imposition of the controlling groups over non-controlling groups, even if the latter do not want it. Unequal control over expansion of capital (e.g. investment) does lend some appeal to the idea that the state will be structurally biased in favour of the controlling group. Instrumental factors may also be operative for similar reasons. Growing centralization of capital, and intensified class struggle and labour demands to ensure accumulation *with* legitimization, also add a new insight to the issue of government failure (fiscal crisis) – ideology – on which the mainstream have virtually nothing to offer (North, 1981).

Despite all this, the Marxist theory suffers from a number of important limitations. First, there is no mechanism through which states can *emerge ex ante*. The state's existence is simply assumed. Only the autonomous form under capitalism is explained. This latter explanation, moreover, assumes that capital's need to exploit labour suffices to establish the superiority of their *common* interests over their differences (competition). Second, the possibility of the capitalist state being (Pareto) efficient *ex post* or even desirable *ex ante* by all groups (see the Machiavellian case in the previous section) is downplayed.[22] Third, the possibility of the state functionaries developing their personal interests and pursuing them, often at the expense of both capital *and* labour, is not entertained. More generally, the state is assumed to be 'globally rational'. Bounded rationality, opportunism, uncertainty etc. are not being considered. Thus fiscal crises are simply due to divergence between revenues and expenditures, *not* inability or inefficiencies in running the state.

The above are limitations *vis-à-vis* the mainstream. With the mainstream, the Marxist theory shares the lack of a historical, evolutionary framework in which emergence, objectives and evolution are derived rather than simply examined *ex post*. An attempt in this direction is made in the next section.

5   History and Evolution

From a historical perspective, the capitalist state did not emerge from a Hobbesian state of nature, but from an existing feudal state. In this sense the real questions concerning the emergence of the capitalist state are how the emerging capitalist class conquered, replaced or transformed the feudal state and to what extent this metamorphosis represented an alliance between the merchants and the kings, a victory for the mechants, or even the effect of conscious state policies to further the kings' interests.

In one of the few attempts to discuss the issue, Hymer (in Cohen et al., 1979) asserts that the emergence of the capitalist state represented an alliance between merchants and the feudal nobility based on mutual advantage. This alliance, moreover, was at the expense of the interests of the feudal classes. 'In its early days capital allied itself with the central power of the sovereign against the feudal classes' (p. 90). There seems to be historical support for this contention (Galbraith, 1987), but the alternative view has also been maintained. According to this the emergence of the nation state in this period was because of the state's actions, which cultivated the merchants in service to its higher authority. Thus 'nation building had a separate dynamic of power, and to this the influence and wealth of the merchants were merely contributing factors' (Galbraith, 1987, p. 37).

Resolution of the historical debate is not easy, and will not be attempted here. For my purposes it is inconsequential anyway. For the question both these views raise is: why? Why would the feudal state wish to ally itself with or cultivate the merchants? Was there a distinctive advantage over existing productive relations that the merchants possessed and that motivated the feudal state's interests in them? The answer, I believe, should be in the affirmative. Merchants possessed the power to generate profit through their knowledge of, and ability to sell in, local and remote markets.[23] (In fact merchants were creating markets.) This power to generate income through increasing commercial activities was a lucrative potential source of 'royalties'; for the 'royals', a reason for an alliance or the cultivation of such activities.

At this stage, profit generation was primarily dependent on the existence of products to buy and sell, on the existence of a ready-made and secure source of supply and demand. It also depended on the price merchants had to pay, itself dependent on the existing supply of producers, and thus products, most notably cloth, yarn, wine, leather, shoes, corn (Galbraith, 1987). However, the existence of products and their prices were uncertain and precarious, depending on the whim of the producers and chance factors, and on the supply by producers and demand by other merchants, or competition. An increase in the supply of producers was required, and thus a reduction in their bargaining power, a reduction in prices demanded and a reduction of uncertainty over product availability to a minimum. The increase in supply could be achieved by the state, by releasing labourers from feudal serfdom; the reductions through a change in the organization of production, such as the putting-out system.

The reason for the feudal sovereigns' participation was expected revenue which they could not otherwise generate. But did the merchants need the state? Indeed they did, for three reasons. First, the release of serfs from their lords would otherwise require direct confrontation with the aristocracy, who 'still retained their special instinct for armed conflict and associated self-destruction' (Galbraith, 1987, p. 32); an ominous prospect. Second, and perhaps more importantly, if the state did not support the merchants, it could choose to support the feudal classes. Third, there were efficiency, including transaction costs, reasons. Creating an enforcement mechanism would necessitate potentially excessive costs of information, communication, contracting and self-enforcement on the part of the merchants. Such a mechanism, being a public good, would also face the possibility of free riding by the sovereigns. Alliance with the latter was the merchants' only realistic action.

The need to increase security of supplies led to the putting-out system: cottage labourers employed by a merchant-manufacturer and producing exclusively for the latter using raw materials provided by him, but often their own capital equipment, and under his direction on the basis of a piece-rate payment (Landes, 1966). This primitive form of the employment relation (the firm) represented a revolutionary improvement in efficiency through the establishment of security and direction, however imperfect, over the production process. Industry was here in spirit and so was the commodification of labour power and the source of surplus through production. Capitalism was born, and so was the proletariat. Merchant-manufacturers and the sovereign,

> working in complex ways, helped to drive the population off the land to become a free wage labor force in the towns and cities. People became unencumbered by property in the twofold sense. They were free of feudal claims on their time and had no property of their own, and therefore had no alternative to working for others. (Hymer, in Cohen et al., 1979, p. 90)

The merchant-manufacturers' comparative advantages in knowledge and ability to trade, and their organizational knowledge, which arose in the process of their transformation from merchants to merchant-manufacturers, as well as through conscious attempts on their part to retain such advantages (Marglin, 1974), greatly restricted the ability of cottage-labourers to become merchant-manufacturers, despite their ownership of capital equipment and thus the absence of a capital barrier to entry. The manufacturers' new-found invention, an increased source of profit through increased quantity (length of working day) and intensity of work, offered them social recognition and power, gradually transforming them to the new rulers. But it also gave them a problem: conflict with labour over the work process.

There is no reason to assume that the population was against these processes. The opposite is more likely. Freedom from feudal claims may well be preferable to serfdom, even at the expense of freedom from property, which was not extended to all – certainly not the cottage labourers. In this sense it is more likely that the emergent capitalist state constituted a (Pareto) improvement, both *ex ante* and *ex post*. This is not to suggest that the improvement was due to individuals seeking efficiency, other than the merchants and the kings. For them efficiency in production and trade was the source of profit and power. For the rest, it was the road to freedom, which was a reason to support it, or at least not oppose it.

In terms of my typology in section 2, the capitalist state's emergence was akin to my Machiavellian case. The merchant-manufacturers, the feudal lords and the rest all wanted it, but for different reasons: the first two to advance their profit and power related interests; the last because this was the better alternative under the circumstances, albeit not the best *possible* scenario, or even the best under Rawls's (1972) 'veil of ignorance'.[24] Thus, the capitalist state emerged, for both *power and efficiency* reasons (efficiency in both its technical and Pareto sense), but driven by the distributional interests of the merchants and the sovereigns. What is more, the separate pre-existence of the feudal state implied a relative autonomy *vis-à-vis* merchants' interests to start with, but of a sectional nature. To the 'populace' they showed a united front: the state was their instrument. This 'instrumental' nature of the state in these days is also noted by Galbraith: 'In the merchant towns the great merchants were not merely influential in the government; they *were* the government' Galbraith, 1987, p. 32, emphasis in original). Although the separate dynamic of the sectional interests of the sovereigns cannot be discarded, Galbraith observes that 'no one seriously questions the influence of the merchants in the new national states' (p. 37).

What followed is a well known story. The efficiency disadvantages of putting-out (Landes, 1966; Marglin, 1974; Williamson, 1985), from the point of view of merchant-manufacturers, led to manufacture, with the associated benefits from division of labour, which so impressed Adam Smith, and team production, which so impressed Marx (but also Alchian and Demsetz, 1972), and more importantly the increased control over the work process, with its associated efficiency gains for capital, which so impressed Coase (1937), Williamson (1985) and Marglin (1974). The removal of the need for a separate body (the state) to exercise force over the production process (the internalization of the task by capital) led to the 'autonomous' form of the state. With the need to exercise force over production removed, all the state needed to do was to ensure the legal protection of property rights and to provide a framework amenable to the continuation of the accumulation process. The capitalist state's relative autonomy was born.

The emergence of manufacture created not only conflict over the labour process but also competition between different merchant-manufacturers. The drive for profits, power and recognition now obtained a separate dynamic: accumulate or die, run to stand still. Marx's accumulation drive, his 'Moses and all the prophets', came into its own. Conflict with labour and competition with rivals necessitated an expansion of the production base (more labourers, more profits to be, less powerful labourers) and the market (more markets, more to sell, reduced competition with existing rivals). The state's role was to provide exactly this: freedom to more labourers and expanded markets, including foreign. Imperialism was born. 'If in the first world economy (sixteenth and seventeenth centuries) foreign commerce created industry, under the symbiosis of capital and crown, in the second (late nineteenth and early twentieth centuries) industry created commerce' (Hymer, in Cohen et al., 1979, p. 91).

The drive to accumulate, 'capital's self-expansion', led to continuous technological developments to outrun rivals, and new organizational forms to enhance control over labour. The resulting process of concentration and centralization of capital gradually gave rise to the national (joint-stock) corporation, with its separation of ownership from management, the socialization of capital ownership through shareholding to remove financial constraints (Pitelis, 1987a), the M-form to remove constraints to expansion and low-level management discretion (Chandler, 1962; Williamson, 1981) and the transnational corporation (Hymer, 1976). However, accumulation also expanded the proletariat – in numbers and in strength through ease of organization resulting from concentration of labour into large units. Labour's demands increased; so did wage levels, now well above the necessary physical subsistence minimum.

Market failure to provide quasi-public goods, which is the unprofitability to private capitalists of doing so, generated the need for state provision of infrastructure. The availability of labourers' incomes in excess of subsistence minima allowed the state to provide infrastructure through socializing its costs of production. Taxation became a means of obtaining surplus value *directly* from labourers, rather than from capital. Increasing needs of capital through concentration, and similarly increasing demands from labour, plus the availability of tax revenue from workers, add a new dynamic to the nature and role of the state. First, the increasing role of the state requires the expansion of state personnel. The numbers of politicians and bureaucrats grow by leaps and bounds. State functionaries gradually start to be drawn from people other than the manufacturers. A separation of control from management takes place, very much like that in the theory of the firm, and for broadly the same reasons namely, the need to administer the far more complex system, something that manufacturers themselves could no longer do and be manufacturers. The process, however, is under the control of the manufacturers, a specialization of tasks. The relationship is still one of agency, of state functionaries working for capital. But this is not the same. Agency always involved the discretion of the agent, and so it does in the case of state personnel. Although still under the control of capital, state functionaries now obtain some discretion *vis-à-vis* capital to pursue interests potentially divergent from those of capital.

The increasing demands from the proletariat strengthen this process. From battle after battle, strike after strike, universal suffrage is gained, modern democracy is born. Parties emerge, to represent the differing interests of different groups of capital and labour. Universal suffrage and the multi-party system put further constraints on the state functionaries' ability or willingness to operate instrumentally. Votes have to be won for re-election. Actual and potential competition from other parties puts on further pressure, to satisfy labour's demands, such as sickness and unemployment payments. The welfare state is born. The state functionaries' interests are brought nearer to those of labour. Even when alternative parties have no real alternative to offer (as argued, for example, by Bowles and Gintis, 1982, for the USA), from the point of view of the incumbent party, loss of elections is undersirable. The vote constraint becomes an important one.

Taxes on labour are another factor increasing the relative autonomy of state functionaries. To the extent that the system works and reproduces itself smoothly, employment generates a source of revenue for both labour and the state. The state acquires an interest in the maintenance of high employment levels to increase its own revenues. The link between capital and

state functionaries becomes more tenuous. But this is only part of
the story. For the economy is capitalist and capitalists its driving
force. Employment requires investment: by capital. Therefore,
the only source of revenue is capital. This puts structural constraints on the state's ability to offer concessions to labour. Space
for manoeuvre is limited. Legitimization investments are a solution: they can be economic (focus on growth given distribution)
or ideological, in education, family, religion, 'success' and thus
individualism. Economic growth and the individualistic pursuit of
success (induced Hobbesianism) are the state's counterpart to the
capitalist division of labour in production.

To the extent that international competitiveness increases
national welfare, the cultivation of nationalism becomes a powerful legitimizing force: attention is shifted from distribution within
to 'relative performance' without. Nationalism has another major
benefit: it restricts the option of exit, that is the possibility of
labour exiting the country because of rival states' superior performance. Voice becomes labour's alternative.[25] The possibility
that monopolies are internationally competitive offers additional
legitimacy to the cause of capital: 'What is good for General
Motors is good for the nation'.

The emergence of monopoly capital, a result of increasing
concentration and centralization within nation states, puts
instrumental-type constraints on the state's functionaries.[26] The
sheer wealth and power of big capital can, more often than not,
ensure that they have their way on all matters of importance,
against labour but also against small capital and often the sectional interests of state functionaries – in cases, against their own
long-term interests too, because of the erosion of the state's
relative autonomy, and thus the erosion of its legitimizing power
and its ability to serve as a factor of cohesion of capitals. International production by big capital offers a temporary respite and
potentially an eventual intensification of the problem. To the
extent that such production brings benefits home (repatriated
profits), it assists legitimization by keeping labour happy at home.
However, to the extent that internationalization releases capital
from the need to produce at home, it provides a massive blow to
the nation state's relative autonomy, legitimizing power and even
its ability to pursue independent policies. For some, it implies the
end of the nation state (Kindleberger, 1973).

The increasing participation of the state in the production process (nationalized industries, utilities etc.) in the monopoly phase, the increasing needs of capital and demands from labour, and the sectional interests of state functionaries, all contribute to the remarkable growth of the public sector. Given transaction and other costs involved with state intervention, particularly of the redistribution type, government policies in a capitalist economy can often lead to inefficiencies. So can bounded rationality and 'rent seeking' (opportunism) by politicians and bureaucrats. The combined needs of the three, capital, labour and state functionaries, can lead to a fiscal crisis where revenues cannot cover required expenses. International production by TNCs can add new dimensions to this process.

6 The 'Nation' State and the Transnational Corporation

The long years of mercantilism (merchant capitalism), extending from the mid-fifteenth to the mid-eighteenth century, experienced the birth and consolidation of the *nation* state. They also saw the rise of 'national rivalry – the competitive zeal of European nations to possess themselves of the products of Asian and the treasures of American, and the colonial system, a basic propelling force, giving the nascent capitalist class a wider market and the chance to make a fortune' (Hymer, in Cohen et al., 1979, p. 90). Since, capitalism has developed within the 'protected' shell of the nation state; an often precarious protection afforded through 'investments' in military expenditures and wars.

The historical fact of the development of the capitalist state in the form of nation states adds important new dimensions to the analysis of the capitalist state. First, the emerging merchant-capitalist class require the state not only for support of its economic role, as described so far, but also for protection from foreign threats. Being a public good, such protection ('defence') could be under-provided. More generally, the (transaction) costs involved in building up a private army might be prohibitive. This and the pre-existence of a feudal army add additional weight to the concept of the merchant–crown alliance. Second, the existence of other rival states introduces the need for economic success (and legitimization) to the sovereigns as a means of preventing their subjects from voting with their feet (exiting); an idea which adds weight to the need of the sovereigns to support the merchants, through whom such success was achieved.

The concentration and centralization of capital that followed within *nation* states can be, and has been, argued to be one of the major factors that led to internationalization of production and the emergence of the transnational corporation (see chapter 3). In its turn, the emergence and growth of the TNC has raised the question of whether the *nation* state is viable and/or necessary in the presence of TNCs; I address these issues here.

The idea that rivalry between firms within a nation state could be seen as an incentive for *national* firms to undertake international operations, with an eye to eliminating conflict, goes back to Hymer's (1976) PhD dissertation, which was completed in 1960. This industrial organization, oligopolistic reaction type approach was pursued and developed by many, most notably Vernon (1971), Knickerbrocker (1973) and Graham (1978). Particularly insightful, in this line of analysis, was Hymer's subsequent observation that while firms' growth within nation states (particularly the USA) was providing an *incentive* for firms to look abroad as well as the ability to do so, given 'monopolistic advantages' (M-form, technology, finance etc.), it was the growth of *potential* rivalry by other nations' firms (particularly those of Europe and Japan) that actually triggered the dramatic expansion of US TNCs after the Second World War. In this connection, Hymer and Rowthorn (1979) observed the higher growth rates of US rivals and concluded that US direct foreign investment (DFI) abroad in this period was of a *defensive* nature.

This dimension of international competition remains at the (oligopolistic) *firm* level. International competition, however, also involves states. Nation states that are 'home' bases to TNCs, for example, can benefit from the latters' expansion abroad in a number of complex ways. First, the use of foreign, cheap, labour, when available, by TNCs can result in cheaper products back home. Second, to the extent that the state can tax TNCs of its national origin, revenue can be generated from overseas operations. Third, to the extent that the country's products become established abroad, via TNCs, the international competitiveness of the country as a whole improves, and so does its export surplus and thus domestic effective demand. More generally, transnationalization, from the point of view of the home state, appears to be a virtuous dynamic process. It presupposes efficiency-monopolistic advantages and through their exploitation leads to their maintenance and enhancement and thus to continuous improvement of the state's international economic position.[27] For this reason, home bases of TNCs are likely to favour their expansion and facilitate it, through, among other things, state aid, government purchases etc.

This 'symbiotic' and cooperative scenario is likely, because of other inherent advantages. It enhances the income (*ceteris paribus*) of domestic consumers, including labour. In this sense international competitiveness through TNCs is one of the most important legitimization devices possessed by nation states. From the point of view of the domestic economy as a whole, international competitiveness appears to be a positive sum game; its absence to be a vicious circle of decline, a negative sum game for the whole nation state. From the point of view of the government of the day, moreover, international competitiveness appears as the road to re-election. Overall, therefore, it has to be pursued at almost any cost, such as the consumer surplus reductions due to domestic monopolization envisaged by the neoclassical theory. A mechanism to defend these interests abroad also develops as a result in the form of 'investments' in the support and development of military technology, armaments expenditures etc. Neo-imperialism (the economic dependence of host nation states) is here in embryo.

Appearances can be deceptive. Some nation states might have learnt this the hard way. The idea is that once TNCs emerge and grow their relative power *vis-à-vis* nation states increases to such an extent that the powers of the nation states are eroded significantly, necessitating that states be replaced by international organizations; the withering away of the capitalist nation state! Exclamation marks apart, the position has been proposed and debated and received some currency for some time. Furthermore, the relationship between TNCs and *their* home base is just the tip of the iceberg. The relationship between TNCs and countries other than their base ones ('host' countries) is at least as important. Within this latter category the relationships between TNC and host state could vary depending on the latter's economic strength, and degree of economic development.

In the mainstream tradition the argument that the nation state could be finished as an economic unit because of the TNCs was posed by Kindleberger (1973) and Vernon (1971). The approach here is TNCs on the one hand, nation states on the other, and the question one of relative bargaining strength. For Vernon, 'The basic asymmetry between multinational enterprises and national governments', that is the capacity of the enterprises to shift some of their activities from one location to another, as compared with the commitment of the government to a fixed piece of national turf, 'may be tolerable up to a point, but beyond that point there is a need to reestablish balance' (Vernon, 1981, pp. 517–18). Beyond the point in question, Vernon (1971) argued, nation states would find their 'sovereignty at bay'. The flexibility of operations of TNCs would put severe limits on governments' ability to pursue autonomous policies.

At the other extreme of the spectrum, the Marxist Monthly Review school views the US TNCs as the result of US imperialism, which is 'the process by which the corporation and the state team up to expand their activities, their interests and their power beyond their borders' (Sweezy, 1978, p. 2). The relationship between the parties involved, for Sweezy, is one where

> the corporations are completely dependent on the state for their very existence, and the state in turn lives off the surplus produced by the workers and accruing to the capitalists, which means in the first instance to the corporations. The *state and the corporations thus exist in a condition of symbiosis*, each deeply dependent on the other. (Sweezy, 1978, emphasis added)

The reason for imperialism is capital's need to expand: 'Considered as a whole, capital *must* expand; the alternative is not a happy and relaxed condition of zero growth . . . but convulsive contraction and deepening crisis' (Sweezy, 1978, p. 5, emphasis in original).

An unexpected ally of the Vernon–Kindleberger idea is Murray (1971), in the Marxist camp. Murray also suggested that TNCs erode the power of the nation state and went on to suggest that increasing transnationalization of capital necessitates the support of capital by nation states other than its home base, or by international organizations. This weakens the bargaining power of not only the home nation state but also nation states in general; TNCs could play off one nation state against the others in the states' attempt to attract TNC investments. The opposite point has been made by Warren (1971). He observed the nation state's own participation in assisting the creation of giant firms *and* in instituting international bodies as well as in the very process of internationalization. These, the fact that under state monopoly capitalism the state's participation in the economy increases, and the fact that monopolization implies fewer firms and thus easier to control, suggested to him that the power of the nation state was on the increase.

While the Vernon–Kindleberger–Murray–Warren debate is concerned with TNCs *vis-à-vis* nation states in general, the US imperialism idea introduces the relationship between one nation state's TNCs on the one hand and the power of different nation states (and their TNCs) on the other. This latter focus presupposes that the USA is the undisputed imperialist world power, an idea criticized by, in particular, Mandel (1967) and Rowthorn (1971). Both claimed that competition from Europe and Japan was challenging US hegemony, which led to an intensification of conflict between these 'nation' states to defend 'their' TNCs, and thus to increased international rivalry. The underlying assumption is still that of Sweezy: that there is a one-to-one relationship between interests of nation states and their TNCs and also, to a lesser extent, that the stronger the nation state's TNCs are, the stronger the nation state will be.

Hymer's position was a more qualified one. He suggested that the increasing bargaining power of the TNCs threatens the autonomy of all nation states, but asymmetrically. Weak states' autonomy (for example, 'host' states of less developed countries, LDCs) is eroded to a higher degree than strong states' autonomy (typically developed countries, DCs). Among the DC TNCs, the situation is not of US imperialism but rather of interpenetration of investments, leading to increasing global collusion by TNCs (the world's wealthy few, including the wealthy from the LDCs), who share the common aim of increasing the total surplus. The increasing complexity of the world economy necessitates the emergence of international apparatuses, such as the EC, to coordinate the needs of international capital. This, however, does not suggest the end of the nation state. For one, Hymer observed, international apparatuses lack the important controlling and legitimizing device of nationalism. Given this, nation states and international organizations are more likely to co-exist, both in support of the needs of international capital.

What can we make of all this? The Vernon–Kindleberger original thesis has now been severely qualified by their own original proponents. Vernon (1981, p. 521), for example, observes the increasing 'spate of expropriations and nationalisations of the foreign properties of the multinational enterprises that occurred during the first half of the 1970s' and the increasing demand for and prices of raw materials such as oil, and concludes that 'I might better have entitled my 1971 volume Everyone at Bay'. The symbiosis and imperialism ideas, on the other hand, found it very difficult to explain the direction of US DFI, after the Second World War, towards other DCs. In a criticism of Magdoff (1969) of the Monthly Review school, Kindleberger (1984, p. 176) observes that the USA 'has aided Japan, Japan has access to the US capital market, uses the dollar and gets its self-defence from the US military. Is Japan a puppet of the United States? The answer is . . . assuredly no.' He goes on to explain this in terms of US inability to knock off Japanese tariff barriers, among other things, and concludes that the imperialism idea looks curious in the light of not only US–Japanese but also French, German or Swedish relationships.

Similar considerations apply to Murray's position as to that of Vernon. Warren's argument, on the other hand, as Fine and Harris (1979) observe, is rather impressionistic. For one, states facilitating the establishment of international bodies need not necessarily imply increasing power of the nation state. Next, the reduction in the number of firms implies the potential ability of states to control them but not the necessity to do so. Finally, the assumption of a one-to-one relationship between a state's TNCs and this state's strength has been qualified by Rowthorn (1980) himself, in view of the obvious and disturbing counter-example of the relative decline of the UK; see Coates and Hillard (1986) for an extensive collection of readings. This decline, despite Britain being the home base of many of the world's most powerful TNCs, Rowthorn attibutes to the international orientation of British capital.

Hymer's interpenetration idea has fared better, as witnessed by a substantial body of empirical literature; see, for example, Trajtenberg and Vigorito (1983) and Jenkins (1987) for surveys. Such interpenetration also lends support to Hymer's other idea that some erosion of state power is taking place, even in DCs. A reason is that interpenetration makes it far more difficult for any nation state to pursue protectionist policies lest other nation states retaliate. The erosion of state's power to exercise control on their economies need not imply erosion of power *vis-à-vis* other states, in particular LDCs. Moreover, it does not cast doubt on Vernon's idea that up to a point the interests of nation states and TNCs go hand in hand. Indeed, it does not even question Sweezy's idea of imperialism (up to the point in hand) as a symbiotic relationship between a state and its TNCs. It only questions the idea of *US* imperialism. However, imperialist policies, in the sense of 'symbiosis', could exist in a number of DCs, all supporting their TNCs and all trying to share in the global surplus generated through TNCs' operations.

The interpenetration idea, in fact, seems to be more consistent with this latter scenario. As Nye (1988) observes, the US share of world product has not been lost to the US 'enemies' but to political allies, particularly Germany and Japan. The Soviet share, in particular, declined from 12.5 per cent in 1920 to 11.5 per cent at the end of the 1970s. On top, Nye observes, US power is still very impressive. With nearly a quarter of world military expenditure and product, the USA is still the single most powerful nation state. He concludes that some erosion of US power to control *outcomes* has taken place, in part because of TNCs and in part because of the emergence of other major players.

Another indication in line with both the observed interpenetration and the idea that, up to a point, the TNCs–states relationship is symbiotic comes from the American versus non-American challenge debate. It was observed in the 1960s that European industry was less developed technologically than US industry, and that gradually European industry was becoming dependent on the USA; see Schreiber-Servan (1968) for the classic statement of the American challenge thesis. Schreiber-Servan suggested a European industrial policy favouring greater size, through mergers between European firms, in the expectation that increased size would allow European firms to compete on an equal basis to American ones. It was indeed the case that

European policy was very permissive (and encouraging) to increased size in the 1960s and early 1970s. There was a 'merger mania', which led to the creation of many European TNCs (Tugendhat, 1971). Whether such policies did help towards the closing of the gap between Europe and the US, the non-American challenge (Rowthorn, 1971), is very difficult to tell. Recent consensus on the unprofitability of mergers (Cowling and Sawyer, 1989) and the overall disadvantages of increased size (Geroski and Jacquemin, 1989) do not seem to support this idea. More importantly, the fact that, among the European states, the one that had one of the worst performances was the UK, despite it being home base to many powerful TNCs, indicates the limits of the symbiosis idea. Still, particularly interesting here is that both industry and the European states, particularly the French, at the time were favouring increased size, which Swann (1988) observes to have influenced the EC Commission's own attitude.

The above discussion seems to be in line with Hymer's idea of the interpenetration of investments, with the idea that Japan and Europe have increased their relative economic role *vis-à-vis* the USA, and with the idea that nation states perceive that their interests go hand in hand with their TNCs' interests, up to a point. Beyond this point, their fortunes (and interests) may part company. The UK seems to be a case in point. This is also in line with Hymer's observations of differential erosion of power, and thus raises interesting questions concerning TNCs and host LDCs.

Seen within the context of the discussion of the state in general in the previous sections, all the ideas and debates discussed in this section suffer from two major problems. First, there is a rather crudely deterministic perception of the relationship between states and TNCs, where the two parties are seen either as independent and bargaining with each other (the mainstream case) or as totally fused (the imperialism case). Second, there is an absence of dynamics and historical specificity, of an examination of the extent to which circumstances and relationships were changing through time.

First the state. To assume that this is independent from capital and TNCs, and bargains with the latter on the basis of a utilitarian calculus, is to ignore the possibility that community of interests may be endogenous; that is, capital's interests are expressed through the state to start with (Poulantzas, 1975). To assert that TNCs dominate the state (or that their interests are the same) ignores the influence of other classes, in particular labour (Fine and Harris, 1979), and the possibility that these classes' interests and demands might differ from those of transnational capital. Similar considerations apply for other groups, such as non-transnational capital. Such interests will be reflected through the state's actions, given, for example, that otherwise the government of the day may face electoral defeat (Fine and Harris, 1979). Such possible constraints need to be considered. Related are the needs and interests of state functionaries *per se*.

In brief, labour's long-term interests are adversely affected by TNCs, given that the locational flexibility of the latter reduces the bargaining power of unions (Sugden, 1990). This puts an upper limit to the symbiotic interests between the two that can potentially accrue to labour through TNCs' foreign operations. This is reinforced by the fact that such benefits, to the extent that they exist, are not obvious unless investment in 'education' by TNCs and the state is involved to make the point. This 'antipathetic' attitude of unions to TNCs might well be reflected in state policies. Similar considerations may apply for non-transnational capital, to the extent that its relative competitiveness *vis-à-vis* TNCs declines, and subject to it not operating as, for example, TNCs' subcontractors, thus depending on the latter.

Such 'discontent' has a dynamic of its own. It is reflected through the state directly, but also indirectly because it affects TNCs own interests in legitimization. As Hymer (in Cohen et al., 1979) observed, nationalism is the one 'product' TNCs are unable to offer. Indeed, can one doubt that to be an American carries with it much more than to be an IBMan? TNCs need legitimization, they need nationalism, they need the nation state. Thus labour interests affect state policies through their effects on capital interests. Furthermore, the need and special interests of governments have a role to play. Governments are interested in re-election, but also in governing! This has implications for the extent to which TNCs' preferences can dominate government policies.

My discussion so far has interesting implications for the state–TNC international state apparatuses debate. First, it suggests that nation states and TNCs should be seen as complementary rather than substitutes. Second, constraints imposed on nation states by, for example, labour, put an upper limit on the erosion of their power to control their policies, a limit reinforced by state functionaries' own dislike of seeing their powers eroded. A solution that kills two birds with one stone is for states to facilitate and support the emergence of international state apparatuses, in part so as to be able to bring TNCs' actions in line with their own interests, through orchestrated actions. This explains (rather than asserts) Warren's observation, which is an everyday life one, that it is through state initiatives that international bodies appear to be set up.

International bodies are of absolute importance to TNCs. For they can provide all those public goods, such as defence, international law and order, stability and regulation of the global system, that any one single nation state might find itself unable or unwilling to offer.[28] In this sense, and generalizing the earlier theoretical discussion and subject to qualifications there, it could be suggested that international bodies are the result of institutional failures; of both nation states and TNCs. From the point of view of both capital and the state they have the advantages of being further removed from the locus of class struggle (Fine and Harris, 1979), and are thus a more *efficient* means of achieving international coordination than any single (imperialist) state: an 'imperialism failure' idea! Enough has been said to make the point that states, TNCs and international bodies are alternative but complementary capitalist institutional devices aimed at achieving an efficient exploitation of the division of labour and team production, with an eye to furthering the interests of their principals, and subject to constraints. Concerning TNCs and international institutions in particular, the issue is international team production and international division of labour.[29]

The other limitation of the theories discussed so far concerns the historical specificity of the relationships involved. The observation, for example, that US TNCs developed at an earlier stage than European and Japanese ones, suggests that the US imperialism idea is not valid or invalid. It could be both, namely US imperialism first, followed by non-American challenge and interpenetration later. More importantly, the relative decline of US imperialism (*vis-à-vis* the whole world) need not imply the absence of imperialism in general; this could have now taken the form of DC imperialism, with an eye to exploiting the advantages offered by operating in LDCs. The debate concerning the relationship between DC TNCs and LDC nation states is one of the most heated, and for obvious reasons. To have your power eroded by 'your' TNCs is one thing. To have it eroded by someone else's is different. Emotions, nationalism and all that goes with it are involved here. Even within Europe, the fear of the south becoming *les garçons* of the north is a topic of everyday discussion and academic interest. Still, views on the issue are diametrically opposed in a way that cuts across different ideologies!

The mainstream view on the *economic* effects of TNCs globally is a rather sanguine one. The transaction costs perspective, for example, emphasizes the efficiency properties of TNCs, regarding them as advantageous to global welfare (Buckley and Casson, 1976; Caves, 1982; Pitelis and Sugden, 1990). The monopolistic advantage theory, at least as developed by Kindleberger (1984), sees the negative aspects of TNCs, such as their ability to close markets, but expresses the belief that the long-term benefits of TNCs are positive and suffice to outweigh any short-term losses. The same view is expressed by Warren (1973), who claims that the international expansion of capital and the TNC have been instrumental in a remarkable development of the LDCs' manufacturing sector, an idea which is traced back to Marx; see also the survey in Palma (1978).

At the other extreme, theorists of the dependency school choose to emphasize the dependent nature of the development process of LDCs. Palma (1978) identifies three different perspectives within this school. First is the 'development of underdevelopment' approach, particularly associated with the work of Frank (1972), which emphasizes the exploitative nature of the metropolis–periphery relationship. Second is a reformulation of this thesis, which distinguishes between economic growth and economic development and claims that the two need not coincide and in fact have not coincided in LDCs. Third is the 'concrete situations of dependency' analysis, which stresses that the emergence of TNCs has transformed the centre–periphery relationship in that industrialization (formerly seen as an antiimperialist struggle) has now become the goal of foreign capital. Accordingly, dependency and industrialization cease to be contradictory, allowing for a path to 'dependent development'.

This approach comes close to Hymer's views (see Cohen et al., 1979). Following Marx, Hymer observed that TNCs were leading to the development of LDCs; but this was both a dependent and an uneven development. Its fruits were shared unequally in favour of DCs and the wealthy of the LDCs. Although TNCs' operations in LDCs provided these countries with benefits, such as skills, technology etc., the real issue was one of control: of who controls the development process. When TNCs do, the LDCs lose their economic independence and enter a process of self-perpetuating dependency. TNCs, moreover, tend to shape the world to their image, the 'correspondence principle'. They create 'superior' and 'inferior' nations by using a pyramid of power, a centre and a periphery (the hinterland), which involves decentralized decision-making but centralized control, the latter concentrated in few metropolises in the centre. New York, London, Frankfurt and Tokyo concentrate on strategic decision-making. New products are first introduced in the centre and then diffused to the periphery through an international trickle down and an international 'demonstration effect'.

Although the periphery might have been better off choosing an independent path to development, the chances of this happening through a national capitalist class were not high. The wealthy of the LDCs, for Hymer, are only seeking promotion within the transnational capitalist order, and for good reason. Being a shareowner in their ex-firm (and still running the branch) is an easier alternative than competing. This way, they are no longer locked into *their* firms, being able to join the world's wealthy by diversifying their portfolios so as to get a share of the general social surplus. This gives rise to a branch plant outlook in the LDCs. Hymer further argued that it is not technology that leads to uneven development but the centralization of control by TNCs. This, in turn, increases TNCs control over the 'labour aristocracy' at home, for the threat arising is the possibility of TNCs drawing on the 'reserve army of labour' in the LDCs.

The dependency school has been criticized by, among others, Fine and Harris (1979) on a number of counts: in particular for its viewing of the whole world as capitalist, for a reliance on 'exploitation through unequal exchange' (Emmanuel, 1972) and, in the case of Frank, for asserting that development in the core necessarily leads to underdevelopment in the periphery. These last theses in particular, Palma (1978, p. 29) argues, are 'mistaken, not only because they do not "fit the facts" but also – and more importantly – because their mechanistic-formal nature renders them both static and unhistorical'. The Warren (1973) thesis has been subjected to detailed criticism by McMichael et al. (1974). In their view, a geographical fragmentation of the processes involved in industrial production has taken place under the aegis of the TNCs: 'each industrializing colony or semi-colony partakes of a part of the industrial process but not the whole. Much of what Warren has euphemistically referred to as "industrialization" has been in large part the development of "assembly plant operations"' (McMichael et al., 1974, p. 86).

All these appear to lend support to Hymer's view of dependent development, although not necessarily to his view of uneven development and inequality, unless the latter is interpreted purely in terms of a class-theoretical perspective (world rich on the one hand, world poor on the other). Even this would require more than assertion to substantiate. From the purely economic point of view, the uneven development thesis is hard to generalize. This is not surprising given the complexity of real life. In discussing the new international division of labour, for example, Cowling and Sugden (1987, p. 69) note that 'Nowadays manufacturing is observed throughout the world. Thus whereas the traditional manufacturing nations have been in relative, even absolute, decline, the "newly industrializing countries" have grown very rapidly'. But, they observe, control is still located in a handful of metropolises.

In would appear fair to conclude that the dependent development thesis is hard to dispute. It is not contrary to the mainstream focus either, to the extent that TNCs are seen to erode the power of states, DCs and LDCs alike. No more than this can be asserted. Hymer's position that dependence will necessarily be self-perpetuating should be taken with a pinch of salt. There is no *a priori* reason why *initially* dependent development could not lead to independent development. The LDCs' 'wealthy' may have an inherent pecuniary interest in joining the 'wealthy' of the world, but this ignores non-economic factors, such as nationalist and religious opposition to 'foreign imperialists'. This and chance factors, such as OPEC's ownership of a crucial raw material, could in cases lead to nationalization, to the amassing of fantastic wealth by the wealthy of the LDCs and, potentially, in certain cases to independent industrialization, as Marx and other 'classics' of Marxism foresaw (see Palma, 1978): 'the country that is more developed industrially only shows, to the less developed, the image of its own future' (Marx, quoted in Palma, 1978, p. 7).

To conclude, reality seems to be far too complex to allow any sweeping generalizations. In part what allows the theorists examined above to derive such generalizations is an inadequate analysis of the nature (and constraints) of nation states and TNCs, as I have suggested. In particular, the role of class dynamics in LDCs is downplayed as are any non-economic considerations, and the potential historical specificity and dynamic change of the relationship involved. All considered, I think I might concur with Kindleberger (1984, p. 31) that 'The most serious charge one can level against the international corporation is that it produces a homogenized world culture, of wall to wall carpeting, tasteless meals, Americanized English, traffic jams and gasoline fumes'. On further reflection, I might wish to add ITT's involvement in overthrowing Allende in Chile (see Radice, 1975).

7 Concluding Remarks

I have claimed that the capitalist state is an institutional device for complementing the market and the firm in exploiting the fruits of the division of labour and team work, with an eye to furthering the interests of its principals and subject to a set of constraints. Historically, it has emerged from and replaced the feudal state, through an alliance between merchants and the crown, to further their mutual advantage, and given their mutual dependence. These two (the principals) have lived symbiotically since. Feudal serfs might also have favoured the emergence of the capitalist state, a progressive one compared with the feudal state, as it provided them with 'freedom' from slavery (and property). In this sense the emergence of the capitalist state might have been (Pareto) efficient both *ex ante* and *ex post*. However, it was driven by distributional-power and not efficiency considerations. Constraints to the principals are competition by other states, and later other parties, and state functionaries' sectional interests, in particular electoral defeat.

International state apparatuses perform a similar role to that of the nation states. They have the additional advantage (for capital) over the latter that they provide international public goods (defence, stability, coordination) while being more distant from the locus of class struggle. In this sense, they do not face the constraint of 're-election needs'. They can also assist state functionaries in their (class struggle mediated) concern with controlling the excesses of TNCs. TNCs effect a more 'efficient' division of labour, in part by dividing labour, thus reducing its bargaining power, both in DCs and in LDCs. TNCs and nation states (as well as international bodies) are complementary, TNCs with a comparative advantage in effecting division of labour, national states in providing legitimization through ideology, such as nationalism. DCs are assisted in this by TNCs to the extent that their actions in LDCs could enhance the welfare of the DCs' 'labour aristocracy'. In this sense, the nation state is not through yet. The current relation between TNCs and LDCs is one of dependent development to start with. This need not preclude independent economic development at a later stage. This has an important implication. It allows labour's (and national capitalists') demands potentially to effect through the state a socio-political climate conducive to seeking independent industrialization, against the apparent strictly pecuniary interest of the local bourgeoisie, which is to join the world's wealthy.

My historical approach to the emergence of the capitalist state does not adequately address the issue, of whether *originally* (in general) states emerge for efficiency (cooperative or prisoner dilemma type games) or predatory reasons (distribution-power, or inequality preserving games). Indeed the issue is not soluble on *a priori* grounds. If any generalization is possible, it is likely to be that states in class societies replacing other states in class societies are likely to be of the inequality preserving type, while in classless societies the cooperative, contractual outcome is possible. Even this cannot be supported without specific analysis of the specific circumstances. The Athenian democracy was apparently the pinnacle of a contractual (city) state, yet based on the existence of slave labour: a cooperative inequality preserving game!

Notes

1 The agreement of no less than both Marx and Marshall on the market and the firm being two alternative institutional devices for the exploitation of the division of labour is noted by Hymer (in Cohen et al., 1979). Ludwig von Mises, the father-figure of the Austrian tradition, also defines the market in this way (Hodgson, 1988). My reference to principals is taken from the neoclassical institutional economic historian Douglas North (1981). My inclusion of the state here is a natural extension of the Marx–Marshall–Mises consensus. 'Principals' are taken as (groups of) individuals whose relation with other groups (agents) is one of authority and control. Agents, that is, have to work for (the achievement of the objectives of) the principals (Jensen and Meckling, 1976). My 'maximum possible' is intended to convey the meaning that the principals' derivation of maximum benefits is subject to constraints. These issues are developed further below.

2 My term 'new right' is borrowed from David Green's (1987) book title. His treatment also includes the liberal tradition and anarcho-capitalism, to which only passing reference is made here.

3 For a critique of the 'free riding' and non-revelation problem and real-life examples of private provision of public goods see Cullis and Jones (1987). Olson (1965) is the classic analysis of compliance through rewards and sanctions in cases where formal statements of what constitutes the 'public interest' are required because of the size, mobility and/or heterogeneity of the 'communities'.

4 Other instances of market failure commonly discussed are incomplete markets, informational failures, uncertainty, unemployment, inflation, disequilibrium, merit goods and economic crises (Stiglitz, 1986; Cullis and Jones, 1987; Karageorgas, 1977).

5 Possibility rather than certainty, given that potential competition may still result in competitive pricing, as suggested by Austrian theorists and by Schumpeter (1942), and the more recent theory of contestable markets (e.g. Baumol, 1982).

6 See, for example, the discussion in Pitelis (1990).

7 The case examined here is that of structural failure (Bator, 1958). Monopoly, however, may also be the result of transaction costs reductions (cognitive or natural market failure) (Dunning and Rugman, 1985). In this case monopoly is a solution to market failure, thus there is little need for the state (Williamson, 1987). In practice it is not easy to distinguish structural from cognitive failures; the latter's solution, for example, often giving rise to the former (Malcolmson, 1984).

8 Concern with positive freedoms goes back to Marx. More recently it has been revived in the work of Berlin (1969) and taken up by a number of economists, such as Dasgupta (1986), Sen (1988) and Lindbeck (1988). What they observe is that freedom in neoclassical economics is normally of the negative type, e.g. freedom from coercion, including state coercion. Positive freedom, on the other hand, refers to individuals' ability to function (choose) consciously, willingly, purposefully, actively and responsibly, and to explain their choices by reference to their own ideas and purposes (Berlin, 1969).

9 They can also be inconsistent. If, for example, saving in market transactions leads to (monopolistic) firms, solutions to natural market failures would give rise to structural failures (Malcolmson, 1984). If so, attempts by the state to control monopoly power would simultaneously increase and reduce efficiency!

10 It is worth noting here that Axelrod's findings have been used by industrial organization theorists to support the likelihood of the prevalence of collusion in oligopolistic markets (Cubbin, 1988), lending support to structural market failures ideas.

11 Inequality-preserving social institutions are defined to be institutions created to preserve the status quo position of inequality between agents. Coordination problems exist where agents always have the incentive to coordinate their activities with others, yet try to have the coordinated strategy that is best for them (Schotter, 1981).

12 In fact, non-market institutions are seen by Schotter as often arising in order to compensate for informational insufficiencies of market prices, and thus complement the market (see also Hodgson, 1988).

13 As Tullock (1976, p. 2) puts it, individuals in government 'serve their own interests within certain institutional limits'.

14 The similarities here with the 'managerial' theories of the firm are obvious, particularly with Baumol's (1959) sales revenue maximization theory. See also Mueller (1989), who notes some differences.

15 For a typology of government failure see Wolf (1979). He considers internalities and private goods (e.g. bureaucrats' 'more is better' approach), redundant and rising costs (e.g. because of X-inefficiency), derived externalities because of government action and distributional inequities (because of government actions). See also Cullis and Jones (1987) for a detailed survey.

16 Additional support for the 'government failure' idea has been provided by a number of macroeconomic theory developments, such as: Friedman and Schwartz's (1963) attempt to explain the Great Depression of the 1930s in terms of 'policy mistakes' (see

Bleaney, 1985, for a critical assessment); the 'rational expectations revolution', e.g. Lucas (1975), who asserts market clearing and the impotency of government policy in the absence of surprises, because of rational expectations by agents (see Tobin, 1980, for a critique); and the Feldstein (1974) hypothesis of saving, according to which social security programmes have depressed total saving and capital accumulation in the USA by around 50 per cent. Tobin (1980) provides a critique of this view; see chapter 5.

17 Compare with Baran and Sweezy's (1966) conception of the 'managerial' group as the upper echelon of the capitalist class. Mills (1963) also uses the concept of power elite, but views it as effectively similar to Domhoff's ruling class.

18 The term is to denote their focus on price categories rather than value categories and the associated emphasis on exchange relationships at the expense of production which instead is the focus of the so called 'fundamentalists', see Fine and Harris (1979) for a discussion.

19 The development of the German debate was in effect an attempt to criticize the so-called 'critical theory' of the state, associated in particular with Habermas (1976) and Offe (1972), whose views, although different to those of Miliband and Poulantzas, also took the line of looking at politics separately from the 'economic base'; see Gerstenberger (1985) and O'Connor (1987) for discussions.

20 O'Connor's work has been criticized extensively (see, for example, the exchange between Moseley, 1978, 1982, and O'Connor, 1978, 1982), most notably for relying on an underconsumptionist theory of crisis and for the functional–ahistorical theory of the state (Hadjimatheou, 1976). Miller (1986) has tested the hypothesis that legitimization expenditures exceed those for accumulation derived from O'Connor's theory of fiscal crisis and concluded that in the post-war USA this was not the case. Heald (1983) notes the resemblance between O'Connor's and the Austrians' perception of the state. Finally, O'Connor's productivity arguments are reminiscent of Bacon and Eltis's (1976) arguments, which attribute Britain's poor performance to public sector growth, as well as Baumol's 'law' (Baumol, 1967), which notes the relatively small productivity growth potential of public services (Cullis and Jones, 1987).

21 For critical accounts of Gouph's theory from a similar (neo-Ricardian) perspective, see Harrison (1980). Fine and Harris (1979) criticize Gouph's (1975) concept of 'productive and unproductive labour'.

22 North (1981) makes a parallel point from a neoclassical exchange-

ex post perspective. He distinguishes between the 'contract' theory of the state and the 'predatory' or 'exploitation' theory. He observes that, while 'the contract theory explains the gains of initial contracting but not the subsequent maximizing behaviour of constituents with diverse interests, the predatory theory ignores the initial gains from contracting and focuses on the extraction of rents from constituents by those who gain control of the state. Nevertheless the two theories are not inconsistent. It is the distribution of "violence potential" that reconciles them' (North, 1981, p. 22).

23 The absence of developed markets implies that merchants could generate profit by buying cheap and selling dear, i.e. in the exchange process alone. Although, from a classical point of view, value was still created by embodied labour, no direct exploitation in the production process is involved here. Accordingly, and subject to demand–supply conditions in the labour and product markets, products could be sold permanently for above their 'value'. It is only in a developed capitalist market that equivalent changes for equivalent, and thus profit cannot be made in exchange, as Marxism claims. In its absence there may not be a notion of equivalence at all.

24 The best possible scenario could be the establishment of perfectly equitable distribution or, even better, themselves becoming nobles or sovereigns. Rawls's 'veil of ignorance' scenario removes this latter possibility. Under a veil of ignorance they would not wish such a possibility to exist lest they found themselves in the position of the unprivileged.

25 See, for example, the analysis by Hirschman (1970), where voice and exit are seen as two alternative means of expressing dissatisfaction, the former more akin to hierarchies and the latter to markets.

26 In Pitelis and Pitelis (1987), for example, the point is made that even assuming structurally induced neutrality of the neoclassical type, increasing concentration and monopolization would tend to generate both structural and instrumental constraints on the state; given the increasing importance of monopolies for investment and the sheer power and resources of their controllers.

27 Non-economic considerations also apply here. A country's culture and value system (subjectively perceived to be superior) and the political and cultural influence of this country in the world are improved; see Hood and Young (1979) for a discussion.

28 Kindleberger's hegemonic stability theory, for example, makes this very point that such stability is a public good and thus likely to be under-provided (Kindleberger, 1986). From a purely theoretical economic point of view, Kindleberger's idea is a plausible one.

It does, however, downplay significantly the many tangible and intangible benefits of hegemony. Going at least as far back as Alexander the Great, shortage of very willing hegemons does not seem to have been a problem; rather the opposite. See Nye (1988) for more criticisms of this theory.

29 From a different perspective, Nye (1988) criticizes the hegemonic stability idea and observes that corporations and nations are complementary institutions with different power resources: wealth for one, legitimacy and force for the other. Given this, incentives for bargaining will be expected, even in the absence of an effective interstate regime.

5

Theory of Capitalist Institutional Failure and Crisis

1 Introduction

Crisis is Greek for 'judgement'.[1] Capitalist institutional crisis is a moment of judgement of the adequacy of capitalist institutions to perform their normal functions under prevailing circumstances. My focus here is on what are arguably the three most important institutions of capitalism: the market, the firm and the state.[2] It is also on two major competing views: the Keynesian–monetarist orthodoxy,[3] on the one hand, and the Marxist alternative(s) on the other.

Orthodox economic theory does not have a theory of institutional crisis as such. This is not very surprising. The neoclassical *magnum opus*, 'general equilibrium' analysis, of the Arrow–Debreu type (see Eatwell et al., 1989b), is based on the assumptions of prices clearing all markets (including contingent futures) and utility-maximizing households over all goods. Given this the market determines everything. Once equilibrium is established (through the Walrasian auctioneer) and given certain assumptions, the existence and optimality of equilibrium can be obtained. In this world the market is the only institutional form and it is failure-free. The firm (private hierarchy) and the state (public hierarchy) are institutional *data*. There is little need for separate *economic* analysis to explain their *raisons d'être* or roles. Indeed there is no *raison d'être* for them at all.

Market clearing precludes the existence of involuntary unemployment. Keynes's (1936) *General Theory* was the major theoretical macroeconomic attack on this idea. Saving and investment, for Keynes, are undertaken by different groups of agents: the former by households, the latter by firms. Their plans need not coincide, but may coincidently. Even when they do, it need not be the case that effective demand (planned demand backed by purchasing power) will be at the full-employment level of output. If it is below, involuntary unemployment will arise, for demand-side reasons. If it is above, there will be inflation. Importantly, there is no inherent mechanism in capitalist economies to return to the full-employment equilibrium level. Involuntary unemployment is both possible and here to stay. Say's (notorious) law, that supply creates it own demand, is rejected (it is hoped) for good. Keynes's is the first and major mainstream theory of (macroeconomic) market failure. It establishes the possibility of such a failure, and the possibility of correcting it: government intervention. Given the latter, the possibility of failure also implies its non-necessity. If present, it is the result of 'policy errors'.

Monetarist economists, most notably Friedman, share the Keynesian belief that economic crises can be explained in terms of errors in policy. Here, however, it is government interference itself that creates, or exacerbates, temporary disturbances. Left to its own devices, the market is well capable of solving any temporary difficulties, provided that government does not interfere so as to worsen the situation. It is government failure, *not* market failure, that explains crises, such as the Great Depression of the 1930s (Friedman and Schwartz, 1963). Such failures are due to government's self-interested behaviour, with its associated dependence on powerful pressure groups such as business leaders and trade unions, but also to sheer inefficiency. Given this, and the superior properties of the market, crises are only possible where there is government intervention. This implies a non-necessity, provided that governments limit their functions to the bare essentials required and prescribed by monetarists, such as a steady growth rate of money.

Government intervention can also be the culprit in more general problems, such as a decline in the rate of capital accumulation, which for the mainstream is aggregate saving. For Feldstein (1974), the saving rate in the USA has declined substantially because of the introduction and expansion of social security pay-as-you-go schemes. Rational households consider their contributions to social security schemes as their saving in the expectation of future benefits. However, as contributions are used by government to finance current benefits, so that no fund is available, total capital accumulation has declined by the rate of substitutability between social security saving-wealth and personal saving-wealth. Growing social security contributions can thus be responsible for a secular decline in the rate of saving (capital accumulation). Government can generate (let alone exacerbate) crises.

The above presupposes that government policy has the power to affect economic outcomes. For the new-neoclassicists (the 'rational expectations' school), such as Lucas (1975), this is far from obvious. If individuals hold rational expectations (i.e. form expectations by making best use of all the information they have), any predictable policy by the government will have the same real consequences as any other, which is no systematic effects at all! Individuals with rational expectations will ensure that they offset any government action by appropriately modifying their behaviour. Social security contributions, for example, will not displace personal saving. In terms of Barro's (1974) Ricardian equivalence, for example, debt finance (social security, for example) by government and current taxes are equivalent from the point of view of rational intertemporal utility-maximizing households, whose optimal consumption–saving pattern accordingly is not affected by the choice of debt finance by the government, versus current taxation. The government non-potency idea of this school rejects the possibility of crises *due* to government policies, such as in the case of social security contributions. It also rejects the possibility of government *correction* of market failures *à la* Keynes (1936). It rejects their necessity too. Markets are assumed to clear continuously. Market failures simply do not arise. Arrow and Debreu are back with a vengeance!

The three mainstream approaches to capitalist institutional failure reviewed above – market failure, government failure and non-failure – will be critically reviewed in the next sections along with other contributions in this tradition. My main claim will be that mainstream approaches, as they stand, lack a *micro-micro*-foundation. Such a foundation can be provided in terms of transaction costs, as in Coase (1937, 1960), Arrow (1970) and Williamson (1975). Such an analysis will be shown to reject the Arrow–Debreu rational expectations scenario, in favour of *both* Keynesian market (and firm) failures *and* monetarist government failures. This establishes the *possibility* of a theory of *institutional failure* (crisis) well within the mainstream scenario; not, however, the necessity of such a failure. This is the Marxist task.

The possibility of, and necessity for, crises in capitalism has been one of the major fields of enquiry within the Marxian perspective. This again is hardly surprising. Unlike the mainstream, Marxism regards capitalism as a transitory phenomenon, a system to be replaced by another: socialism (it is hoped). In this sense, the focus is on the 'present as history'. If capitalism is not here to stay, then crisis may well be a factor that eventually leads to capitalism becoming history. It does not need to. But it may. Even if not, crises are particularly interesting for another reason. They prove that besides being a system of class exploitation (or because of it) capitalism is not virtuous. It does not deliver the goods. Accordingly it needs to be replaced. Thus, through collapse and/or class struggle, capitalism's demise and crisis are inextricably linked.

The *possibility* of crisis in Marxian theory results from such characteristics of capitalism as the existence and role of money, in particular credit money, the co-existence of *social* production and *private* appropriation, and thus the associated unequal distribution of incomes, and the 'anarchy' of the market, which can generate sectoral disproportionalities. Such *conditions* of crisis need to be triggered by a causal factor in order to establish the *necessity* of crisis. Three such causal factors have received the lion's share in Marxist theory: underconsumption and realization failures; a declining rate of profits resulting from a rising organic composition of capital; and the rising strength (or militancy) of labour. The first attributes crises to deteriorating conditions of profit realization, which in mainstream terms implies a secularly declining effective demand. The second suggests that competition leads firms to introduce labour-saving technological advances, which increases the organic composition of capital (the capital to labour ratio), and thus reduces the rate of profit. The third suggests that a similar reduction takes place, but because of the relative improvement of labour's position *vis-à-vis* capital in the class struggle. Realization failures and declining profit rates are then seen as the causal factors that necessitate the crisis. This *necessity* is seen in a dual sense: in terms of inevitability but also as a requirement for a new round of successful accumulation.

These theories are critically appraised in section 3. Following this it is suggested that, at the theory level, they do not contradict each other, as is often claimed (particularly concerning realization failures and rising labour militancy). Rather, they can be synthesized in one general theory of Marxian *economic* crisis. This synthesis at the *logical level* between the three theories is provided in this section, where disproportionalities and other aspects of Marxian economic theory are also discussed.

The above theories are centred on the private sector. The state is usually brought into the analysis *ex post*, a *deus ex machina* to correct the situation, much in line with the Keynesian conception. Unlike in Keynes, the state is seen as acting primarily on behalf of capital for structural (capitalist control of investment, thus national welfare) or instrumental reasons (links of capital with, and influence on, state functionaries) and thus within fairly tight constraints. In all cases it attempts to remove private sector failures. In so doing, it becomes increasingly more involved in the economy, becoming part and parcel of the system. This is particularly the case in the monopoly capitalism stage because of the increasing demands and needs of capital, and the associated needs of the state to legitimize its role (and the system) to workers. This can lead to fiscal crises, seen as a structural gap between revenues and expenditures at the expense of the former, and more generally to the politicization (and socialization) of crises, which now become political (and social) crises (O'Connor, 1973). This endogenization of the state in the analysis of crisis allows us to introduce and appraise critically another major approach to Marxian crisis theory, the theory of 'regulation'. According to this, capitalist institutional configurations, which in one period are both necessary and sufficient conditions for profitable and uninterrupted accumulation of capital, can become institutional fetters when historical conditions change, necessitating institutional reforms. For example, the crisis of the late 1960s onwards is seen as resulting from the crisis of Fordism as a technical, social and economic organizational principle (Boyer, 1986). In similar vein, Bowles et al. (1983, 1986) analyse the current crisis in the USA in terms of the rise and demise of the 'institutional peculiarities' of the current capitalist epoch, what they call the social structure of accumulation (SSA). Again, the erosion of a SSA is seen to require institutional restructuring in order to re-establish the undermined conditions for accumulation. We discuss these issues in section 4.

The internationalization of production, the emergence of the transnational corporation (TNC) and the associated 'new international division of labour' raise important additional questions concerning the possibility for, necessity of and nature of crisis, in particular the question of de-industrialization and relative decline. Particularly interesting here is the case of the UK, a country experiencing signs of severe de-industrialization and relative decline, despite being second only to the USA in terms of direct foreign investment overseas by its home based TNCs; or perhaps because of it? I examine these issues too in section 4. In particular, the relationship between crisis and internationalization and the TNC is examined. Following this, I discuss the impact of internationalization and TNCs on (the analysis of) crisis, the 'new international division of labour' and de-industrialization and relative decline. I suggest that all these issues are inextricably linked, crisis contributing to internationalization and TNCs, the latter to de-industrialization and the new division of labour and all to the social structures of accumulation and regulation globally, and thus the possibility of relative declines. 'Contributing' is the crucial word, as the multiplicity of the factors and issues involved here is prohibiting of any attempts at generalization.

The above analyses are largely static. In section 5 an evolutionary approach is pursued in which changes in capitalist institutional forms are derived, in a dynamic framework, from capital's attempts to remove constraints to profitable accumulation. Capitalist institutions are seen to emerge, fail and reconstitute themselves, in a continuous attempt to allow successful capital accumulation to proceed. This theory of capitalist institutional crisis brings together most elements of the mainstream and Marxian perspectives in a dialectic (and not eclectic) manner. Some of its major 'missing links' are empirically tested in this section, where some other existing empirical evidence is also discussed.

2 Mainstream Theories of Capitalist Failure . . . and Success

General equilibrium theory is the jewel in the crown of neo-classical economics. It represents an ingenious construction, in which private agents are taken to receive price signals and assume they can exchange at that price whatever they want. Their expressed demands and supplies ('notional') are functions of these price signals. Equilibrium is the set of prices that clear all markets (demand equals supply). Transactions accordingly are equal to the demands and supplies at the equilibrium price (Benassy, 1989b). No less than Arrow and Debreu (1954) were instrumental in the development of this construct. Uncertainty is also accounted for: by multiplying the number of commodities to be traded, specifying the date and contingency ('state of nature') when each good will be delivered. Assuming a utility function over such commodities by households, and a single market for such (contingent futures) commodities, the market takes care of everything: 'the famous Walrasian auctioneer has a big job finding the equilibrium, but he has to perform it only once' (Tobin, 1980, p. 23).

Under the now conventional microeconomics assumptions, the existence and optimality of general equilibrium can also be proven; see McKenzie (1989b) for detailed discussion. In McKenzie's words, 'The institution whose phenomena are the primary subject matter of economic analysis is *the market*, made up of a group of economic agents who buy and sell goods and services to one another' (1989b, p. 1, emphasis added). The optimality of general equilibrium is the optimality of the market. This optimality implies non-market failure and thus no need for other institutions in capitalist economies.

At the macro level, the theory was to be attacked by 'disequilibrium theorists', who based their critiques on Keynes's (1936) classic *General Theory*. Keynes's work had provided an apparently fatal blow to Say's law (that supply creates its own demand, so that market failures, such as involuntary unemployment, are inconceivable). Important in Keynes's argument was that aggregate demand determines the level of economic activity (income). An important aspect of such demand is investment by firms. Such investment may fall short of the full employment level of output, leading to a situation of an unemployment equilibrium.

A reason why investments could fall short of what is required for full employment is that saving (for investment) is undertaken by households, *not* firms. Saving and investment plans need not coincide. When this happens the market fails. And this is an *equilibrium failure*, without a self-correcting (market) mechanism. Given involuntary unemployment, the labour market fails to clear. The price of labour (money wage) does not fall in the face of excess supplies, in part because of the unemployed persons' inability to signal their availability for work at a lower real wage, in part because job specific skills of internal workers mean that wage rates are determined by employers and *their* employees (Tobin, 1980). Azariadis's 'implicit contract' theory (see his survey in Azariadis, 1989a) appeared to have provided support to this observation.[4]

Keynes's is a theory of quantity adjustments: given the non-necessity of *ex ante* equality of (planned, notional) saving and investments, *ex post* equality is established through changes in income. Such quantity adjustments are conspicuously absent in general equilibrium theory. Building on this idea, the re-interpretation of Keynes by, in particular, Clower (1965) and Leijonhufvud (1968) provided the basis for 'disequilibrium models', where rationing in a market (e.g. the labour market) can affect agents' behaviour in other markets (e.g. consumption–saving) on the basis of the 'rule of the minimum', which sees aggregate transactions being determined by the minimum of supply and demand. In this model, equilibrium in the goods–money markets, as exemplified by the conventional Hicksian *IS–LM* model, obscures the disequilibrium nature of the model. Benassy (1989a), who originally formalized these ideas, provides a comprehensive account and discussion. Most important in these models is the re-invention of the Keynesian ideas of notional versus effective demands, which in the absence of an auctioneer re-establishes the apparent radicalism of the Keynesian theory: market failure. Market failure, however, need not imply capitalist failure (crisis). Where the market fails, the government could intervene. Through the use of appropriate fiscal and monetary policies, aggregate effective demand could be brought to equality with aggregate supply. The possibility of depression thus implied its non-necessity, through government intervention. Capitalism was freed of the trade cycle. This was celebrated in classic economics texts, such as Samuelson's *Economics*, which did so in the ninth edition, only to reconsider soon afterwards! Why?

Monetarists, such as Friedman (1962), provided an answer. State intervention to correct for market failures presupposes that the government is both willing and able to do so. More importantly, it must be the case that the government is not itself responsible for apparent market failures. Friedman's attack on state interventionism is comprehensive; see, for example, the discussion in D. G. Green (1987). Government intervention can fail because of the sheer inefficiency of politicians, but also because of politicians' dependence on the votes of powerful groups, such as business people and trades unions. Given this, although external *shocks* could have displaced the economy from the 'natural rate of unemployment',[5] and possibly for long periods, and despite the workability *in principle* of discretionary government policies, the latter are neither necessary nor desirable.

The monetarist attack on government intervention was certainly not a new one. Demery et al. (1989, p. 27) quote J. S. Mill, claiming from as far back as 1861 that 'the very principle of constitutional government requires it to be assumed, that political power will be abused to promote the particular interests of the holder'. The Friedman attack was novel for the claim that government intervention can be responsible for market failures, most notably the Great Depression of the 1930s. In his famous reinterpretation with Ann Schwartz (Friedman and Schwartz, 1963) he claimed that the Depression was *caused* (or at least severely exacerbated) by monetary policies. Between 1919 and 1933, the quantity of money in circulation was reduced by one-third, the largest and fastest decline in the period under consideration, 1917–60. An unsustainable speculative bubble in October 1929 led to a stock market crash, which, had the Federal Reserve System expanded money supply to offset the contraction caused, would probably have had no further consequences. Instead, money supply was allowed to decline further throughout the 1930s. This exacerbated the situation and led to the Great Depression. The Federal Reserve's failure to perform its role adequately was attributed to power struggle between the Federal Reserve Bank in New York and the Federal Reserve Board in Washington.

The monetarist conclusion is one of government failure. This is not to deny the possibility that the economy can be out of its natural rate for often prolonged periods. The fairly recent phenomenon of 'slumpflation' (high inflation accompanied by unemployment higher than expected by the natural rate hypothesis) is a case in point. However, this is attributed to a volatile economic climate arising from haphazard government interventions, which preclude market forces from functioning (D. G. Green, 1987). To reiterate the point, it is government failure, not market failure, that leads to capitalist failures (depression, crises). The 'political business cycle', in which booms can occur before elections and recessions soon after (Nordaus, 1975), can be seen as a particular manifestation of such state-induced market failure.

Despite apparent disagreements, Keynesians and monetarists share the belief that crises are caused by policy errors. In the Keynesian story, the state (expression of the general will) fails to pursue correct policies, such as increasing expenditure in depressions. This explains not the crisis, but its non-correction. For monetarists, on the other hand, policy errors can explain both initiation and non-correction. Thus in the last resort they are two fundamentally different views on market and the state: one views the market as fallible and the state omnipotent; the other vice versa. Given the existence of the Great Depression, they cannot both be correct concerning the infallibility of states (Keynesians) *and* markets (monetarists). They could both be correct concerning the fallibility of both the market and the state. I will come back to this point later.

The above theories establish the possibility (empirical reality) of institutional failure, but no mechanism is provided to link government policies (persistent errors) with secular declines in economic activity. An interesting possibility within the mainstream tradition is provided by Feldstein (1974). Feldstein's insight was that household contributions to social security schemes would be viewed by them as a form of wealth, a perfect substitute for other forms of wealth, such as their personal saving. This is the asset substitution hypothesis. Depending on the degree of substitutability, this takes the form of perfect substitution, imperfect substitution or independence.[6] With any degree of substitutability, increases in social security contributions, Feldstein argued, would tend to reduce aggregate saving. The reason is that unlike funded pension schemes, social security schemes are pay-as-you-go (PAYG). Namely, contributions from households are used by the government to finance *current* benefits. Accordingly no actual fund exists. To the extent, therefore, that personal savings are being reduced because of social security schemes, such reductions also represent a one-to-one reduction in aggregate saving, which Feldstein equates to capital accumulation.

Feldstein's attack on government is a serious one. His empirical evidence, obtained within a version of the life-cycle hypothesis of Ando and Modigliani (1963) that was extended to include social security wealth and pension wealth (Feldstein, 1978), did appear to support the idea that in the USA the introduction and growth of social secruity schemes led to a substantial replacement of personal saving and thus to reduced capital accumulation. To the extent that social security contributions increase over time (e.g. because of population growth or increasing contribution rates), this can be taken to imply a secular decline in the rate of capital accumulation, and thus private sector failure *due* to state intervention.

The 'Feldstein hypothesis' has generated a remarkable flow of studies intending to support, criticize or test the hypothesis, in a variety of countries. Kessler et al. (1981) have a detailed survey of the early contributions. On theoretical grounds, even accepting Feldstein's hypothesis, it has been observed that social security contributions may lead to early retirement, and thus more saving during active working lives. This 'induced retirement effect' could offset (partly, fully or even more than fully) the possible Feldstein-type displacement effect (Munnell, 1976). Munnell's empirical finding suggested a change in the structure, not the level, of saving as a result of social security contributions. Tobin (1980) observed that for low-income liquidity-constrained households the issue is not so much whether personal saving will be reduced, as whether such households will be able to maintain their consumption by borrowing when their contributions are increased. This Tobin finds unlikely: 'opportunities for borrowing against future earnings from labor are limited' (p. 57), even in countries with sophisticated financial institutions. This reduces the potency of the Feldstein argument. Indeed Tobin's idea seems to be in line with the empirical evidence, which, on balance, is against the Feldstein hypothesis (Kessler et al., 1981).

If induced retirement and liquidity constraints question the potency of the Feldstein effect, new-neoclassical economists, such as Barro (1974), attacked its very logic. For Barro, social security contributions are seen as taxes. Current benefits fail to stimulate consumption, because of households' anticipation of future contributions (taxes) to social security. If consumers' horizons are infinite, their intertemporal budget constraint will not depend on the timing of taxes, provided government bonds bear the same interest rate as that at which households can perform intertemporal consumption shifts. If each generation's utility function includes the utility of the next generation along with consumption, the resulting 'overlapping generations' model does render household horizons infinite. As a result the substitution of debt finance by governments (e.g. social security contributions) for current taxation will leave households' optimal consumption saving unchanged.

The 'Ricardo equivalence' between finance through current taxation and debt finance effectively represents an extension of the Modigliani–Miller theorem for corporate finance to government.[7] The central idea is consumer sovereignty, the prevalence of households' preferences, notwithstanding the existence of corporations and governments, and thus 'the downgrading of social institutions' (Tobin, 1980, p. 50). Not only the Keynesian belief in the effectiveness of government policy is questioned (e.g. the futility of deficit spending), but also its long-run ability to do any harm (the monetarist belief). Only households matter. Governments cannot help, but they cannot harm or fail either.[8] Such dramatic claims could not go unchallenged. Tobin's (1980) detailed critique, for example, points to problems associated with the chain of overlapping generations (childless families, indifference of parents to the utility of successors), liquidity constraints and non-neutrality of consumption–saving plans with respect to the timing of tax payments, to suggest that the Ricardo equivalence idea is rather far-fetched. His view is that households will invariably prefer to defer tax payments given the opportunity, so that they will tend to increase current consumption, even when they (or their children) have to pay the taxes later. Accordingly there is scope for (deficit spending) fiscal policy. Again, this in itself need not imply the validity of the Feldstein view, the potency of which is also reduced by liquidity constraints.

The Barro critique is part of a more general attack on the Keynesian–monetarist orthodoxy by the rational expectations school, most notably Lucas (1975).[9] Rational expectations are said to exist when agents do not make systematic errors in forecasting the future (Begg, 1982) – the 'weak version' of the hypothesis – or when agents form expectations on the basis of complete knowledge of the model of the economy or its reduced form mechanics (Hodgson, 1988) – the 'strong version' of the hypothesis. On the basis of this assumption and, more importantly, universal and instantaneous market clearing, the rational expectations people conclude that economic fluctuations are simply 'moving equilibria' that result from temporarily incomplete information concerning wages and prices. Labour markets, in particular, are said to clear always, so that observed employment levels are full employment levels, or at least the 'natural rate'.

Detailed criticisms of the 'Lucas critique' are provided in Tobin (1980), Begg (1982) and Hodgson (1988), among others. The latter also provides a survey of early criticisms. Not surprisingly such criticisms focus on the *assertion* of almost universal market clearing, and the idea that agents are virtually omniscient. Interestingly, Tobin observes, such assumptions are not based on any additional empirical evidence in their favour, just the notion that this is 'the only game in town'. All in all rational expectations can be seen as an attempt to re-establish the Arrow–Debreu conclusions without their restrictive assumptions concerning contingent future markets. Still, Tobin (1980, p. 46) concludes, 'The view that the market system possesses . . . strong self-adjusting mechanisms that assure the stability of its full employment equilibrium is supported neither by theory, nor by capitalism's long history of economic fluctuations'. This establishes the need for, and efficacy of, government intervention.

It is hard not to agree with Tobin, particularly when one observes that at the same time that new-neoclassicals were expressing their belief in omniscient agents, mainstream economics were experiencing a forceful re-introduction of the concept of bounded rationality in the work of Williamson (1975). Such limits to rationality are seen by Williamson as one of the reasons for market failure and the replacement of markets by private hierarchies (firms). Similarly, at this time Arrow (1970) was emphasizing the importance of market transaction costs as a cause of market failure, and thus the need for state intervention.[10] Granting this, what explains the economic fluctutions that Tobin alludes to? 'Shocks . . . in policies, or in other exogenous events' (Tobin, 1980, p. 25) are one answer. Such shocks have in fact constituted, with supply-side constraints, the main elements of an explanation of the end of the post-war boom and the current recession.

The simple monetarist position attributes the end of the boom to excess demand caused by mistaken expansion, which led to accelerating inflation (through the expectations augmented Phillips curve). Restrictive policy is here seen as the cure for earlier laxity. State interventions and regulations contribute to the worsening of the situation. The exogenous shocks idea focuses primarily on the oil price increases in 1973–4 and 1979–80. This is seen to increase inflation and energy prices, and thus to lead to cautionary policies and unemployment, and to the substitution of labour and capital for energy, which reduces labour productivity and productive potential because of the obsolescence of capital equipment (Bruno, 1982). Maddison (1980) has a synthesis of these (and other) views. Bleaney (1985) provides a critical account.

An endogenous theory of financial fragility (thus potential crisis) in the Keynesian tradition is provided by Minsky (1978). For Minsky, the development of fragile financial structures is not due to accidents or policy errors. Instead fragility is systemic, and fragile and crisis-prone financial structures are developed endogenously. The source of this fragility lies in flaws in the capitalist market mechanism, the basis of which is the financial system. This is why the capitalist market mechanism does not lead to price stability and full employment equilibrium. Full employment equilibria are unsustainable because of changing expectations in an uncertain environment. Overheating emerges out of temporary full employment periods, and increasing fragility characterizes the boom. This eventually leads to financial crises, which, if not quickly aborted, can culminate in depressions as in the 1930s. State intervention, through fiscal policy and central bank intervention, can provide the necessary infusion of funds, which can abort financial crises and avoid depressions; see Pollin (1986) for a critical assessment.

Other factors, such as excessive growth causing disequilibrium (Kindleberger, 1973) and price rigidities (Means, 1935), have also been proposed to explain the Great Depression; see the critical assessment by Dumenil et al. (1987). The growth of the public sector, in particular the expansion of the services sector, is seen as a reason for the UK's relative decline by Bacon and Eltis (1976). All are in line with the idea that for internal or external reasons capitalist economies can fail. Differences arise when the question emerges of who to blame: the market, the state or both.

A problem with all the above mainstream macro theories is that they lack foundations at the micro-micro-level. Although the possibility of market or firm failure is considered, no consideration is given to the possible reasons for such failures. This is rather paradoxical when one considers the substantial input in the areas of *market* (and *firm*) and *government* failure in industrial organization theory and the theory of public and welfare economics.

Starting from the theory of the firm, the Coase (1937) and Williamson (1975, 1981, 1986) tradition have emphasized the failure of the market because of excessive market transaction costs, such as costs of information, negotiating, contracting, enforcement etc. Such market failure, explained in terms of bounded rationality, opportunism and asset specificity, is seen as the reason for the emergence of firms. The latter should thus be seen as efficiency enhancing devices, economizing in market transaction costs. Coming to the theory of the state, Arrow (1970), Dasgupta (1986) and Stiglitz (1986), among others, have emphasized the pervasiveness of market failure due to high market transaction costs, but as an explanation of the need for state intervention. Here the state, not the firm, is seen to result from market failures. Strangely the market in this approach is seen to include firms, so that market failure is tantamount to private sector (market, in the sense of price mechanism, and firm, in the sense of private hierarchy that supersedes the price mechanism) failure.

The possibility of state failures has also received wide attention in recent years, in main part owing to Friedman's efforts, but also because of the public choice school; see the survey in Mueller (1989). Government failure are seen here to result from a multitude of factors: self-interest seeking politicians and bureaucrats, inefficiency etc. The possibility of government failure has more recently acquired wide acceptance in the mainstream and Marxist theories too; see Cullis and Jones (1987) for a survey. Here again, however, such government failures are not given a micro-foundation in terms of transaction costs. Following the Coase (1960) and Arrow (1970) contributions it could be possible to suggest that government exchanges also involve transaction costs, like firms and markets. These can arise, for example, from bounded rationality and the opportunism of politicians and bur-eaucrats.[11] Such transaction costs can, in cases, exceed those of allocating resources through the market or the firm, which would suggest a return to the private sector (firm, market) when such government failures occur.

This type of argument is circular and does not take us very far. Its interest, I think, lies in that it allows for the possibility of both the private sector and the government sector failing simultaneously. When this occurs a theory of *institutional failure* can be said to emerge. I believe that this type of institutional failure theory is in line with the combined insights of Keynesians and monetarists and provides a transaction costs foundation in line with recent advances in the mainstream tradition. This allows for a neoclassical theory of institutional crisis. It would suggest that generally capitalism is stable when the right institutional mix (firm–market–state) exists: a mix that allows maximum economy in transaction costs. When private sector failures are not solved by government actions, but rather followed by govern-ment failures, overall transactions costs are too excessive for exchange to take place. Exchange breaks down and so does capitalism, at least temporarily. External shocks can accentuate this process. Keynesian and monetarist arguments concerning market failure and government failure are easily cast in terms of the above transaction costs framework. For example, high trans-action costs could preclude households and firms from negotiating to reach a decision on the mutually desired level of saving and investment (a variant of the Coase, 1960, theorem). Similarly, such costs could preclude government departments from deciding to adopt the best policy – money supply expansion in the case of the Great Depression. Once again, the possibility of both happening simultaneously allows for the possibility of capitalist institutional crisis in a mainstream vein.

Building upon his earlier 1973 contribution, Kindleberger

(1986) has more recently provided an interesting interpretation of the recent crisis based on the notion of 'hegemonic stability'. Stability in international markets is viewed by Kindleberger as a public good, subject to the usual problems, including the possibility of under-provision by markets. While national stability is provided by the government, when many governments are involved free-riding may arise, and thus under-provision. A 'hegemonic power' may well provide stability, but hegemons decline: Britain, for example, after 1913, and the USA after about 1971. Concerning earlier crises, Kindleberger concludes 'that the existence of an international lender of last resort made the financial crises of 1825, 1836, 1847, 1866 and 1907, more or less ephemeral, like summer storms, whereas its absence in 1873, 1890 and 1929 produced deep depressions' (Kindleberger, 1986, p. 9). The USA lost the appetite for providing international public goods, such as open markets, supplies in times of acute shortage, last resort lending and coordination of macroeconomic policy, after 1971, which contributed to the recent crisis.

In appraising Kindleberger's views, Nye (1988) observes that divisibilities and appropriability in international economic rules may be enough to allow bilateral bargaining, which can provide a significant component of second best management. Free-riding may not be as extensive as Kindleberger assumes. Whatever the relative merits of the two arguments, Kindleberger's insight is an important contribution to the mainstream theory of crisis, for it allows both markets and governments to fail – albeit maintaining the Keynesian belief that a hegemon can provide to the world what the Keynesian state provides to the nation. Interesting from my point of view here is that the hegemonic stability idea can be re-interpreted in terms of transaction costs. For example, bounded rationality and opportunism on the part of national governments can lead to excessive bargaining costs, no agreement between governments and, in the absence of a hegemon, international 'closure': crisis. When one considers that similar problems can be associated with the hegemon as with the nation state (a possibility allowed by Kindleberger), the possibility of international capitalist institutional crisis re-emerges with or without a hegemon.

To conclude, a mainstream transaction costs based theory of institutional crisis can be developed along the lines suggested above. Once the possibility is allowed, external shocks, policy errors, factors such as financial fragility and increases in the growth of the public sector, and international public goods can be used to explain the *cause* of international capitalist institutional crisis. But not the necessity. The transaction costs approach is still in line with the idea that, in the absence of shocks, policy errors etc., the possibility of crisis need not lead to a crisis. There are no theories of inevitable capitalist crisis in the mainstream, unlike the Marxist approach, to which I now turn.

3   Marxian Theories of Economic Crisis

For Marxism, capitalism is a transitory situation: a 'mode of production' or a 'social formation' which is, but is not to be.[12] Like other modes of production, such as feudalism, capitalism will eventually be replaced, by socialism, a system where the means of production will be collectively owned and the fruits of labour collectively enjoyed, by each according to his or her contribution or work. Going a step further, socialism is expected to be replaced by communism, where unlike in socialism the state will no longer exist. It will wither away and be replaced by the administration of things, where each will receive according to his or her needs.

For this great vision to rest on scientific foundations, one needs a theory explaining which factors lead to, and necessitate the appearance of, socialism. In Marxist economic theory, the existence of social production but private appropriation (that is, most are involved in production but a few appropriate a disproportionate part of the social product) is a condition which leads to socialism; provided socialization of production is gradually increasing, but appropriation remains private. This is because socialized production makes it easier for the proletariat and its vanguard, 'the party', to take over the already socialized (means of) production and 'correct' for distributional inequities. In this sense, increasing socialization of production facilitates the transition to socialism. This very same contradiction – social production with private appropriation – is simultaneously the source of class struggle (rivalry between producer-labourers and appropriator-capitalists) *and* a condition that allows crises to occur, because of inequities in the distribution of income. Under certain circumstances this may hinder capitalists' ability to sell products at a profitable price.

The above focuses on 'capital in general'. It does not take into account that in capitalism production takes place by many capitalists and firms, whose plans are not coordinated in the market. This 'anarchic' nature of capitalist production provides another *condition* of crisis: *disproportionality*. In Marx's reproduction schemes, two departments are assumed, one producing means of production, the other means of consumption. This can be written as follows,

$$C_1 + V_1 + S_1 = Q_1 \quad \text{(department I, production goods)}$$
$$C_2 + V_2 + S_2 = Q_2 \quad \text{(department II, consumption goods)},$$

where Q_1 and Q_2 equal the total value produced in departments I and II respectively, C_1 and C_2 are the values of constant capital (buildings, raw materials, machinery), V_1 and V_2 are the values of variable capital (the value of labour power) used up in production, and S_1 and S_2 are the values of surplus product (product above that necessary for the reproduction of labour power).

Given the two departments, for equilibrium to occur under conditions of simple reproduction (i.e. no expansion of capital), the condition

$$IC = II \, (V + S)$$

needs to be satisfied, that is in each of the two departments demand and supply need to be balanced. No investment takes place here, which implies that the entire surplus value (S_1 and S_2) is consumed by capitalists. For expanded reproduction, the equilibrium condition is similar, although investment by capitalists (accumulation of both constant capital and variable capital, ΔC and ΔV) is allowed; see Howard and King (1985) for detailed exposition.

The essence of the reproduction schemes, which as Bleaney (1976) observes can be viewed as an elaborate version of Say's law, is that, provided the equilibrium condition is satisfied, capitalism is capable of reproducing itself without any crisis tendencies. A number of Marxists, most notably Tugan-Baranovski, relied on these reproduction schemes to argue that disproportionalities due to the anarchic (and antagonistic) nature of capitalism were the main way through which crises can arise, a view also supported by Hilferding (1981); see Shaikh (1978) for more on this, and Kalecki's (1971) critique. One such type of disproportionality arises when, in the case of simple reproduction, capitalist consumption falls short of the entire surplus value (S_1 and S_2). In this case *under-consumption* can be seen as a form of disproportionality crisis, arising from the anarchic nature of capitalism.

The existence of money, which means that capitalism is not a barter economy, provides another *condition* of crisis. Under capitalism capital accumulation takes the form

$$M - C(LP, MP, RM)\ldots P\ldots C' - M',$$

where M is money spent by a capitalist on commodities C, i.e. labour power (LP), means of production (MP) and raw materials (RM). After production (P) has taken place, commodities produced (C') are sold to 'realize' money (M'). M' needs to exceed M for the capitalist to have any incentive at all to produce. M', in its turn, could be thrown back to production for more money to be realized. But it does not need to be. Money can be hoarded, for whatever reason. This possibility provides another condition for capitalist crisis.

Overall, therefore, (1) the co-existence of social production and private appropriation, and the associated existence of distributional disparities, (2) the existence of many uncoordinated capitals (firms), and thus and anarchic nature of capitalism, and (3) the fact that capitalism is a monetized economy, are the three major conditions that establish the *possibility* of crisis in Marxian economic theory. Unlike mainstream theorists, however, Marxists go further in asserting that the possibility will tend to become reality because causal factors tend to transform conditions into actual tendencies and outcomes. Such causal factors give rise to *theories* of crisis. Among them, three have received most of the attention of Marx and Marxist economists: the rising organic composition of capital–declining rate of profit theory; the theory of underconsumption and realization crisis; and the rising militancy, and strength, of labour. Despite explicit reference to the declining rate of profit by one theory only, all three theories are based on this very idea; but they differ as to the reasons why the rate of profit tends to decline, and the form that this tendency takes, as explained below. Further, and following from the above, crises are seen as interruptions in the accumulation of capital, which are *inevitable*, not just possible (O'Connor, 1987).

The 'law' of the tendency of the rate of profit to fall (TRPF) is, according to Marx (1959), the most fundamental law of modern economy. In terms of the definitions introduced so far the value rate of profit can be written as $r = S/(C + V)$ where $C + V$ is total capital stock (K). According to the law of the TRPF, this ratio will tend to decline as capitalism develops, because of a tendency for a rising organic composition of capital (ROC). Organic composition of capital is the ratio of C/V, that is of constant capital to variable capital.

Two other compositions of capital are considered by Marx: the technical composition (TCC) and the value composition. The first is the ratio of the mass of the means of production expended per production period to the mass of wage goods expended. The second is the same as the first but measured in terms of values of productive means and wage goods expended. The organic composition is then defined by Marx as the value composition in so far as it is determined by its technical composition and mirrors changes in the latter. The difference between value and organic compositions lies in that, while changes in the former may not always be proportional to changes in the TCC – because of changing values potentially at differential rates, per unit of wage goods and production means when the TCC increases and more productive techniques are employed – the organic composition abstracts from these changes (exchange and distributional) and focuses on production alone (Fine and Harris, 1979).

Dividing through by V, the profit rate formula can be rewritten as $r = (S/V)/(C/V + 1)$, which suggests that the rate of profit is positively related to the rate of surplus value (or the degree of exploitation) and negatively related to the organic composition of capital. The latter now tends to increase because of conflict between capital and labour in production (to appropriate highest possible surplus value by increasing labour productivity), and rivalry between many capitals in exchange (to gain a competitive edge over rivals). Both necessitate labour-saving technical progress. The expulsion of living labour from production increases the organic composition of capital, and thus reduces the rate of profit unless the rate of exploitation has increased sufficiently to compensate for increases in the organic composition. This is unlikely to happen, at least in the long run. There are definite limits to S/V (both technical, e.g. 24 hours in a day, and socio-political, e.g. labour strength), which is not the case for C/V. Thus eventually increases in C/V will not be offset by increases in S/V, and the TPRF will manifest itself.

Increasing labour exploitation is only one of the ways in which the TRPF can be counter-balanced. Other such counter-tendencies considered by Marx are depression of wages, foreign trade, increases in joint-stock capital, relative overpopulation, which tends to reduce wages, and the cheapening of the elements of constant and variable capital. These counter-tendencies, Fine and Harris (1979) suggest, are associated with the formation of the value composition (thus they account for exchange and dis-tribution), while the law as such is associated with the rising organic composition (production only). Focusing on all these, and given that the same factors that lead towards the TRPF also call forth countertendencies, the TRPF should be seen as 'the law of the tendency of the rate of profit to fall and its counteracting influences' (Fine and Harris, 1979, p. 64).[13]

The 'law' of the TRPF has an interesting history. Despite Marx's own conviction of its utmost significance, most early Marxists preferred to focus on 'disproportionalities'; for example, Hilferding (1981) or under-consumptionist theories. It was in the 1930s, following the systematic treatment of the law by Henryk Grossman in 1929, that interest in it revived (O'Connor, 1987). This revival also gave rise to a number of criticisms, regarding the theoretical and empirical validity and usefulness of the law. Three such criticisms are: that increases in the technical composition need not given rise to increases in the value composition; that technical change can be capital saving *not* labour saving, so the technical composition may not increase as a result of technical progress; and that increases in the technical composition may reduce the costs of, for example, raw materials, which may prevent the TRPF.[14]

For the first criticism to follow, increases in technical com-position will have to reduce the value of the means of production by the same degree as, or more than, the value of the means of consumption. Despite its apparent logic, O'Connor (1987) observes that this criticism fails to grasp the fundamentally different social origins of the demands for commodities produced for production goods and consumption goods. In particular, capital is able to increase simultaneously the exploitation rate *and* the size of the 'basket' of workers' consumption goods, by lowering the value content of the average consumption basket.

For the second criticism to follow, there must be an excess of capital-saving over labour-saving technical progress. This, Yaffe (1973) observes, is unlikely if the size of exploitable labour is the ultimate limit to capital's self-expansion. On the other hand, Shaikh (1977) and O'Connor (1987) observe that limits in the supply of labour are not obviously the typical case in capitalist developments. Marglin's (1984) exposition of the Marxist theory of growth is based on the opposite assumption, of unlimited labour supply, and claims this to be Marx's own interpretation. Furthermore, Wright (1977) suggests that if we focus on many capitals then rivalry between firms will induce them to reduce costs, any costs, so that the assertion of labour saving technical progress need not follow. O'Connor (1987) also observes that in modern capitalism firms do not have the incentive to reduce the organic composition, especially when it is already very high. Both Wright (1977) and O'Connor (1987) agree that if the law is to be salvaged, appeal must be made to the fact that 'machines do not go on strike', which implies a higher incentive by capital to expel living labour from production, thus unintentionally increasing the organic composition.[15]

Concerning the third critique, O'Connor (1987) suggests that Marx appears to have underrated capital's 'genius' in that twentieth-century history has proven the ability of capital, so far, to both produce and make more efficient use of raw materials and energy. In this view it is capital's unwillingness to 'internalize' the costs of accumulation (such as to the environment) that will eventually tend to increase the price of most, if not all, the elements of constant (and variable) capital. This will tend to increase the organic composition, thus, under the assumptions involved, reducing the rate of profits.

In summary, and following on from Fine and Harris (1979), it can be suggested that focus on production alone suggests that increasing organic composition definitionally implies declining profit rates. On the other hand, focus on exchange and distribution implies that the law may not manifest itself empirically because of counter-tendencies. Focus on all three together would suggest that the law and the counter-influences may be seen as enjoying equal status. To these, it is worth adding that, given Marx's own emphasis on production and the related idea that it is what happens in production that triggers counter-influences in exchange and distribution, it is 'correct' to regard the 'law' as a tendency of fundamental importance, quite independently of its actual realization empirically. Regarding its realization, views are as divided as they could be. Mandel (1975) among others asserts that the organic composition has increased and given rise to the TRPF. Critics, such as Rowthorn (1976), dispute this. Wright (1977) observes that the evidence is at best indecisive. Shaikh (1977), however, suggests that this 'evidence' is based on non-Marxist categories, and that the use of Marxist categories has confirmed the Marxian scenario.

The other major Marxist theory of crisis is 'underconsumption'. Underconsumptionism has historically been very popular, claiming adherents such as Malthus, Sismonde de Sismondi and Hobson; see the survey in Bleaney (1976). Common to these authors and underconsumptionism in general, Bleaney observes, is that they regard depressions as a state towards which the economy tends, in the absence of offsetting factors, and not simply as a phase of the business cycle. This tendency is the result of a tendency towards insufficiency in the demand for *consumption* goods. Both elements are viewed as necessary for the definition.[16] There are certainly 'quotes' in Marx that could be taken as underconsumptionist, and are so by Sweezy (1942) and Wright (1977), among others. On the other hand, most 'orthodox' Marxists today (e.g. Mattick, 1969; Yaffe, 1973; Mandel, 1975a; Shaikh, 1977) reject the ideas that Marx was 'underconsumptionist' and that 'underconsumptionism' is more than a *condition* (or the expression, the result) of crisis. This rejection is shared by others, such as Bleaney (1976) and Fine and Harris (1979).

Although what Marx really meant is of no interest other than to the history of economic thought, it seems worth reproducing some of the quotes in question to let the reader get a flavour of what is involved. The quotes Sweezy cites are from *Capital*, Volumes I and III respectively. The first suggests that 'The ultimate reason for all real crises always remains the poverty and restricted consumption of the masses' (Marx, 1954). The next says:

> The conditions of direct exploitation, and those of realizing it . . . diverge not only in place and time but also logically. The first are only limited by the productive power of society, the latter by the proportional relation of the various branches of production and the consuming power of society. But this last named is . . . determined . . . by the consumer power based on antagonistic conditions of distribution which reduce the consumption of the bulk of society to a minimum varying within more or less narrow limits. . . . But the more productivity develops, the more it finds itself at variance with the narrow basis on which the conditions of consumption rest. (Marx, 1959)

On the other hand, Marx in Volume II suggests that 'It is purely a tautology to say that crises are caused by the scarcity of solvent consumers, or of a paying consumption. The capitalist system does not know any other modes of consumption but a paying one, except that of the pauper or of the "thief" ' (quoted in Bleaney, 1976, p. 108). Add on this Engel's view that underconsumption is a prerequisite of crisis and it tells us just as much about today's crises as about why they did not exist before (Wright 1977). Add Marx's own characterization of the TRPF as the most important law of 'modern' political economy and one gets the message: that getting *the* message is not easy.

Had someone else produced these passages he or she would find it hard to find a publisher. With Marx you can find publishers for their exegesis! But exegesis is not my aim here. On this score, I would go along with Wright's (1977) observation that the TRPF proponents have the upper hand; that is, from an exegetical point of view the passages are more in line with the idea that underconsumption is a condition, prerequisite, or expression of the crisis than a theory. This is not to say that the condition for cannot become a cause of crisis. Modern versions of underconsumptionism have attempted to do just this. They build upon the ideas of Kalecki (1971) and Steindl (1952), who both provided reasons why underconsumption will tend to become a *cause* of crisis by generating a tendency for effective demand (consumption and investment, as well as export surpluses and budget deficits) to decline over time.

Kalecki's lasting contribution was the 'invention' of Keynes's general theory a few years before Keynes, and importantly the focus on oligopolistic markets; see for example Sawyer (1985) and Reynolds (1987). It is this latter focus that gives Kalecki a *theory* of secular effective demand decreases as opposed to a *possibility* of effective demand deficiencies. As already seen, the latter possibility is considered by Keynes (1936), for whom any income redistribution to favour the rich (assuming a higher propensity to save on their part), and any adverse impact on entrepreneurs' 'animal spirits', which lowers investment, can generate a non-self-correcting demand deficiency. But there is no mechanism there to explain a secular tendency towards such decreases. In Kalecki, the mechanism is there; in terms of the degree of monopoly. In the simplest terms this is the extent to which prices exceed marginal costs of production and it is taken to be determined by factors such as the degree of concentration, firms' advertising and selling promotion activities etc.[17] If there is a tendency for the degree of monopoly to increase over time, a tendency for a secular decline in consumption emerges. Indeed such a tendency is already there and it is Marx's own: 'the law of increasing concentration and centralization of capital'.

Unless investment demand is somehow derived from consumption, the above need not imply a reduction in total demand (consumption and investment, assuming a closed economy with no state for convenience). The reason is that capitalists do not invest for consumption but in order to make profit. Given this, investment expenditure is in principle capable of increasing sufficiently to compensate for any reductions in consumption due to increasing degree of monopoly. Thus underconsumption need not give rise to a 'realization crisis'. Kalecki expounded these ideas in a 1967 article on 'the problem of effective demand with Tugan-Baranovski and Rosa Luxemburg'. As already noted, Tugan-Baranovski relied on Marx's reproduction schemes to suggest that problems of effective demand need to arise given that capitalists produce for profit, not consumption. Luxemburg accepted the logic of the argument, but considered it socially impossible, on the basis of the absence of the 'new consumers' for whom such production would take place. She went on to explain imperialism and (thus) armaments expenditures in terms of the need for new markets. It is such external markets that, for her, are necessary for capitalism's expanded production. Bleaney (1976) and Shaikh (1977) have extensive critical assessments of the debate.[18]

Kalecki's position on the debate is that Tugan-Baranovski rightly addresses the 'antagonistic character' of capitalism, but fails to show 'at all why capitalists in the long run are to invest to the extent which is necessary to contribute to full utilization of productive equipment' (Kalecki, 1971, p. 147). On the other hand, he observes, expanded reproduction does need a supporting factor, which could be innovations, not necessarily external markets. Concerning these, he observes that it is 'net external markets' (i.e. export surplus), the quantitative importance of which is not as big as of exports alone, that are relevant. Concerning Luxemburg's focus on armaments expenditures as external market, broadly speaking, Kalecki approves of her anticipation of this most important source of absorption of accumulation, but criticizes her focus on total government expenditure without regard to its financing. The outcome of the debate overall effectively hinges on the construction of a theory of investment decisions, which 'I always considered to be the central problem of the political economy of capitalism' (Kalecki, 1971, p. 148).

Steindl (1952) provides such a theory of investment. Investment is seen to be influenced primarily by endogenous factors: the rate of internal accumulation (corporate retained earnings), the degree of capacity utilization, the rate of profit and the gearing ratio (total capital divided by own funds). The growth of sales is taken to determine the rate of internal accumulation. Innovations are seen to determine only the form investments take, not the level; a view which he abandons more recently (Steindl, 1979) in favour of the Kaleckian one. On this basis, Steindl suggests that the growth of oligopoly implies that reductions in demand will not result in decreases in profit margins, but rather reductions in output and the degree of capacity utilization, which will further affect investment negatively. Importantly, in the long run the growth of monopoly will tend to increase profit margins and reduce capacity utilization, thus reducing the incentive to invest.

In anticipation of recent developments in industrial organization theory (e.g. Spence, 1977; Dixit, 1980), Steindl also suggested that investment in excess capacity was operating as an entry barrier in oligopolistic industries. The growth of oligopoly, however, would tend to increase barriers to entry in concentrated industries, thus reducing the incentive to use excess capacity for this purpose. This would further reduce the incentive to invest. Overall, the growth of oligopoly would tend to generate stagnation. In his view this was the case in the US economy from the 1890s to the 1930s. Steindl went on to suggest that his views were an organic development of Marx's underconsumption theory, at re-interpreted by Sweezy (1942). This underconsumptionist tendency would tend to manifest itself in the form of excess capacity, and thus wasted resources, because of capitalism's inability to realize all surplus value.

The main tenets of the Kalecki–Steindl scenario are brought together by Baran and Sweezy (1966), easily the most influential underconsumptionist story ever to appear. Here markets are oligopolistic and firms behave collusively to obtain the joint-profit maximum (monopoly profit). This tends to increase the 'surplus', which is all that is usually included in Marx's notion of surplus value (gross profits, rent, interest, income from self-employment), but also wasteful expenditures by firms (e.g. advertising) and governments (e.g. armaments). This is actual surplus. Potential surplus is what could have been produced had all unemployed resources been (efficiently) used. The surplus can be consumed, invested or wasted. Consumption tends to decrease over time, because of joint-stock companies' dividend pay-out policies. These are such that dividends are sluggishly adjusted to their long run (stable) ratio, so that increases in profits tend to reduce the disposable income ratio. For investment to fill the gap, it must be increasing over time. This is unlikely. Although oligopoly does tend to result in non-price competition, including competition in technical progress, the profitability of existing plants provides a disincentive for the adoption of new innovations. The gap remains, unless it is absorbed by wasteful expenditure. Three such kinds of 'waste' are sales efforts (e.g. advertising), armaments expenditures and civilian government spending.

Baran and Sweezy's theory has been criticized very extensively on both theoretical and empirical grounds. The notion of a 'surplus' has been questioned by, for example, Mandel (1967).

Moreover, criticisms have focused on both the generation of the surplus and its absorbtion. The idea of the generation of surplus is based on the assumption of monopolistic market structure adopting monopolistic pricing behaviour of the mainstream monopoly model type. This need not be true. Monopolistic market structures are perfectly compatible with perfectly competitive pricing, as Baumol's (1982) contestable markets theory suggests – others suggest this too, including Marxists; see Mandel (1967) and the discussion in Jenkins (1987).[19] Such Marxists have criticized Baran and Sweezy's reliance on neoclassical-type market structures as well as their use of the firm as the unit of analysis, which is reminiscent of methodological individualism; see Mandel (1967) and Fine and Murfin (1984).

The other criticism concerning surplus generation is to do with whether this arises in production, as Marx claimed, or in exchange through monopoly pricing, as Baran and Sweezy seem to claim. Mandel (1967) and Fine and Murfin (1984), for example, argue that the focus is on exchange, so the labour theory of value is being repudiated. This critique appears to be far too extreme. Surplus value can only be realized in exchange anyway, so that whether prices in exchange are competitive or above competitive levels does not have to do with whether surplus value has been generated in production or not. Perhaps, the criticism should be that focus on prices in general as opposed to values deprives the analysis of a major dimension, that is the relationship between capital and labour (see below).

Concerning the absorbtion of the surplus, Bleaney (1976), following Kalecki's critique of Luxemburg, suggests that not all of the state budget should be included in the surplus or be seen as surplus-absorbing. The issue of the way the budget is financed has to be addressed. This also bears upon empirical estimates of the 'surplus', in which Baran and Sweezy included all state expenditure. If this was not the case, Bleaney (1976) observes, the 'surplus' could have declined in the period in hand. In an empirical assessment of the Baran–Sweezy scenario, Keller (1975) confirms their views on the increase of monopoly power and redistribution of income towards capital, but finds that the consumption to investment ratio was increasing, not decreasing, in the period preceding the Great Depression. This is taken to reject the underconsumption scenario.

More recently, Sweezy (1981) has countered some of the

critiques. First, he takes competition of capitals to lead, via concentration and centralization, to its own negation, monopoly. He then explicitly addresses the issue of barriers to entry, through which monopolists protect their positions, including excess capacity, 'which can be quickly activated in retaliation against unwanted newcomers' (Sweezy, 1981, p. 28). He goes on to counter the criticism concerning monopoly prices and surplus value, observing that such prices are transformed prices of production in exactly the same sense that prices of production are transformed values. From this it follows that monopoly prices are also transformed values. What he concedes to his critics, and a major 'misunderstanding' of his in his 1942 classic, is that 'the centre of gravity, which holds everything else in its place, is the rate of surplus value, and it is *precisely the rate of surplus value which disappears, vanishes without a trace from an analysis made in terms of prices*' (Sweezy, 1981, p. 26, emphasis in original). He goes on to suggest that in comparison to the rate of surplus value, the rate of profit, which neo-Ricardians use (e.g. Steedman, 1977), is both a secondary concept and one that, taken by itself, tends to foster fetishistic thinking. Quite a concession!

Following on from this, Sweezy explains the recent recession in terms of the US hegemony, facilitating the post-war boom but generating gradually, behind the illusion of self-sustaining growth, the building-up of excess capacity. The cyclical downturn of 1974, plus the oil price shock, heralded the new period of stagnation, precipitated in the USA through a credit explosion, which both caused and reflected the leading role of consumption in the current (mid-1970s) recovery. Loyal to his own tradition, Sweezy concludes that without an exogenous factor, this time the debt explosion, 'capitalism would probably long since have sunk into a state of near collapse' (Sweezy, 1981, p. 35).[20]

A formal model of the Kaleckian 'degree of monopoly' has been provided by Cowling (1982), where again increases in the degree of monopoly are shown to generate increases in the *potential* profit share. However, these tend to reduce consumers' expenditure because of firms' retention policies and to increase the degree of excess capacity, which has negative effects on investment. As a result a tendency towards realization crisis manifests itself. As one way for the degree of monopoly to increase is through firm expansion, and given firms' requirements for finance to expand, the emergence of share ownership can be interpreted along these lines (Pitelis, 1987a). Discretionary and compulsory (through occupational pension funds) shareholding simultaneously provides to firms internal finance for expansion *and* reduces the part of private (personal and corporate) income available for consumption. Provided that increases in retained earnings and pension funds surpluses are not offset by reduction in personal saving, as the life-cycle hypothesis would suggest (Ando and Modigliani, 1963), increased finance for expansion provides another source of realization failures. Competition between capitals necessitates seeking finance. When realization failures expressed in the form of excess capacity reduce the incentive to invest domestically, firms with 'excess saving' can seek international markets.

Emphasis on potential increases in the surplus, or the profit share raises some questions about the ability of raw data (even assuming their 'correctness', compatibility with theory etc.) to test the thesis in hand. Some econometric evidence would seem to be required, at the very least. This observation also suggests that a non-increasing surplus does not suffice to prove that the tendency is not there. As in the case of the ROC-TRPF theory, the tendency may itself generate counter-influences, such as overseas investments, 'wasteful expenditures' etc., not allowing the empirical manifestation of the tendency.

To conclude, underconsumption is both a condition of crisis and a cause, at least in the way developed by the Kalecki–Steindl–Baran–Sweezy tradition. This is a consistent story, and one that takes account of all aspects of effective demand, not just consumption. In this sense the theory is one of 'realization crisis'. Consumption is given prominence is most cases, albeit not all (e.g. Steindl). This prominence, however, is negative: consumer expenditure reductions are seen to arise from the accumulation needs of capital. Whether one wishes to distinguish underconsumption from realization crisis on the basis of relative importance attributed to the various parts of effective demand (as Bleaney does by excluding Luxemburg from underconsumptionists, and wondering about Steindl) is a largely semantic issue. For our purposes here, suffice it that under the assumptions of the model a realization crisis is possible.[21] A major criticism, in my view, is that with virtually no exception the post-Kaleckian roots of modern underconsumptionists, that is their near exclusive focus on the level of exchange, result in significant losses in richness of analysis. This is because the shift of the focus away from production effectively results in the loss from sight of labour, and thus endogenous class struggle. This does not imply that focus on exchange is not consistent with acceptance of exploitation in production. It implies that the theorists deprive themselves of a potentially important means of approaching the issues in hand.

The third major Marxian approach to the theory of crisis is the theory of rising labour strength (RLS). Marx used arguments in line with such ideas when explaining the business cycle (Goldstein, 1985). Recent major contributors in the area are Glyn and Sutcliffe (1972), Botty and Crotty (1975) and Itoh (1975, 1988). More recently the number of authors taking this line has increased; Devine (1986) has a survey. The central thesis of the approach is that increasing labour strength tends to reduce the market rate of profit, which eventually leads to a crisis. Glyn and Sutcliffe's version focus on a long run secular decline, while Botty and Crotty have a cyclical version of the argument. Itoh's analysis incorporates the role of credit.

The central argument in Botty and Crotty is that capitalist accumulation gradually leads to increasing labour strength, which implies the ability of the working class to increase its share of income in price terms. As profit share is simply one minus the wage share, increases in wage share definitionally imply reductions in the profit share. This is a major part of the profit rate (see below), so that profit share declines also give rise to decreasing profit rates. Unlike in the ROC variant of the Marxist crisis theory, the reason for the decline is the (periodic) depletion of the reserve army of labour, which manifests itself in the expansion phases of the cycle. This makes labour scarce, thus increasing the bargaining power of labour and the price they can command for their services. However plausible it may be to base a secular theory of increasing labour strength on the reserve army of labour thesis, it is manifestly non-Marxist. Marx, as Marglin (1984) for example observes, considered that labour supply was endogenously determined by the rate of accumulation, which he always regarded as the independent variable. Glyn and Sutcliffe's (1972) secular rising labour strength theory does not rely on the reserve army idea. Rather the theory is presented as an attempt to explain the relative decline of the UK in particular. The increase of trade union power after the Second World War is seen as responsible for the UK's documented decline in the rate of profit. The other major factor is seen to be increasing international competition, which disallowed British capital from effectively competing in international markets.

Itoh's (1975) theory is more elaborate. The central idea is that during the expansion phase of the cycle fixed capital will be replaced by capitalists only exceptionally. The reason for this resistance is the non-exhaustion of the value of fixed capital, through either depreciation or a fall in its exchange value due to market conditions. In crises, instead, the opposite will be true: fixed capitals will be replaced and productivity increased. The replacement of fixed capital in the crisis sets off a quantitive expansion of capital, which paves the way for a new revival. As it is the crisis that results in the replacement of fixed capitals, accumulation proceeds at a more or less given ratio of constant to variable capital, and reaches its limit when the reserve army is depleted. In the crisis again, labour is expelled from production, so the size of reserve army increases again, and so on. During the expansion, as the reserve army contracts, there is an upward pressure on wages, Itoh's 'overproduction of capital in relation to the labouring population' (unlike Marx's other under-consumption-type 'excess commodity theory'). Rising wages increase the demand for money-capital, which increases the market rate of interest, and squeezes the profits of firms by the rise of both wages and interest rates. The result is a 'credit crisis', which is transformed into a full-blown crisis.

The RLS thesis has received a mixed response from critics. It is often suggested that its good aspect is that it emphasises the role of class struggle, which, for example, is not the case in underconsumption-realization crisis theories (Wright, 1977; Shaikh, 1977). Fine and Harris (1979) view this as both a strength and a weakness, while Weeks (1979) rejects this view, and describes the theory as a 'great leap backwards' (p. 259). Critiques are of two major types: those that focus on particular aspects of particular theories, and those that are general.

Specific theoretical critiques have been advanced against the Glyn and Sutcliffe version, by, for example, Weisskopf (1979). The problem Weisskopf observes is the absence of a *source* of secular growth in working class power. In this sense the theory is a description of a particular case, the UK, and not a theory of general secular decline in profit rates resulting from RLS. Fine and Harris (1979) observe the exclusive focus on the price rate of profit, wage rates etc., which makes the theory's view of class struggle partial; its focus is confined to conflict over distribution in the exchange sphere. Wright (1977) makes the related point that the level of productivity plays almost no role in the theory, therefore no role in Glyn and Sutcliffe's view of the rate of exploitation. This he partly attributes to the definitions of labour and capital shares adopted. Labour share is defined by Glyn and Sutcliffe as the share of national income that goes to wages and salaries, which does not correspond to the value notion of variable capital, and thus has no necessary relationship to the rate of exploitation. Variable capital is seen here to refer to *productive* labour, labour that contributes directly or indirectly to surplus value creation.[22] Much of the growth of total wages and salaries is, however, due to increases in unproductive labour (e.g. government employment, advertising), which implies that wage shares can increase without exploitation rates being reduced. In this sense, to the extent that crisis due to increasing wage shares, this is because of the increase in unproductive labour.

A more general detailed attack on the theory has been made by Shaikh (1977) and, particularly, Weeks (1979). Shaikh observes the affinity of the RLS theory with mainstream theories (e.g. Nordhaus, 1975), and then follows Wright (1977) in elaborating on the failure of profit-squeeze theorists to see the potential difference between the profit share and the rate of exploitation. In this case, it is assumed (which is not obvious in Glyn and Sutcliffe, for example) that profit-squeeze theorists base their theory on the theory of surplus value, yet fail to see the difference between surplus value and market price profit. In this sense, declining profit shares need not be associated with declining rates of exploitation. Marx is quoted here to the effect that rising real wages are expected to go hand in hand with a rising rate of exploitation, and that profit rates decline precisely because the rate of exploitation increases, not decreases: 'Nothing is more absurd . . . than to explain the fall in the rate of profit by a rise in the rate of wages, although this may be true by way of an exception' (Marx, quoted in Shaikh, 1977, p. 33). With this additional indication that Marx is like econometrics (one can prove virtually everything with him, provided one wants to and subject to time constraints), Shaikh's critique would suggest a need for the 'by way of exception theory of RLS'.

Weeks (1979) is by far the most devastating critic of the RLS theory, and in a way provides a generalization and extension of the Wright and Shaikh critiques. Following the latter he argues that the accumulation process need not reduce the reserve army. Moreover, if the reserve army was to decline and the 'real wage' to increase, this need not imply a reduction in surplus value per worker. If the surplus value per worker was to decline, a slow-down in accumulation, not a crisis, would suffice to solve the problem for capital. Finally, increases in the real wage rate are necessary to the capital accumulation process for the social re-division of labour and centralization, and not constraints to this process. More specifically, it is suggested that profit-squeeze theorists fail to prove that there is a systematic tendency for productivity change to occur at a rate insufficient to replenish the reserve army. They also fail to realize that the standard of living can rise while the labour time necessary to produce it falls; and that a rise in wages does not increase capital's requirements for money, it simply shifts the component parts of total value relative to each other (given that the entire value of commodities circulates as capital, not only the constant and variable capitals advanced). Finally, they do not realize that rising wages are the means through which capital effects redistribution among branches of industry, and thus the social division of labour and the removal of labour from low-wage capitals; for Weeks, cen-tralization proper.

An important point the critics have demonstrated is that a declining share of profits to wages is quite compatible with an increasing rate of exploitation, or that price and value categories need not be equivalent. As a result increasing wage rates can only reduce the rate of exploitation by way of exception. The obvious counter to this criticism is that capitalists may be taking their decisions on the basis of price not value categories, as indeed Robinson (1978) and the (post) Kaleckians, among others, claim. Given that the profit to wage ratio is an important part of the profit rate, capitalist investment (to the extent it is influenced by the profit rate) may well decline as a result. It can also be suggested, in fairness to Glyn and Sutcliffe, that they *are* referring to a special case, the UK (see below).[23]

In the light of the above, the major theoretical criticism to the secular version of the theory would appear to be the absence of a theoretical cause (the source) of increasing labour strength. In line with my critique of the underconsumptionist theory, it could also be suggested that focus on exchange alone (price categories) deprives the theory of an endogenous theory of class struggle, and of state intervention (see below). On the empirical side, the secular version of the theory has been interpreted as requiring a secular decline in the profit share. Given the exclusive reliance of the theory on price categories, and the related difficulty in claiming that the tendency is *potential* (as in the case of the TRPF and realization crisis), evidence to prove the point has been seen as essential. Glyn and Sutcliffe have produced data in line with this scenario for the UK. Such data, however, raise the important question of appropriate definitions, measurement problems etc. I will be returning to this very complicated issue, but it is worth mentioning at this stage that the use of after-tax or before-tax measures of profit shares (the ratio of net-of-depreciation manufacturing operating surplus to national income) makes a big difference. King (1975), for example, found that there is no secular decline in the after-tax profit share. Similarly, Aaronovitch and Smith (1981) report after-tax wage shares that show no secular tendency to increase. These simple observations alone suffice to make the point that a clear conception of the role of the state is required before a decision is made as to whether before-tax or after-tax measures are used.

Conventionally, the three theories examined so far have been treated as rival, despite cautions 'against viewing them as competing alternatives' (Weisskopf, 1979, p. 348). Weisskopf has been instrumental in providing a general theoretical framework through which empirical tests of the (non-competing) hypotheses can be tested. This consists of decomposing the profit rate (in price terms) to three constituent parts as follows:

$$r = \frac{\Pi}{K} = \left(\frac{\Pi}{Y}\right) \left(\frac{Y}{Z}\right) \left(\frac{Z}{K}\right) \tag{1}$$

where Π is the volume of profits, Y is output or income and Z is potential output or capacity. Thus the rate of profit is seen as definitionally equal to the profit share, times the share of capacity utilization and the capacity to capital ratio. The three variants of crisis theory are then identified with the three constituent parts of equation (1). The ROC variant is identified with the capacity to capital ratio. The reasoning is that ROC requires constant income shares (degree of exploitation) and does not hinge on capacity utilization changes, but requires increases in the capital to surplus value (wages) ratio, thus reducing the capacity to capital ratio.[24] The RLS version is identified with a declining profit share as the initial source of decline.[25] The realization failure (crisis) variant is identified with the capacity utilization part of the profit rate.

On the basis of this framework Weisskopf develops a more elaborate theoretical analysis to account for the potential impact of utilization effects on the profit share, for offensive versus defensive labour strength and for the deterioration of the terms of trade. His conclusion for the 1949–75 period for the US non-financial corporate business sector rate of profit, is that the secular decline of the latter can be almost exclusively attributed to RLS, which, however, was defensive, i.e. not commensurate with the growth of true productivity. Labour simply succeeded in defending itself better than capital against a long-term deterioration in the terms of trade. The evidence did not support any impact of the ROC variant on the profit rate, while the realization failure variant contributed modestly to the profit rate decline. In line with Glyn and Sutcliffe, the before-tax profit measure was used, but Weisskopf considers this a major limitation of the analysis:

> Most important of all it is essential to go beyond the analysis of the before tax rate of profit to consider the role of the state and the after tax rate of profit; . . . insofar as capitalist behaviour . . . is influenced by after tax rather than before rates of profit, any analysis confined to the latter is bound to be incomplete. My study must therefore be considered pre-liminary if only because of the role of the state. (Weisskopf, 1979, p. 374)

The Weisskopf study has been extended by Henley (1987) to account for the 1975–9 period. The author provides evidence in line with the idea that realization failures can explain the (secular) decline in the profit rate during this period. The strength of the effect is such that the RLS and realization failures variants contributed in equal proportions to the overall post-war decline in the profit rate. Funke (1986) provides econometric support for Weisskopf's finding that capacity utilization and cost pressures give a reasonable explanation of the cyclical profitability pattern, but fails to support the idea that declining international competitiveness is responsible for the profit squeeze.

In a more recent paper, Weisskopf (1985) himself provides econometric evidence for the determinants of the profit rate in the manufacturing sector of eight OECD countries (UK, France, West Germany, Italy, Japan, Canada, Sweden and the USA) that rejects his early findings. In particular it is found that in every country the profit rate is positively and significantly related to the rate of capacity utilization, which is taken to reflect the overall strength in demand. It is also positively related in most countries with the (lagged) rate of unemployment and negatively related with the extent of import penetration. Weisskopf interprets his findings as seriously questioning the high employment profit-squeeze theory of secular declines in profitability, as for example restated and defended in Weisskopf et al. (1983), although not the applicability of the cyclical version of the theory. He concludes that the sources of profitability decline in many – if not all – advanced capitalist countries should be traced to the forces that have slowed down the growth of demand and heightened the intensity of international competition throughout the capitalist world.

To summarize, the empirical evidence based on pre-tax profit rates and shares for the manufacturing sector of the economy appears to support strongly the idea that capacity utilization is a positive and significant determinant of the profit rate, offering support to the underconsumptionist–realization failures story. Importantly this is even suggested by authors favouring different hypotheses, such as Weisskopf. The evidence also seems to argue against the secular version of the profit-squeeze theory, but is indecisive as regards the cyclical version of the theory and the role of international competitiveness. No support is found for the ROC variant of the theory. Given my focus here on secular tendencies, it is fair to conclude that the evidence is in line with the secular realization crisis story.[26]

An important element of the realization crisis theory, as expounded in this section, is the tendency for the profit share to rise. It is this increasing profit share that is seen eventually to reduce productive capacity utilization, thus decreasing the profit rate. Initially the increase of profit shares would tend to exert upwards pressure in the profit rate and increase investment (assuming that the profit rate does affect investment positively). In this sense Weisskopf's focus on the capacity utilization term to test the realization failure variant presupposes that the problem has been there for long enough to have already rendered the tendency of the profit share to rise *potential*, so that focus on capacity is justified. However, this scenario raises doubt about the extent to which realization failures and secular profit-squeeze theories have different implications.

The main idea of the last-mentioned theory is that increasing labour strength tends to increase wage rates, thus *ceteris paribus* the wage share. This assumes that because of booming conditions employment will also be increasing, or at least not declining. In the cyclical context this is not unrealistic, although arguments to the contrary can be made: such as 'workers pricing themselves out of jobs' because of high wage rates, or employers maintaining an optimal pool of unemployed; see, for example, the discussion in Putterman (1986). In the secular context, however, the assumption of constant employment levels is patently unrealistic. Indeed it contradicts the very notion of a crisis due to high wage rates, and thus declining profit rates. The latter, according to the theory, should lead to decreasing investment, output, capacity utilization and employment levels. Reduced employment in turn may well suffice to reduce the wage share (a product of wage rates and employment levels), thus increasing the profit share. In this sense the secular version of the profit-squeeze theory may well be consistent with an increasing profit share, in line with the underconsumptionist–realization failures scenario. In both cases the end product hinges upon the extent to which the impact of increases in profit shares on the profit rate, thus investment, is offset by decreases in capacity utilization. In the underconsumptionist story, this is achieved through reductions in effective demand *due to* increasing profit shares. The argument is perfectly compatible with the profit-squeeze theory, although not taken up by profit-squeeze theorists.

The above synthesizes, logically at least, the predictions of the secular profit-squeeze and realization failures theories. Given tl.is, the two theories are also consistent with the ROC-TRPF theory; to the extent, that is, that ROC reduces the capacity-to-capital ratio, which reinforces the capacity utilization effect, thus potentially offsetting the impact of the increasing exploitation rates, and thus *ceteris paribus* (see Shaikh, 1977; Weeks, 1977) the profit share in price terms. In this sense all three variants of Marxian theory can be seen to operate simultaneously on the profit rate, by exerting a positive impact on the profit share and *eventually* a negative one on capacity utilization and/or the capacity to capital ratio. Again it must be the case that the impact of the last two on the profit rate should be sufficient to offset the impact of the profit share. It is also crucial for the theory that profit rates (determinants) do have a positive impact on investment.

The increasing profit share leading to reduced capacity utilization and profit rates through realization failures scenario can also be seen as a type of *disproportionality* (Shaikh, 1977) between effective demand and *potential* supply. So interpreted, the disproportionality thesis can also be incorporated in the analysis. Surprisingly, the observation of an increasing profit share, seen here to be consistent will all three main variants of Marxian crisis theory, provides support to another prediction by Marx, the *relative* impoverishment of the working class – see the discussion in Catephores (1989) – even from the purely *economic* and *national* point of view, that is disregarding socio-political, personality and environmental issues, as well as global distributional trends. These latter issues are not my interest here; see, for example, O'Connor (1987) and Wallerstein (1980) for discussions. The above 'synthesis' of the secular versions of the theories casts some doubt on empirical attempts such as Weisskopf's (1979); which is not to deny their invaluable contribution to the debates in hand.

4   Crisis, the State, Regulation and De-industrialization

The only institutional form present in the above theories is the market, which is seen to comprise interrelationships between individuals and firms (i.e. through both hierarchy and the price mechanism). No attempt at special theory of the firm is made. The state does not figure in the theory either, except *ex post*. The common case for proponents of the three variants discussed so far is to introduce the state in the theory *post festum*, as a *deus ex machina*. Its aims and functions are seen as attempts at crisis resolution. Thus theories based on the ROC-TRPF variant (e.g. Mandel, 1975a; Gamble and Walton, 1976) see the role of the state primarily in terms of an attempt to restrain the rise of the organic composition. A similar (instrumentalist) view is taken by underconsumptionists (e.g. Baran and Sweezy, 1966), although the state now is seen as attempting to absorb the 'surplus' via wasteful expenditures, in particular in armaments. Profit-squeeze theorists (e.g. Glyn and Sutcliffe, 1972) take a very similar position, but the role of the state is here seen in terms of an attempt to increase the price profit rate. In some cases this involves state-administered reductions in unemployment, so as to reduce the bargaining power of labour, and thus increase the profit rate (Gouph, 1979).

Yaffe (1973) provides a more elaborate theory, in that the state is now seen to be involved in the accumulation process as a result of the ROC-induced TRPF. The latter tends to increase unemployment which, contains the seeds of a social crisis because of increased labour unrest. To avoid this, the state attempts to increase employment through increasing state expenditure. However, such attempts eventually intensify the crisis, because most state expenditure itself is unproductive, in that it realizes surplus value but does not produce additional surplus value. This further reduces the profit rate, thus rendering the crisis inevitable. A similar view is taken by Gamble and Walton (1976), although the result of state policies is here seen as intensified inflation. Fine and Harris (1979) provide a detailed critical assessment of these theories. They observe the affinity of such ideas with orthodox Keynesianism, except that here 'the state exercises its Keynesian policies on behalf of capital as opposed to a neutrality conceived notion of society in the orthodox theory' (p. 103).

As noted in section 2, monetarist theorists, in stark contrast to Keynesians, stress government failure as opposed to market failure as the source (or a facilitating factor) of the crisis. There are two major counterparts of this idea in the Marxist tradition,

Kalecki's (1943) 'political business cycle' and O'Connor's (1973) 'fiscal crisis' of the state. The former is the political counterpart of the profit-squeeze hypothesis, in which increased employment increases the economic bargaining power of labour, and thus wage rates and shares. Kalecki (1943) considers both economic and political factors. The main claim is that full employment has political implications detrimental to capitalists. Generally, 'industrial leaders' are seen by Kalecki to oppose government spending for a multitude of reasons: dislike of government interference with employment as such; dislike of the direction of spending to public investments and subsidization of consumption; and dislike of socio-political changes resulting from the maintenance of full employment. 'Under a regime of permanent full employment the sack would cease to play its role as a disciplinary measure. The social position of the boss would be undermined and the self assurance and class consciousness of the working class would grow' (Kalecki, 1943, p. 326). As a result 'the workers would "get out of hand" and "the captains of industry" would be anxious to teach them a lesson' (p. 329). The result, Kalecki suggests, is a political business cycle, whereby full employment will only be reached at the top of the boom, while relatively mild and short-lived slumps will follow, as a result of conscious government policies (see also Feiwell, 1974).

The concept of a political business cycle has gained influence among mainstream theorists too (e.g. Nordhaus, 1975). This, I think, is hardly surprising. Not only is the concept in line with the monetarist belief of government failure, but it also shares with Keynesians the belief that the government is always capable of achieving full employment. The only reason it does not do so is opposition by capitalists. The state is again seen as an 'instrument of capital' in line with Baran and Sweezy (1966), Glyn and Sutcliffe (1972) etc., and this is where the theory departs from Keynesianism. The departure, however, is towards monetarism, albeit with a major difference: total disregard of supply-side constraints, unlike the monetarists. This does not necessarily cast doubt on the simple idea that the *economic* bargaining power of labour can increase because of high employment levels. Rather, it points to the insufficiently developed treatment of the institutional form of the state in the theory.

O'Connor's (1973) theory goes further than Kalecki's, in that the state is seen as relatively autonomous, and specifically concerned with ensuring uninterrupted accumulation for capital, but also legitimization for labour. The growth of needs and demands by capital and labour necessitates increases in both types of expenditures, such as socialization of infrastructure costs for capital and 'social wages' (such as unemployment benefits) for labour. However, difficulties emerge with financing these expenditures, which gives rise to a structural budget deficit, what O'Connor calls the fiscal crisis of the state; see also the debate between Moseley (1978) and O'Connor (1980). In this sense, the O'Connor thesis sees fiscal crises as linked with the more general sociopolitical condition of monopoly capitalism (concentration and centralization of capital, and thus rising labour demands), but not a simple result of the economic crisis. This idea is developed further by Poulantzas (1978). O'Connor (1987) provides a detailed account of political and social crises resulting from the 'new and close affiliation between the economy, the state and ideology' (O'Connor, 1987, p. 133, quoting Poulantzas).[27]

The close articulation between economy and the state, particularly in an era of monopoly capitalism, is seen by a number of Marxist authors as a further reason for state failures: a crisis of crisis management. Structural inflation is seen to arise from a number of sources, such as conflict over production and distribution of income, and oligopoly pricing leading to such conflicts (Kotz, 1982) or to stagflation (Sherman, 1977). All these make it more difficult for the state to pursue crisis management policies. For Wright (1977) it is the dominant role of the state in regulating the economy that weakens the role of crises as restorative mechanisms (particularly when corporations are locked in production for the state); see Fine and Harris (1979) and Devine (1986) for further discussion of these issues.

All the theories of economic (and fiscal) crisis discussed so far are largely non-historical. Although explicit or implicit reference to the particular capitalist era under examination is always present, there is no discussion of the extent to which crisis tendencies can be historically dependent, and thus transformed in the various stages of capitalist development. Wright (1977) is the exception and makes a major contribution in this direction. The attempt is to trace historical transformations of crisis tendencies, in a framework of emergent structural solutions to historically specific constraints on accumulation. Wright identifies six stages of capitalist development, along with their structural constraints on accumulation and the emergent structural solutions to these constraints.

In brief, at the early stage of 'primitive accumulation' the *mass* of surplus value is seen to be the constraint, because of the restricted size of the working class and lack of close supervision of labour. Institutional changes designed to solve the problem (immigration, enclosures, factories) are seen as the solution. In the second stage, manufacture, the constraint is the *rate* of surplus value, because of the low productivity of the technology and (relatively) high value of labour. Labour-saving technical innovations are seen as the solution. As a result, in the machinofacture stage, the ROC-TRPF manifests itself. The solution is seen as business cycles, which devaluate capital and lead to increasing concentration, and labour-saving innovations to expand the reserve army, thus undermining labour's power. Increasing concentration leads to the next stage, monopoly capital. There the tendency is seen as one of rising surplus, and thus the underconsumption–realization crisis, and a more militant labour movement. Keynesian demand management, particularly military spending, is seen as the solution, along with complex promotion structures, job hierarchies, collective bargaining etc. In the next stage, advanced monopoly capital, the reproduction cost of the system is seen to increase because of contradictions in the accumulation–legitimization roles of the state. This results in stagnation with chronic inflation; tendencies exacerbated by the growth of monopoly and internationalization. Active state intervention in production, designed to increase productivity ('post-industrial' state policies), is seen to be the solution here. Finally, in the next stage, state-directed monopoly capitalism, an ever-deepening politicization of the accumulation process is said to emerge, the possible solution being a fully fledged repressive state capitalism.

Important, I believe, in Wright's analysis is the introduction of dynamics, although not history as such despite claims to the contrary. Similarly important is the endogenization of 'periodization of capitalism' in terms of emerged structural solutions to accumulation problems in each particular phase. Obviously, there is scope for disagreement in virtually every particular aspect of the scenario. For example, why a particular variant of the crisis theory, such as ROC-TRPF, ceases to operate even as a tendency following the emergence of monopoly capital is not obvious. As I have already indicated all these theories, at least in their secular versions, are consistent with each other. Furthermore, no real analysis is provided of the potential effects of imperialism (as Wright himself admits) and no evidence is provided to support the claims made. Despite such criticisms, Wright's analysis is an improvement over previous theories, for the reasons explained. It bears close affinities to the French regulation school, most notably Agglietta (1979) and Boyer (1986), and to the social structure of accumulation (SSA) model, which is particularly associated with a number of contributions by Samuel Bowles, David Gordon and Thomas Weisskopf in the USA (Weisskopf et al., 1983; Bowles et al., 1983, 1986; Bowles and Gintis, 1982).

The SSA approach is explicitly concerned with analysis of the 'institutional particularities of the current capitalist epoch, by applying the concept of the social structure of accumulation (SSA) as a historically specific expression of the capitalist mode of production' (Bowles et al., 1986, p. 133). The idea is to develop a model of the rise and demise of successive SSAs. The establishment of a set of socioeconomic institutions comprising an SSA is seen to provide the necessary and sufficient conditions for capital accumulation and stable growth rates. However, internal and external shocks gradually erode the SSA, undermining its effectiveness in promoting profitability, investment and growth. It enters a period of crisis, during which political struggles develop over the structural restructuring necessary for the emergence of a new SSA and thus of another round of successful accumulation.

The affinity with Wright's analysis is obvious, although the aim here is not as ambitious; only specific social formations are being considered, in this case the USA. The central idea is that three major elements of the postwar US structure, Pax Americana (i.e. US hegemony), the (limited) capital–labour accord, and the capitalist–citizen accord, contributed to an SSA, which allowed the post-war boom to take place. This worked because it secured the dominance of the private profit-making capital-accumulation logic over the whole economy.[28] However, conflicts gradually emerged 'from *within* each of these three relations of power and privilege, challenges rooted in the spreading refusal . . . to accept the subordination required by the structure of the postwar, corporate system' (Bowles et al., 1983, in Edwards et al., 1986, p. 385). External shocks also contribute to the erosion.[29] In this light, the RLS variant of crisis theory is seen as nearer to explaining the erosion of post-war SSA, and econometric evidence is provided in apparent support of this view (but not by Weisskopf, 1985, himself) as explained above.

The regulation school has a far more elaborate analysis than the simple (one might say simplistic) line taken by SSA theorists. In Agglietta (1979) the aim at the very outset is a grand one: the development of a theory of regulation of the capitalist economy, as a total alternative to 'general equilibrium' theory. Instead of focusing on abstract 'laws of motion', the aim is to study the transformation of social relations, which creates new economic and non-economic forms that are organized in structures and that reproduce a determining structure, the mode of production. Growth and crises are seen to be changing in time and space here, and this change is considered a crucial issue for economic analysis (Boyer, 1986). Crises are basically seen as representing the exhaustion of a previous regime of accumulation. Institutions and the need for institutional reforms are seen as important, and the endogeneity of distribution is stressed, in line with Kaleckian approaches. An important claim is that intensive accumulation regimes based on mass production tend to face crises of the TRPF type and not the effective demand type (Boyer, 1986).

The forms that crisis takes, more generally, are seen as correlating with the accumulation regimes. In extensive accumulation periods, such as the 1848 crisis, constraints are seen to arise from the supply of labour. In an intensive accumulation period, the crisis of 1929 took the form of realization failures (problems with the self-expansion of department I, along with constraints to the development of demand in department II). As a result, it is no surprise that intensive accumulation with mass production is at least initially different: problems with the profit rate result from the maturing of Fordism and struggles over the distribution of income, but there are also structural efficiency problems. This is the case for the USA of the 1960s and the other OECD countries from 1973 onwards. Neo-Fordism, in the form of more collective working, skill enhancement etc., is seen as a capitalist solution from the labour side. The state's forms also change, following changes of regulation regime. The state is seen to be active in the establishment and crises of regulation regimes.

Boyer (1986) gives an excellent critical account of the regulation school arguments. Lipietz (1982) incorporates the role of credit money in the analysis. In Lipietz, the dynamic equilibrium, including production growth, growth in the technical composition of capital and the real wage, was sustained through a stable intensive accumulation system, through a 'fixed' set of institutional processes defined as 'monopoly regulation'. Crisis, however, has emerged in the form of insufficient increases in the rate of exploitation in productivity *vis-à-vis* increases in the technical composition, and thus a TRPF. External shocks (the oil prices) have exacerbated the crisis. The role of credit money is seen as permitting inflationary crisis. In a more recent paper, Lipietz (1986) interprets the crisis as a victory of the ROC-TRPF over the counter-tendencies. He also provides a succinct survey of the regulation school. The regulation school approach, like that of the SSA, bears close similarities to Wright's (1977) approach: a periodization of capitalism is adopted, defined in terms of accumulation regimes. Different types of crises are seen to correspond to different such regimes. However, unlike Wright's (1977) and the SSA approach, the ROC-TRPF variant of crisis theory is seen to be relevant under monopoly capitalism, or a monopoly regulation regime. Again, the possibility of the simultaneous operation of the three tendencies is not entertained.

Despite a more elaborate analysis, the regulation school suffers along with the SSA and Wright's approach from the absence of an analysis of institutions. The importance of institutions is recognized, but they are seen as data; the firm and the state, for example, exist, function and evolve. Little explanation is offered as to why, and how. Affinities with, for example, Marglin (1974) concerning the firm (Lipietz, 1986), and with the Poulantzian approach to the state (Boyer, 1986) are noted. Boyer provides a discussion of affinities of neo-institutional and other analyses with the regulation approach, but also points to the absence of an exegesis of institutions. He notes A. Noel's critique to the effect that regulation theorists fail to explain the *raison d'être* of capitalist institutional forms.[30] Particularly conspicuous by its absence is any discussion of the firm and the transnational corporation.[31] Explanations of the process through which internationalization of production emerges (with the notable exception of Palloix (1976), whose sympathy towards regulation is doubtful) and of the role institutional forms, such as the transnational corporation, can play in this process are also lacking. By implication these limitations tend to be more pronounced in the 'simpler' economic crisis theories of the previous section.

The link between crisis, internationalization and the transnational corporation (TNC) has a very long history, particularly associated with contributors in the broad underconsumptionist vein. The main idea here is that underconsumption problems domestically generate a need for external markets, which leads to imperialism. Imperialism is seen as a solution to the inability of capitalism to achieve expanded reproduction in the absence of external markets. Brewer (1980) makes a critical appraisal of this line of thought. The two major problems, as already explained, lie in the near exclusive focus on the exchange side and the non-consideration of the possibility of internal stimuli to department I's production (e.g. Kalecki's, 1971, technical change notion). Another problem is the implication that, in the absence of underconsumption, imperialism and internationalization of production might not have arisen.

The above need not be true. Palloix (1976), for example, has persuasively argued that internationalization of the three circuits of capital (commodity, money and productive) is inherent in capitalism, a result of the self-expanding nature of capital, which itself is a result of competition with labour and between capitalists. In this scenario the recent growth of TNCs is associated with the internationalization of productive capital, the TNC being the institutional manifestation of the tendency towards internationalization. That internationalization and TNCs can be explained by focusing on production alone (or production *and* exchange) casts doubt on the underconsumptionist idea that external markets are needed for effective demand reasons. Add to this the possibility of internal stimuli to demand, and the critique is really damaging; with two reservations. First, that underconsumption need not be a necessary and sufficient condition for internationalization need not imply that effective demand problems, if present, cannot facilitate an inherent tendency towards internationalization, that is provide an additional stimulus. Second, the possibility of underconsumption operating simultaneously with other secular crisis causes on the rate of profit could itself be seen as a contributory factor to internationalization, one incorporating both production and exchange-side aspects.

Observations such as these, I believe, render premature the total rejection of the potential importance of effective demand or declining profit rates in explaining the process of internationalization. Concerning effective demand issues, for example, I have indicated elsewhere (Pitelis, 1991b) that the USA was experiencing effective demand (and excess liquidity) problems before the dramatic growth of direct foreign investments (DFI) in Europe in the 1950s. Demand was more buoyant at the time in the UK, the major recipient of such investments. Moreover, effective demand problems in the UK also manifested themselves before the growth of DFI. Given this, the total disregard of such issues by all mainstream and radical theories of the TNC (see the collection in Pitelis and Sugden, 1990) is, I believe, unjustified. Effective demand problems and declining profit rates are certainly not the only cause of internationalization; they can however, facilitate the process (see also Cowling and Sugden, 1987).

Internationalization of capital, in its own turn, has dramatic implications for the various crisis theories examined here. First, it can help to ameliorate the consequences of crisis tendencies and to a certain extent offset the causes. In the ROC variant, for example, internationalization can reduce the technical composition of capital if overseas investments are more labour-intensive. This was noted by Marx. Effective demand problems can be resolved, to the extent that increased export surpluses are generated from overseas investments. The strength of labour can be substantially reduced as a result of the mobility of TNCs *vis-à-vis* the immobility of labour (Sugden, 1990). The exploitation of (the division of) overseas labour and markets can also provide an explanatory factor in the emergence of SSAs and regulation regimes: to the extent that such exploitation provides the material conditions for the prevalence of a growth ideology, such growth can bring together states, citizens labour and TNCs in an 'unholy growth alliance'. This in turn can be broken when (or if) changes in the underlying factors establishing the SSA arise (see below). Importantly, internationalization can also be associated with the continuance (or even emergence) of crisis. In the realization failure case, for example, the availability of overseas markets and possibility of DFI can provide an explanation of why effective demand problems domestically do not lead to reduced prices, but reduced output and capacity utilization. The 'monopoly power-pricing' idea commonly adopted by underconsumptionists is in itself insufficient. If the alternative to reducing prices, for mon-opolists, was to reduce output and thus the mass of their profits, prices *might* be reduced in an attempt to stimulate demand and raise total revenue. The existence of international markets for export or DFI provides the missing link, a supporting factor for domestic monopoly pricing.

The importance of international production and the TNC has been widely acknowledged and discussed more recently, in the form of a particular type of national crisis theories: theories of relative decline. Such theories address the issue of the relative deterioration of the economic performance of some industrial-ized countries *vis-à-vis* their rivals. The USA and especially the UK are the two primary examples. In the case of the USA, a number of studies have attempted to explain the crisis in terms of de-industrialization, and this has been linked with the 'flight of capital' (see, for example, Bluestone and Harrison, 1982). The main idea here is that the changing international scene since the Second World War, in particular the rapid growth of Japanese and European capital, and their associated ability to compete with the USA, marked the end of the country's pre-eminence in industry. Faced with declining international market shares, capital sought a short-termist profit-maximizing approach, through capital restructuring and flight overseas.

A theory of relative decline emphasizing the international orientation of British capital, or particular sections of it, such as financial capital or the City of London (see Minns, 1981b; Coackley and Harris, 1982 among others), has also been proposed for the UK. The central idea here is that different orientations between sections of British capital (international for the City, national for the manufacturing sector) have been resolved in favour of the international. The City's policies deprive domestic capital of investment funds, thus giving rise to de-industrialization.

International orientations need not be the prerogative of financial capital alone; manufacturing capital can also be inter-nationally oriented, if better investment opportunities are offered abroad (Hobsbawm, 1968; Aaronovitch and Smith, 1981). The idea is an old one, with Hymer (in Cohen et al., 1979), for example, having provided a particularly interesting scenario for the role of TNCs in the 'new' international division of labour. Unlike in earlier relationships between the developed and less developed countries (core and hinterland), which were based on the extraction of raw materials and primary products from the hinterland for the core, in the new situation production takes place in the hinterland. This Hymer describes as a process of dependent development, which is unequal too, in that its fruits are divided unequally in favour of the core (see chapter 4).

It is only one step away from this to argue that de-industrialization of the core may in some cases emerge as the result of TNCs' attempts to minimize global production costs.[32] For Cowling and Sugden (1987), for example, while the new situation can be stimulated by a myriad of causes, it seems that 'an all pervading general influence would be the existence of and changes in, unit labour costs differentials, reflecting differences in the relative power and militancy of labour. By extension an increasing tendency to switch production and investment away from the advanced industrial countries to the unindustrialized or newly industrialized countries' (p. 87). In line with Hymer this industrialization process is seen as being dependent (see also Palloix, 1976). There is a link with the Glyn and Sutcliffe scenario here in that to the extent that the UK, for example, has a particularly strong labour force, it could be de-industrialized because of capital restructuring. The relative decline of the country, despite its being second only to the USA in terms of total DFI, would appear to lend some support to this scenario. Unlike in Glyn and Sutcliffe, however, de-industrialization and relative decline are viewed as contributing to a crisis, itself induced by effective demand problems due to an increasing degree of monopoly and socialization of capital. Thus crisis leads to internationalization and this in turn to de-industrialization (Pitelis, 1985, 1987a).[33] It is not an international orientation as such that leads to de-industrialization, but a more complex crisis–internationalization–de-industrialization articulation. To the extent that a particular capital, such as the UK, has special links overseas (e.g. because of the Empire) the process can be facilitated.

The observed chronic deterioration in UK manufacturing competitiveness has been said to have led to a demand constraint, which in turn led to reduced investment, rate of technical progress and (thus) output, exports and employment. This led to a process of cumulative decline (see Blackaby, 1979). Stafford (1986, 1989) observes the lack of an explanation of the origin of this cumulative process, in a critical assessment of this post-Keynesian story. He attempts to synthesize it with the Kilpatrick and Lawson (1980) observation of the particularly strong labour movement in the UK, resulting from organization at factory level, which is said to have thwarted many of capital's attempts to increase productivity. This factor is seen to provide a cause of the origin of the decline in competitiveness, which then leads to cumulative decline.

Like the international orientation thesis, the post-Keynesian–Kilpatrick and Lawson thesis can be seen within the more general framework of a crisis-induced internationalization, where failures by particular capitals (such as the UK) could explain the relatively more acute crisis. A problem with this scenario and the thesis in general is that it assumes a one-to-one correspondence between the success of a country's capital and the success of the country itself. This need not necessarily be the case. TNCs may be privately successful and still based in relatively declining countries like the USA and the UK. That this is indeed the case would appear to argue against the post-Keynesian–Kilpatrick and Lawson story.[34] In an empirical study Martin and Rowthorn (1986) test three different hypotheses of de-industrialization: the maturity hypothesis (that continuing economic development leads to increasing, stable and then decreasing manufacturing employment), a trade specialization thesis (the non-requirement by UK manufacturing to have a surplus in order to supply the world, unlike in the earlier Empire period), and the failure thesis, broadly associated with the post-Keynesian scenario discussed here. They conclude that the first two factors can explain virtually all decline in manufacturing empolyment. Stafford (1989) has a critical review.

An additional problem with the post-Keynesian (and Glyn and Sutcliffe) thesis of reduced competitiveness is that it fails to explain international crises, such as in the 1930s and the 1970s. The focus is on a particular case and its particular peculiarities. Still, there is scope, I believe, for raising the observations of rising labour strength to a theory of crisis, simply by observing that increased capitalist development creates the proletariat, and contributes to its organization in labour unions. A standard Marxian proposition in this framework, the tendency towards increasing concentration and centralization of capital, can be seen to lead to increasing labour *economic* bargaining power, with internationalization being a (partial) response to this tendency, and de-industrialization and relative decline the eventual outcome. To the extent that the UK reached 'maturity' earlier than other countries, as Martin and Rowthorn (1986) show, it is also the first to experience these tendencies. Given that the tendency is for TNCs' actions to be induced by the crisis, there is no reason for TNCs to be unsuccessful if the country declines. Once internationalized production is the norm, TNCs need not have strong nationalistic allegiances. Profits will simply do, from whatever source.[35] Ironically, *trans*nationals tend to become *multi*nationals!

To summarize, internationalization tendencies can be facilitated by crises, seen here as possibly resulting from the effects of a synthesis of secular ROC-TRPF, underconsumptionist and rising labour strength crisis variants on the rate of profit. In turn internationalization can facilitate a process of de-industrialization. In both cases many other factors are involved. It is important that internationalization can explain the maintenance of a monopoly regulation regime or SSA, by providing the material conditions for a growth accord. De-industrialization (in part due to, and through, internationalization) can explain the demise of the monopoly regulation regime.

My arguments so far provide, I hope, a logical synthesis of Marxian crises theories, and their links with the state and the internationalization of capital. However, this is at the level of static logical possibilities. There is no analysis, so far, of the dynamic evolutionary process through which capitalist institutions emerge, evolve, fail and reconstitute themselves; this characterizes all existing work in the area. A first step in this direction is contained in the next section.

5   Theory of Capitalist Institutional Crisis

The price mechanism (market), the firm (private hierarchy) and the state ('public' hierarchy) have been argued to be three alternative, but complementary, capitalist institutional devices for the exploitation of the division of labour and team work, aiming at furthering the interests of the principals. Historically, the early *capitalist* institutional device through which division of labour was performed was the price mechanism.[36] Through it the emerging capitalists, the merchants, were able to profit by the simple act of buying and selling, by turning products into commodities, or use values into exchange values. Product availability in often remote markets and (thus) demand and supply considerations were the means through which a source of revenue was generated for the merchants in the process of exchange.

Use of the price mechanism was an inherently uncertain and (thus) imperfect means of satisfying the merchants interests: profit and (thus) power. Neither the availability of producers nor the price of products and commodities to be could be guaranteed for the merchants. Alternatively, such availability could only be guaranteed at the price of excessive market transaction costs; that is, the costs of finding producers, negotiating with them, contracting with them and policing such agreements. Such costs could endanger the very existence of a satisfactory profit. In this sense, the price mechanism was failing to deliver the goods to the merchants. The firm was the way out. In its earliest form, the putting-out system, the merchant-manufacturer replaced the price mechanism with an employment relation, where labourers worked for the merchant-manufacturer for a compensation, a wage, initially at their own place (and pace) and by making use of their own capital equipment.

Within the capitalist logic of profit generation for the principals, the employment relation is transactionally superior to the price mechanism, and thus a more efficient means of labour division. In this sense the transactional properties of firms are not *per se* the reason for market failure; the reason is the transactional properties needed for capitalist control to be established. Such control is easier under the employment relation, which renders the latter transactionally superior from the capitalist point of view. Given this, (transactional) efficiency cannot in itself explain the existence of firms; the principals' objectives (thus distribution) also need to be considered. Efficiency and distribution are inseparable, as are existence and objectives. This need not necessarily imply that firms are *not* Pareto inefficient *ex post*. Given efficiency gains, from tighter control and reduced transaction costs, the opposite is more likely, at least from a pure pecuniary point of view. In a historical context, moreover, whether labourers to be preferred the status of labourer to (the uncertainty of) being free peasants is a thorny question, leaving unanswered the question of whether the firm was Pareto efficient or not *ex ante* too. Important, however, in my context is that the driving force has been efficiency for profit (distribution) and not efficiency for efficiency's sake (economizing) as the Coase–Williamson neo-classical institutionalism suggests.

The emergence of the employment relation does not remove the market *in toto*. It replaces the use of the price mechanism with a hierarchical device, for a particular type of transaction relating to the employment of labour. Outside this relation, the price mechanism remains. Going further, it can be said that the firm emerges *for* (the production of commodities for sale in) the market. The replacement of putting-out by the factory system, which initially at least brings together labourers on one site under the direct control of the capitalist, who now owns the means of production too, further enhances efficiency for profit, by solving two problems of imperfect control (and thus transaction costs) associated with putting-out: imperfect supervision of labour and imperfect control over organizational knowledge, which would allow some labourers to join the ranks of capitalists, given their ownership of capital. The factory system both solves these problems and fully frees labour from property. It also brings about the benefits of team work. From the point of view of the capitalist, the factory system represents a futher efficiency gain. Whether it is Pareto efficient is doubtful. *Vis-à-vis* the putting-out system, labourers lose control over their lives, for an uncertain increase in their wage, as their share in the efficiency gain (chapter 2).

In the above framework, the price mechanism and the firm complement each other in the principals' efforts to further their profits by achieving a more efficient division of labour. The price mechanism in itself is an imperfect and insufficient means of achieving this aim because of the excessive transaction costs associated with its inherent reliance on voluntary exchanges. The private hierarchy, the firm, solves some of these problems, but not all. The availability of labourers to be (the freeing of the peasants from their feudal lords) and the enforcement of the labour contract necessitate substantial expenses and suffer from public goods characteristics, and thus from potential free-riding. No individual capitalist may be willing or able to undertake the role of providing such goods. In this sense the firm (and the market, thus the private sector) fails. A third party, the public hierarchy or state, can be the way out. This undertakes the provision of goods necessary for capital to achieve its aims, for a share in the resulting benefits. Transactional difficulties associated with capitalists trying to establish a private means of creating free labour and enforcing contracts at the aggregate level (containing labour unrests) are one reason for private sector failures to control labour directly, as capital *per se*. Historically, the pre-existence of a feudal state, with a ready army and, initially at least, on better terms with nobles than merchants, led to an alliance between the merchants and the crown, so as to share in the profit generated by the merchants; an alliance based on community of interest. In this sense, merchants and the crown can be seen as the principals in the early stages of capitalism. A state 'instrument', living symbiotically with capital, was instrumental in creating the proletariat and establishing the 'rules of the game' allowing capitalism to function; that is, protection of (capitalist) property rights and freedom in exchange of commodities, including the one commodity *par excellence*, labour power. The control of labour at the workplace in the factory system rendered direct intervention by the state in production unnecessary, and provided a reason for the apparent *autonomous* form of the capitalist state.

The apparent community of interest between capital and labour, as income receivers, allows for the *possibility* of the apparently autonomous state. From the point of view of capital, the emergence of the capitalist state represented a transaction costs gain and thus enhanced efficiency. Again whether the capitalist state was also Pareto efficient is an open issue. Considering the existing alternative, the feudal state, it might well have been. However, the driving force was efficiency gains for distributional gains, much in line with the case of the firm. The issue, once more, is not efficiency versus distribution, but efficiency versus efficiency for distribution. While the capitalist state saves private sector transaction costs for the principals, it has costs of its own, mainly arising from the need to derive an agreement among the principals (initially the merchants and the crown) on how to distribute the profits. Such problems of opportunism, to use conventional language, but also the inefficiency of state functionaries (for example, because of bounded rationality) establish the possibility of state failures too. The possibility of the co-existence of private sector and state failures allows for the case of an institutional failure (crisis) which can be seen as a variant and extension of the neoclassical institutional approach; but one that derives efficiency for distribution, not for efficiency's sake (chapter 4).

Transactional problems related to the control of labour are one of the forces explaining institutions and their forms. The more basic underlying reason is the extraction of more output from given number of labourers, by increasing the productivity of labour (degree of exploitation). For every individual capitalist (firm) this introduces the additional (and related) need of technological improvements, as well as improvements in their organizational forms, designed to achieve the joint aim of extracting more profit. The existence of capital in the form of many capitals (firms) introduces a further element of competition, besides conflict between capital in general and labour in general; namely, competition between firms (rivalry) to distribute the profit derived from the exploitation of (the division of) labour and team work. This rivalry renders the conflict between capital and labour a means through which competitive advantages can be gained. Increasing efficiency in the exploitation of labour (division), but also in every other conceivable form, becomes a matter of life and death. In the competitive struggle the more efficient, talented and innovative firms will survive. Much of this, however, involves the application of this ingenuity in achieving a more efficient exploitation of the source of more profits: labour power.

Conflict with labour and rivalry with other firms become the *economic* driving force of capitalist accumulation, the reason why profit derivation and realization is not the simple expression of a sociological need for power, recognition or a religious ethic, but rather a condition of survival. Conflict with labour necessitates technological and organizational improvements, which, ideally, achieve the simultaneous enhancement of control over labour and of the degree of exploitation, work intensity and (thus) productivity of labour. Competition with rivals (rivalry) necessitates a reduction in unit costs, so that competitive advantages are gained. *Ceteris paribus*, the need to increase control over labour and simultaneously gain competitive edges over rivals tends to favour labour-saving technical changes. Both capital-saving and labour-saving changes can achieve reductions in unit costs, but 'machines do not strike'. The very threat of the introduction of labour-saving changes can be a powerful discipline device for the workforce. This creates the demand for such changes. Once the supply is there all the incentives are also there for the threat to be realized. To the extent that this happens a tendency towards a rising organic composition (ROC) of capital and (thus) a declining profit rate manifests itself. Given that one of the main reasons for the introduction of labour-saving technical changes is the control of labour and (thus) an increase in the degree of labour exploitation, the tendency towards a declining profit rate will, initially at least, be expressed in and thwarted by an increasing profit share.

Conflict with labour and rivalry with other firms also tends to increase the concentration and centralization of capital. In the competitive struggle, the fittest will survive. Fitness is measured in terms of exploitation of technical and transactional economies and labour, in order to reduce unit costs and increase profits. The attempt to minimize unit costs from all sources, so as to increase long-term profits, becomes each firm's objective. Under uncertainty, it is achieved through the pursuit of growth, both internal and external (mergers). The attempts by firms to remove constraints in growing, such as financial, organizational and managerial constraints, can explain firms' evolution and organizational changes, such as the socialization of capital ownership in the form of the joint-stock company, the managerial and pension funds revolutions, and the M-form organization, see chapter 2. Firms successful in introducing and exploiting such innovations are the winners in the competitive struggle; the others are taken over, disappear, become a competitive fringe serving the successful, or work directly for the successful, through, for example, subcontracting or licensing. This process introduces a tendency towards increasing concentration and centralization of capital (see chapter 3), which *ceteris paribus* tends to increase the profit share and thus the profit rate. This tendency also counteracts the tendency towards declining profit rates through ROC.

The emergence and growth of capitalist firms is tantamount to the emergence and growth of (the strength of) labour. Increasing monopolization facilitates the organization and power of labour against capital. This tends to counteract the ability of firms to increase the degree of exploitation in the production process and, to the extent that labour opposes labour-saving technical changes, it tends to thwart the tendency towards ROC. Monopolization through growth becomes the *sine qua non* of capitalist success. Giant firms can satisfy labour's demands by granting higher wage rates than smaller firms, by shifting increasing costs to consumers through increased prices. Monopolization and increasing wage rates for the monopoly sector's labour can therefore go hand in hand with increasing economy-wide unemployment as smaller firms go bankrupt and labour in the competitive sector (less well organized) is laid off. Thus increasing monopolization gives rise to increasing labour strength over wage rates, but simultaneously reduced levels of employment. In this sense increasing labour strength is perfectly compatible with increasing profit shares, despite increasing wage rates.

Overall, the dynamics of capitalist evolution imply a tendency towards increasing profit shares; through increased labour exploitation of the early phases of capitalist development (*laissez-faire* or competitive phase) and through reduced employment as the economy moves towards the next (monopoly) stage. This tends to counteract the tendency towards declining profit rates through ROC and increasing labour strength. Increasing prices and increased socialization of capital ownership enhance this tendency at the monopoly stage (Cowling, 1982; Pitelis, 1987a). Monopoly pricing in the monopoly stage achieves what supply of labour does at the competitive stage; namely, the maintenance of the overall wage share at near subsistence (socially defined) levels. As wage rates tend to diverge from subsistence because of rising labour strength, but also inter-firm rivalry, monopoly pricing becomes an alternative means of surplus value derivation, in the process of exchange this time.

Taxation by the state is a similar means of such surplus value derivation. In the early phase of capitalism near subsistence wage rates imply that all taxation is paid by capital. This is a reason for the *laissez-faire* attitude of the state in this period, as its role is limited to sharing the surplus produced in production by firms. State autonomy in this phase is only in the state's *form* – autonomy in the sense of existing independently of (but symbiotically with) capital. Divergence of wage rates from subsistence imply the possibility of surplus value derivation from labour in exchange through taxation. This renders the state's relative autonomy more substantive; it enjoys relative autonomy from capital. This induces a preference of the state for high employment levels, a source of taxation. It is also an incentive for the undertaking of direct productive activities by the state to produce surplus value, which is state monopoly capitalism. Such functions by the state are, to differing degrees and depending on the particular activity, beneficial to both capital and labour: to capital because of the socialization of the cost of, for example, infrastructure; to labour because of the security of employment in nationalized industries or increased welfare expenditures, such as unemployment and sickness benefits. The state (functionaries), capital and labour all favour increased state participation in the economy, to start with. However, such participation tends gradually to erode the power of capital *vis-à-vis* the state and labour, and to decrease the profit rate, given that certain state functions, such as welfare contributions, can only realize and not produce surplus value, at least not directly (Gouph, 1979). This, the increased share of surplus value going to state functionaries as a result, and the increased confidence of labour resulting from the removal of the potency of the threat of the sack, gradually generate capital's disenchantment with the state's increased participation in the economy. Demands for a return to *laissez-faire* capitalism are the 'natural' reaction of capital.

The increasing participation of the state in the economy in the monopoly phase of capitalism tends to reduce the profit rate in two ways: through its 'unproductive' expenditures but also through increased employment levels, thus wage shares, thus reduced profit shares. While these tend to enhance the realization of profit by capital through increased aggregate demand, they undermine the control of capital over investments and labour. Along with declining profit rates tendencies, this suggests capital's eventual dissatisfaction with state interventionism, particularly when alternative forms of profit realization are available; internally (innovations) and externally (foreign markets). Given capital's control of a substantial part of production, and thus the threat of *domestic* investment strikes, which in a capitalist economy would harm all stakeholders, in particular the state and labour, the continuation needs of the system ensure the existence of an upper limit to the economic role of the state under capitalism. This itself creates the need for an increasing ideological role of the state, in part to justify to labour the maintenance of the system, given the evident *possibility* of the state undertaking an increasingly higher share of productive activities, turning itself into a socialist state, or a 'national socialist' one.[37]

The tendency towards increasing monopolization puts constraints on the state's autonomy, both instrumental (increased wealth of firms, etc.) and structural (increased control by few private actors of investment decisions etc.). The practical expression of this is a tendency towards favourable tax treatment of (retained) profits, and thus a facilitation by the state of the tendency towards increasing profit shares in the monopoly and state monopolist stages of capitalism.

The tendency towards increasing monopolization and (through the) socialization of capital ownership, generates a tendency towards increasing profit shares, which exists alongside the tendency towards declining profit rates through ROC of capital and rising labour strength. The last two, as already suggested, tend to be offset by the increased degree of labour exploitation and increased unemployment, thus allowing the tendency towards increasing profit shares to dominate under monopoly capitalism. State policies favouring (retained) profits tend to ensure the prevalence of the tendency even when counter-tendencies (increased ROC, rising labour strength) are strong enough to offset the (pre-tax) tendency. After-tax profit shares therefore tend to increase under monopoly and state monopoly capitalism. Given that all such tendencies can be explained by exclusive focus on production level conflict between capital in general and labour in general, leading to capital introducing labour-saving technical changes, it can be suggested that the ROC-TRPF notion is more fundamental than the alternatives. This need not mean that it is inconsistent with or even that it prevails over such alternatives. Indeed my claim is that the tendency towards increasing profit share is prevalent (albeit in a sense derivative), particularly at the (state) monopoly capitalism stage.

Capital is strengthened *vis-à-vis* labour and the state by its ability to undertake overseas operations. These operations cushion firms from the adverse impact on them of, for example, 'investment strikes' domestically. Such strikes can take the form of choosing to operate overseas (and not domestically). Monopolization and organizational forms such as the M-form make such operations possible. Conflict with labour and rivalry with other firms (domestic *and* overseas) make them necessary, as suggested by Hymer (in Cohen et al., 1979). This is a supply-side motive for transnational corporations (TNCs) to appear. The possibility or threat of a 'capital flight' tends to enhance the power of domestic monopolies *vis-à-vis* labour and the state.

The benefits from the exploitation of the factors leading to increased monopolization (capital abundance, advanced technology, etc.) create oligopolistic advantages to domestic firms, which initially tend to facilitate the conditions for an export-oriented improvement of the domestic standard of living. International competitiveness at this stage becomes the reason for the possibility of the establishment of a stable social structure of accumulation or regulation system. All this means is that the benefits to all (the nation) through exploitation of competitive advantages over foreigners are such that they allow an accord of capital and labour. This allows uninterrupted growth and accumulation. Countries that enjoy the advantage of earlier development also reap its benefits in terms of conditions allowing a focus on growth *given* distribution. What is good for the monopolists is good for the nation too here, a statement which is for some time much more than a legitimizing slogan.

Crisis and international operations of firms through direct foreign investment (DFI) put an end to the euphoria and undermine the conditions of the regulation regime. Crisis is the apparent direct product of the tendency towards increasing after-tax profit shares. Such increases tend to reduce the ratio of consumers' expenditure to private sector disposable income through two mainly overlapping routes: smaller propensities to save wages than profits, and/or imperfect substitutability between corporate retained profits and personal saving; see Pitelis (1987a) for a detailed discussion. In oligopolistic industries operating below the full capacity level of output, reduced consumer spending will tend to lead to reductions in output not prices (Rowthorn, 1981).

As a result, reductions in consumers' expenditure will reduce demand for consumer goods industries, and *ceteris paribus* the output and capacity utilization in such industries and the economy as a whole. Increases in excess capacity will tend to reduce the rate of profit, offsetting the tendency for an increasing profit rate owing to increasing profit shares. This tends to reinforce the similar tendency operating through ROC and increased unemployment owing to increasing labour strength. To the extent that capacity utilization decreases also adversely affect individual firms' decisions to invest (expand capacity), underconsumption will be reflected as excess capacity and, through the effects of the latter (itself an element of the profit rate, one of the most important determinants of investment), will tend to give rise to a 'realization crisis'.

Reduced effective demand, the manifestation of the realization crisis, tends to increase unemployment and provides a demand-side incentive for firms to become TNCs. The existence of financial capital in the hands of giant firms in the form of retained profits will facilitate this tendency from the demand side. Both factors will tend to relieve the firm's pressures on profitability. Unemployment reduces labour's confidence, and thus wage rates, and so does firms' DFI. All these tend to increase the profit rate and investment. However, investment need not take place domestically now; not unless wage rates (weighted appropriately to account for infrastructure, political risks and other such factors) are globally competitive. If not, domestic TNCs can invest abroad and foreign TNCs not choose a particular country. When unemployment and (or because of) TNCs' non-preference for a particular country coincide, the conditions for a stable social structure of accumulation are undermined. Monopolies fail to persuade on the coincidence of their interests with labour's. The state cannot satisfy both capital and labour, in great part because of the ability of TNCs to 'un-nationalize' themselves for tax purposes, by registering in tax havens. The effect is labour discontent arising from the failure of both the private sector and the state to deliver the goods. In this sense, internationalization of production allows the undermining of the SSA and leads to an apparent private sector failure and a fiscal crisis. Both together lead to an economic *and* a fiscal crisis; a failure of the three major capitalist institutions, the market, the firm and the state. As far as the state is concerned, this is expressed as a failure to deliver the goods to the 'citizens', and a legitimization crisis.

A new international division of labour emerges as a result, in which each country's relative attractiveness to international capital, in terms of what it has to offer, becomes the determining factor of the quantity and type of operations undertaken by TNCs in it. Early industrial countries, the 'homelands' of TNCs, become the headquarters, because of the availability of appropriately skilled personnel, but also for what they offer in terms of cultural and other activities to the top executives. Manufacturing is undertaken in or subcontracted to the low cost, high labour exploitation, countries and distributed to the rest of the globe. De-industrialization of early industrialized countries is in part the result of these tendencies. A *dependent* industrialization of some less developed countries results, which, however, does not exclude the possibility of independent industrialization in cases, subject to the economic conditions and the political will of the local bourgeoisie, people and state, as well as the articulation of their interactions (chapter 4).

The crisis and (or caused by) the internationalization of production contains the seeds of inflationary tendencies in de-industrializing developed countries, from three major sources, capital, labour and the state: the monopoly sector of capital through monopoly pricing; small capital (the competitive sector) through increased borrowing from the financial sector, which pushes up interest rates, mortgage rates and the general price level; labour (consumers) through increased demands for high wages to offset inflationary losses, and increased borrowing to re-establish (in the short run at least) their habitual standard of living; the state also through borrowing and spending, in part at least to satisfy the demands of both capital and labour, but also to satisfy its own needs, including the incumbent government's re-election. The co-existence of inflationary tendencies, of both cost push and demand pull type, and increasing unemployment owing to the crisis gives rise to the familiar stagflation. Engineered recessions by the state can exacerbate the unemployment tendencies. Such state actions can often be the only available policy capable of re-establishing competitiveness, and thus making the country more attractive than its rivals to TNCs.

The new transnational phase of capital establishes capital's control over labour and undermines the nation state's relative autonomy. There is a tendency for a new social structure of accumulation, a new regulation regime, based on an '*austerity consensus*' that labour has to understand that success and growth relative to rivals is through TNCs, and thus austerity is part and parcel of the package required to attract TNCs away from 'foreigners'. Austerity consensus is seen as the means through which *we* (e.g. British labour) become 'better' than *them* (e.g. German labour). Nationalism wins over international solidarity of labour. The tendency is enhanced by the economic success of some countries, such as Japan and West Germany. The success of these, in part due to a history- and policy-induced capital nationalism, can apparently be competed away by less successful rivals only through an austerity consensus. Thus both success and failure breed austerity, the new social structure of accumulation of advanced capitalism *and* the world as a whole.

I have tried in this short account to derive capitalist institutional failure evolutionarily. In part such evolution has been attributed to transaction costs, but other costs, particularly labour, are included, within a general framework of principals' efforts to further their interests by achieving a more efficient exploitation of (the division of) labour and the benefits of team work. The tendency from this type of behaviour is seen to be for an increasing profit share, which gives rise to a tendency towards a realization failure, and (in part) to internationalized production. Along with, and in part because of, internationalization, realization crises also lead to fiscal crises, and thus overall to a failure of the three major capitalist institutions: the private sector of firms and market and the public sector of the state. The need for a new regulation regime arises, in the modern epoch the tendency being for an austerity consensus; a direct result of the dominance of international capital over labour and the erosion of the relative autonomy of the nation state *vis-à-vis* capital.

Two issues are worth emphasis here. First, my focus on increasing profit shares is not incompatible with the declining rate of profit tendency predicted from the ROC-TRPF theory or the rising labour strength theory. Indeed the tendencies can operate simultaneously, but be expressed as a rising profit share giving rise to excess capacity, reduced investment and a realization crisis. Second, it is at least implicit in my account that the rising profit share tendency becomes particularly evident in the monopoly phase of capitalism, and even more so in the state monopoly capitalism epoch, with a high degree of internationalized production and TNC activities. This last factor, it is worth stressing, becomes instrumental in the rise and fall of the social structure of accumulation or the monopoly regulation regime.

To test empirically every single theoretical proposition made in this section would be a nearly impossible task, for well known reasons: data availability and reliability, their compatibility with theoretical categories, general problems associated with empirical, econometric work, time constraints – and often sheer lack of interest in so doing! But theory with no evidence is just speculation. My means of balancing these two contrasting considerations is to focus on four major links proposed in my theoretical account and to discuss existing evidence or provide new evidence on them. These links are: first, a tendency towards an increasing after-tax profit share; second, the impact of increasing profit shares on consumers' expenditure; third, the effects of excess capacity on individual firms' decisions to invest; finally, the link between investment and firms' realized profits. To the extent that after-tax profit shares are increasing, that such increases reduce consumption, that (resulting) excess capacity reduces investment and that investment is positively linked with realized profits (implying that the latter decrease when investment expenditure does), I can claim that there is empirical support for the four major propositions of the theoretical account.

I have examined the first two links in detail elsewhere (Pitelis, 1987a) for the cases of the USA and the UK. In both cases the after-tax gross profit share of gross private sector disposable income was steadily increasing in the whole post war period: from 12.42 per cent in 1945–9 to 14.79 per cent in 1980–4 in the USA and from 17.56 per cent in 1946–50 to 24.31 per cent in 1981–4 in the UK. The only exceptions were 1970–4 for the USA and 1961–5 for the UK, when small declines *vis-à-vis* the previous periods were observed. This evidence is in line with my theory. It suggests that existing evidence in favour of declining profit shares is the result of exclusive focus on pre-tax data (as in Weisskopf, 1979), on only one sector of the economy, such as manufacturing (as in Glyn and Sutcliffe, 1972), or on operating rates of return (both studies mentioned above), as opposed to the Kaleckian (and Marxian) measure, which also includes rent, interest and income from self-employment. As my measure is post-tax economy-wide gross (i.e. it includes profit, rent, interest and self-employment income) profit share, it is, I believe, a more reliable one, at least for my purposes here. Room for disagreements obviously exists, and it would take a separate study to compare and contrast different measures of the profit share. All I claim here is that once the state is accounted for, as Weisskopf himself thought necessary but did not do, and a gross (Kaleckian–Marxian) measure is adopted, the US and UK evidence does support the claim of an increasing profit share.

In the period under examination consumer expenditure shares declined: from 82.64 per cent in 1945–9 to 81.39 per cent in 1980–4 in the USA and dramatically from 88.23 per cent in 1946–50 to 74.73 per cent in 1981–4 in the UK. Evidence on the effects of different income types on consumers' expenditure indicate that this decline was in part due to the increase in the profit share. When corporate retained earnings and pensions funds wealth shares are examined, it is found that both these were on the increase in the post-war USA and UK and their degree of substitutability with personal sector saving was minimal. This supports the socialization of capital through shareholding (discretionary and compulsory through occupational pensions) leading to reduced consumers' expenditure hypothesis. The issues and evidence are further discussed in Pitelis (1987a). Suffice it to point out here that through the two in part substitute and in part complementary ways (increasing profit shares and increasing compulsory saving owing to the socialization of capital), a tendency towards decreasing consumer expenditure shares did manifest itself in both the USA and the UK after the Second World War.

As already noted, it is widely believed that decreases in consumers' expenditure will tend to result in increasing excess capacity through reductions in output, and that this in turn will affect negatively firms' decisions to invest. I have elsewhere reported some evidence pointing to a coincidence between reduced consumers' expenditure, increasing excess capacity and relatively stagnant manufacturing investment shares for the USA and the UK (Pitelis, 1987a). This *does not test* the link between reduced capacity utilization and firms' decisions to invest, or aggregate investment. At the aggregate level, there is some evidence in line with the existence of this link; see Cowling (1982) and Stafford (1986) for surveys. The microeconomic relationship is less explored. However, in a recent study on the Western European chemical industry, Paraskevopoulos and Pitelis (1990) report econometric results in line with the idea that capacity utilization has a positive and significant impact on firms' capacity expansion programmes. Moreover, this effect is independent of the effects of a multitude of other micro-level explanatory variables, such as the capacity expansions of rivals, the firms' market share, the minimum efficient scale of output, absolute capital requirements etc. This evidence supports the existing evidence for the relationship at the aggregate level. It points to the conclusion that capacity utilization reductions are in part at least responsible for stagnant or declining investment expenditure shares.

Reductions in investment may in their turn have a negative impact on aggregate realized profits, and the profit share and profit rate, thus turning the underconsumptionist tendency to a full blown realization crisis. The alleged positive link between aggregate investment and aggregate profits has been proposed and tested by Kalecki (1971) as far back as 1934 with US data. Since, there has been no empirical study to test this hypothesis, to my knowledge, save for a recent study by the present author (Pitelis, 1991a). In this study 1955–80 time series data for the UK have confirmed the hypothesis that aggregate realized profits are positively and significantly affected by aggregate investment. Moreover, the effect was independent of other explanatory variables, such as advertising expenditure.

A more important relationship, perhaps, is that between aggregate investment and the realized profit rate. The reason is that realized profit rate is widely acknowledged to be the major determinant of firms' decisions to invest, as already pointed out. Some evidence in line with this idea comes from studies testing the relationship between investment and capacity utilization, given that the latter is one of the constituent parts of the profit rate (Paraskevopoulos and Pitelis, 1990). That investment expenditure may be positively linked with the profit rate is a hypothesis never tested so far, to my knowledge. The profit rate can be written as

$$\frac{\Pi}{K} = \frac{\Pi}{W} \cdot \frac{W}{K}$$

Given this, changes in Π/W are directly reflected in changes in the profit rate (Π/K). We can, therefore, avoid the notorious problem of measuring the capital stock, and focus on Π/W to test the link between investment expenditure and realized profit rates. If this is positive, then we have a scenario of cumulative reduction in investment arising from reduced capacity utilization, to start with, and (thus) reduced realized profit rates subsequently.[38]

The data I used were UK time series for the 1955–80 period. They are explained in Pitelis (1991a), although the focus there is different. Only one equation was run, expressing changes in Π/W as a function of changes in investment expenditure, the previous year's change in investment expenditure, the change in advertising expenditure and also the change in the previous year's Π/W. This equation was obtained by using a Koyck transformation to the simpler static relationship:

$$\Delta (\Pi/W) = f(\Delta I, \Delta A)$$

where Δ denotes the first difference, Π, gross after tax profits, W wage income, I investment expenditure and A advertising expenditure, itself a form of investment expenditure. A constant term, assuming the character of a time trend, was also included in the regression, which on estimate gave

$$\Delta(\Pi/W) = -0.20^* + 0.000015^{**} \Delta I_t + 0.00034^* \Delta A_t$$
$$(2.68) \qquad (1.92) \qquad\qquad (4.05)$$

$$+ 0.00010\Delta I^*_{t-1} -0.50^* \Delta(\Pi/W)_{t-1}$$
$$(2.83) \qquad (2.87)$$

$R^2 = 0.6006$, $DW = 1.737$,* significant at 5% level,** significant at 10% level.

The lagged investment term and lagged dependent variable are the result of the adoption of the Koyck transformation and the assumption that investment affects Π/W contemporaneously, while advertising does so with a geometrically declining lag. Justification for this treatment and the exact mechanics of the equation are discussed in Pitelis (1991a). Suffice it to note here that these two variables could also be included in the absence of the Koyck transformation; for example, for the sake of testing their effect by including them in the simple equation referred to above.

It can be seen from the regression that investment expenditure tends to affect positively and significantly Π/W. This is also true of advertising expenditure. Past years' Π/W, on the other hand, appear to affect negatively the current year's rate. Given the first differences from the explanatory power of the equation is satisfactory. Multicollinearity does not appear to be a problem, judging from the low standard errors. However, autocorrelation's presence could not be excluded given the DW's bias towards indicating no autocorrelation, in the presence of the lagged dependent variable. Subject to this qualification, the equation seems to support the idea that investment expenditure increases the realized Π/W and (thus) *ceteris paribus* the rate of profit. Given the rate of profit's positive link with planned investment, the overall effect is a cumulative decline in investment, resulting from and reinforcing the tendency towards reduced consumers' expenditure, and thus a realization crisis. This itself tends to reduce the income available to the state through taxation, thus tending to exacerbate the tendency towards a fiscal crisis.

The limited evidence discussed and provided here is broadly in line with my theoretical analysis. Evidently, my theoretical points have not all been tested, nor could it be claimed that no other alternative interpretations could be made of the evidence. All I wish to claim here is that the major economic and political institutions of capitalism need to be analysed in more detail, in a more synthetic non-dogmatic way and also dynamically, evolutionarily and historically. Such an approach was pursued here for three major institutions, the firm, the market and the state. I believe this approach provides useful insights on the existence, evolution and crisis of these institutions and, to a large extent, capitalism as a whole. More research needs to be done; both in the direction taken here and towards incorporating more socio-political, psychological and ecological aspects in the analysis of capitalist institutions and the capitalist institutional crisis.

Notes

1 Other meanings of the word, from ancient Greek, are to separate, to divide, to sift, to decide, the turning point of an illness in which it is decided that an organism's self-healing powers are sufficient for recovery, or 'moments of truth, when the significance of men and events were brought to light'; see O'Connor (1987, pp. 54–5) for further discussion.

2 In this sense the analysis is limited to economico-political issues, often at the expense of other (e.g. social, personality, environmental) aspects of crises. This is not to underplay their importance. An attempt to discuss and integrate all potential facets of crisis is indeed a necessary and useful task, but falls beyond the scope of this book. O'Connor (1987) discusses some of the issues involved.

3 Following the 'neoclassical synthesis' and early debates on the relative potency of fiscal and monetarist policy, it is now widely agreed that the two schools can be viewed as broadly homogenous, analysable in terms of the Hicksian *IS–LM* interpretation of Keynesian economics (see Sawyer, 1982a).

4 The possibility that reductions in money wage rates could fail to increase aggregate demand was also discussed by Keynes. See Tobin (1980) for the Keynes–Pigou–Kalecki exchange on the 'real balance effect'.

5 The 'natural rate hypothesis' represented an attack on the Keynesian idea that there is a trade-off between unemployment and inflation (the Phillips curve). Friedman denied this trade-off, claiming that in the long-run the Phillips curve was (near) vertical, at the unemployment level which had no tendency to accelerate. Such a tendency was presumed to exist because, unlike in the Phillips curve interpretation where unemployment was related to price wages, Friedman suggested that because of agents' inflationary expectations, the relationship should involve the real wage rate. The resulting Phillips curve is the 'expectation augmented' one, and the non-accelerating inflation rate level of unemployment, the 'natural rate'.

6 In the case of funded occupational pensions the relationship could also be one of complementarity; see Pitelis (1987a) for a detailed treatment.

7 For a critical exposition of the Modigliani–Miller theorem, see Auerbach (1988).

8 This idea incidentally dents the internal consistency of the Feldstein argument. Loyal to the life-cycle hypothesis of rational intertemporal utility-maximizing households, Feldstein (1973) suggested

that corporate retentions do not add to personal saving, because households 'see through the corporate veil'; that is, realize that retentions are *their* saving, and thus manipulate their personal saving so as to offset changes in retentions. It is only one step from that to argue that households realize that their social security contributions are PAYG. To assert that they do not effectively asserts the co-existence of suprarationality for retentions and near idiocy for social security contributions. In this sense the rational expectations idea re-establishes the internal logic of the Feldstein hypothesis by pursuing it to its logical limit.

9 It should also be noted that the analyses by both Feldstein and Barro and Lucas are non-historical. From a historical point of view social security contributions can be seen as arising from the need to replace (institutionalize) declining family solidarity, the decline itself being due to the development of capitalism and the associated breaking of (extended) families through urbanization etc. (Bowles and Gintis, 1982). From this perspective social security contributions may represent a mere institutionalization of family solidarity. As long as the flows do not change appreciably between the two institutional settings, little has changed because of the introduction of social security schemes; see also Kessler et al. (1981).

10 Tobin (1980) also observes the need for reliance of actors on 'rules of thumb' and satisficing procedures when 'radical uncertainty' is present.

11 For a critique of Friedman's treatment of the concept of bounded rationality in the market, see Kay (1990).

12 For a discussion of the concepts of 'mode of production' and 'social formation', see Fine and Harris (1979). For our purposes here the capitalist mode of production can be taken to refer to all socio-political and ideological relations developed in an economic system based on social production and private appropriation. Social formation includes more than production modes, e.g. feudal remnants.

13 Once the 'law' is defined in terms of ROC-TRPF, as in Weisskopf (1979), the ambiguity concerning whether the counter-influences should be seen as enjoying equal status to the 'law' is solved; given the ROC's exclusive reliance on production. As Marx considered production as the *primus inter pares* (*pares* being exchange and distribution), the Fine and Harris reformulation becomes semantic. It does, however, help us address some of the ciriticisms of the law; see below.

14 More general criticisms are advanced by Steedman (1977) and Hodgson (1974), who question the relevance of value and the

organic composition. For critical assessments of these debates see Fine and Harris (1979) and Howard (1987). A related criticism by, in particular, Himmelweit (1974) is that increases in the organic composition only imply declines in the maximum attainable profit rate, because when V equals zero the rate of profit becomes equal to the reciprocal of the organic composition. This need not imply falls in the actual profit rate when V exceeds zero. This view is criticized by Fine and Harris (1979) and Wright (1977) among others. The latter suggests that *if* the organic composition increases secularly, it becomes increasingly more unlikely that increases in the rate of exploitation will fully counteract rises in the organic composition. Accordingly, he views the organic composition as a significant impediment to the accumulation process.

15 A related criticism is that rational capitalists will not adopt a technique which reduces their profit rate, the so-called 'Okishio theorem'. The problem here is the extent to which technical change is a matter of choice or necessity. If conflict with labour and rivalry with other firms are seen as the main sources of technical progress, the argument does not follow (Shaikh, 1977). See also the Van Parijs (1980, 1983), Clawson (1983) debate.

16 From these early contributions Bleaney (1976) observes that Malthus stressed the mass of saving as a cause of underconsumption, while Sismonde de Sismondi stressed the distribution of income. Hobson combined the two and blamed excessive saving on unequal distribution of income. Hobson explained imperialism on the basis of this idea and his views significantly influenced Lenin's (1917) pamphlet on imperialism. Also important in Hobson's work was that he attributed part of the excess saving to monopoly and introduced the concept of the 'surplus'. Both ideas were crucial for later underconsumptionists, such as Baran and Sweezy (1966).

17 For a detailed discussion of Kalecki's views on and critiques of the degree of monopoly, see Reynolds (1989).

18 On the basis of his definition and observing Luxemburg's focus on both production goods demand and consumption goods demand, Bleaney does not classify Luxemburg as an underconsumptionist.

19 Mandel (1975b) refers to competition by foreign rivals, very much in line with recent proponents of contestability; see the discussion in Pitelis (1990b).

20 In Baran and Sweezy it was 'epoch making' innovations which explained non-collapse. In fact 'debt' explosions could themselves be seen as 'innovations', and epoch making ones too. One wonders to what extent these are exogenous or the result of capitalism's self-preservation abilities.

21   Rowthorn (1981) provides a detailed, careful exposition of the assumptions involved.

22   For a discussion of the productive versus unproductive capital debate, see Fine and Harris (1979).

23   It is this special case that allows Glyn and Sutcliffe through appeal to international competition to explain why increased labour costs are not passed on to consumers in the form of increased prices, as suggested by underconsumption theorists. This appeal to international competition is challenged by Cowling (1982), who observes that a part of imports is in fact controlled by domestically based transnationals. In an attempt to fill this gap in the theory, Goldstein (1985) develops a formal model of cyclical profit squeeze, which also provides microeconomic foundations to the theory. It is found that a mid-expansion profit squeeze can be generated as the result of an optimal cyclical pricing policy of an oligopolistic price leader.

24   It is worth reiterating here that, as Shaikh (1977) and Weeks (1979) stress, the value rate of exploitation S/V, need not coincide with the price share of profit to wage income. As Moseley (1987) observes, the latter varies directly with the rate of surplus value (S/V) and inversely with the ratio of unproductive capital to variable capital. Thus, increases in the S/V ratio are quite consistent with stability or reductions in the Π/W ratio, if the unproductive to variable capital ratio is on the increase. Assuming the Π/W ratio varies directly with the Π/Y ratio, the above implies that constant profit shares are also consistent with increasing rates of exploitation. Moseley provides estimates for the 1975–87 US business sector in line with this view.

25   The reason is that a decline in the reserve army of labour (i.e. increased employment) is seen as increasing real wage rates, thus reducing profit shares. Moseley (1985) observes that profit shares were inversely related to the unproductive to productive capital ratio, and suggests that this rise was responsible for the declining profit share. Moseley (1987) also tests his prediction in the 1985 paper that further increases in the unproductive to productive capital ratio will hinder further increases in the profit share even in the face of increasing unemployment, and offers empirical support for this prediction.

26   For a discussion of cyclical underconsumptionist theories and a synthesis of the cyclical versions of the three theories discussed here, see Sherman (1979).

27   The crucial task of modern crisis theory, for O'Connor (1987) 'is to develop a united "field theory" based on the interpenetration of economic, social and political crisis tendencies in ways which

have not been systematically studied within the framework of modern historical materialism' (p. 133). O'Connor goes on to discuss critically the 'class struggle' theory of crisis, legitimation crises (Habermas, 1973) and personality crises.

28 For a more elaborate analysis of such effects, e.g. individualism, dominant ideologies, etc., see O'Connor (1987).

29 The SSA model was originally proposed as an explanation of the 'long waves', the alternation of long periods of growth and stagnation of capitalism. A number of theories have been proposed to explain these long waves: the theory of innovation and entrepreneurship (Schumpeter and Mench), the capital theory (Mandel, Forrester) the labour theory (Freeman) and the raw materials–food stuffs theory (Rostow). An excellent collection is in Freeman (1984). Delbeke (1984) has a critical survey. Boyer (1986) reflects the feelings of many, in observing that a satisfactory explanation of long waves is still to be found. Mandel's attempt is interesting (see his contribution in Freeman, 1984), in that it endogenizes the stagnation phase of long waves (resulting from declining profit rates) but relies on external factors to explain the growth phase. Eclectic syntheses have also been provided (see Freeman, 1984).

30 Other critiques are also addressed by Boyer (1986). Interestingly, in his response to a criticism concerning the absence of 'analytical method' in regulation theory an institutional and macroeconomic foundation of microeconomics is proposed. Within a resulting holistic framework, which determines the general 'rules of the game', an individualistic approach is seen as acceptable, as in Roemer (1981). Neo-institutional and game-theoretic approaches to institutions, as in Williamson (1975) and Schotter (1981) for example, are briefly discussed. The latter is seen as a potential institutional basis for the exegesis of the emergence of regulation regimes.

31 In this sense, all Marxian crisis theories, including the regulation approach, are less well developed than their neo-institutional counterparts (e.g. Coase, 1937; Williamson, 1975, 1981) on this particular front; but not than their macroeconomic mainstream counterparts (e.g. Keynes, 1936), who also take institutions as data.

32 De-industrialization is normally defined in terms of a process of contraction in a number of manufacturing indices, such as employment, output, trade etc. The tendency for de-industrialization of the UK economy has been well documented by a number of researchers; Coates and Hillard (1986) and Martin and Rowthorn

(1986) have extensive surveys.

33 De-industrialization can be due to a wide variety of causes, and indeed a multitude of them have been proposed. Coates and Hillard (1986) have a collection of articles in the area, from three different perspectives: the right, the centre and the left. At risk of oversimplification, it could be said that the right is seen to blame the unions and too much government, the centre the waste of assets, the Victorian legacy, which led to failure to provide industrial leaders, the imperial bureaucracy etc., and the left the international orientation of capital intercapitalist rivalries, the strength of labour, the weakness of labour, heavy armaments expenditures, demand-side constraints arising from reduced international competitiveness, or a number of these factors pur together (Stafford, 1986).

34 Harris (1986), for example, observes that it was the lack of labour militancy that led to non-modernization. Rowthorn (1981) suggests, in a similar vein, that lack of labour militancy led to the ability of an internationally oriented UK capital to pursue its international activities.

35 This is a rather crude scenario. The TNCs–states relationship is a far more complex one; see Pitelis (1990c) for a discussion, and the collection in Radice (1975).

36 This statement appears to lend support to the Coase–Williamson assumption of pre-existing markets. This is misleading. My claim here is not that the market predated the state, for example, but that the emerging capitalist, the merchant, achieved an early form of capitalist division of labour (division of labour for the production of commodities for sale in the makret) through the price mechanism.

37 Seen in this light, capital's interests and power are in part a constraint to socialism, but also in part a constraint to fascist tendencies of the state functionaries (including the military), themselves a result of the increasing state autonomy.

38 The relationship between investment expenditure and the profit-to-wage ratio is evidently one of interest *per se*.

References

Aaronovitch, S. and Smith, R. (with Gardiner, I. and Moore, R.) (1981) *The Political Economy of British Capitalism: a Marxist Analysis*. London: McGraw-Hill.

Agglietta, M. (1979) *A Theory of Capitalist Regulation*. London: New Left Books.

Alchian, A. and Demsetz, H. (1972) Production, information costs, and economic organization. *American Economic Review*, **62**(5), 777–95.

Altvater, E. (1973) Notes on some problems of state intervention. *Kapitalistate*, **1**, 96–116; **2**, 76–83.

Ando, A. and Modigliani, F. (1963) The life cycle hypothesis of savings: aggregate implications and tests. *American Economic Review*, **53**, 55–84.

Aoki, M., Gustafsson, B. and Williamson, O. E. (1990) *The Firm as a Nexus of Treaties*. London: Sage.

Arrow, K. (1962) Economic welfare and the allocation of resources to invention. In R. A. Nelson (ed.), *The Rate and Direction of Economic Activity*. Princeton, NJ: Princeton University Press.

Arrow, K. (1963) *Social Choice and Individual Values*. New Haven, CT: Yale University Press.

Arrow, K. (1970) The organization of economic activity: issues pertinent to the choice of market versus non-market allocation. In R. H. Haveman and J. Margolis (eds), *Public Expenditure and Policy Analysis*. Chicago: Markham.

Arrow, K. and Debreu, G. (1954) Existence of an equilibrium for a competitive economy. *Econometrica*, **22**, 265–90.

Auerbach, P. (1988) *Competition: the Economics of Industrial Change*. Oxford: Basil Blackwell.

Axelrod, R. (1984) *The Evolution of Cooperation*. New York: Basic Books.

Azariadis, C. (1989) Implicit contracts. In J. Eatwell et al. (eds), *The New Palgrave. Allocation Information and Markets*. London: Macmillan.

Bacon, R. and Eltis, W. (1976) *Britain's Economic Problem: Too Few Producers*. London: Macmillan.

Bain, J. S. (1956) *Barriers to New Competition*. Cambridge, MA: Harvard University Press.

Baran, P. and Sweezy, P. (1966) *Monopoly Capital*. Harmondsworth: Pelican.

Barker, C. (1978) A note on the theory of capitalist states. *Capital and Class*, **4**, 118–26.

Barnet, R. J. and Müller, R. (1976) *Global Reach: the Power of the Multinational Corporation*. New York: Touchstone, Simon and Schuster.

Barro, A. (1974) Are government bonds net wealth? *Journal of Political Economy*, **82**, 1095–117.

Bator, F. M. (1958) The anatomy of market failure. *Quarterly Journal of Economics*, **72**, 351–79.

Baumol, W. J. (1959) *Business Behaviour, Value and Growth*. New York: Macmillan.

Baumol, W. (1967) The macroeconomics of unbalanced growth. *American Economic Review*, **57**(3), 415–26.

Baumol, W. (1982) Contestable markets: an uprising in the theory of industry structure. *American Economic Review*, **72**, 1–15.

Baumol, W., Panjar, J. C. and Willig, R. D. (1982) *Contestable Markets and the Theory of Industry Structure*. New York: Harcourt Brace Jovanovich.

Begg, D. K. H. (1982) *The Rational Expectations Revolution in Macroeconomics: Theories and Evidence*. Oxford: Philip Allan.

Benassy, J. P. (1989) Disequilibrium analysis. In J. Eatwell et al. (eds), *The New Palgrave. General Equilibrium*. London: Macmillan.

Berle, A. A. and Means, G. C. (1932) *The Modern Corporation and Private Property*. New York: Harcourt Brace and the World Inc.

Berlin, I. (1969) *Four Essays on Liberty*. Oxford: Oxford University Press.

Blackaby, F. (ed.) (1979) *Deindustrialisation*. London: National Institute of Economic and Social Research and Heinemann.

Blaug, M. (1976) Kuhn versus Lakatos or paradigms versus research programmes in the history of economics. In S. Latsis (ed.), *Method and Appraisal in Economics*. Cambridge: Cambridge University Press.

Bleaney, M. (1976) *Underconsumption Theories: a History and Critical Analysis*. London: Lawrence and Wishart.

Bleaney, M. (1985) *The Rise and Fall of Keynesian Economics*. London: Macmillan.

Bluestone, B. and Harrison, B. (1982) *The Deindustrialization of America*. New York: Basic Books.

Botty, R. and Crotty, J. R. (1975) Class conflict and macro policy. *Review of Radical Political Economics*, **7**(4), 1–19.

Bowles, S. and Gintis, H. (1982) The crisis of liberal democratic capitalism: the case of the United States. *Politics and Society*, **11**, 51–91.

Bowles, S., Gordon, D. M. and Weisskopf, T. E. (1983) *Beyond the Wasteland: a Democratic Alternative to Economic Decline*. New York: Anchor Doubleday.

Bowles, S., Gordon, D. M. and Weisskopf, T. E. (1986) Power and profits: the social structure of accumulation and the profitability of the postwar US economy. *Review of Radical Political Economics*, Spring and Summer, **18**(1, 2), 132–67.

Boyer, R. (1986) *La Theory de la Regulation*. Paris: La Découverte.

Braverman, H. (1974) *Labour and Monopoly Capital: the Organization of Work in the Twentieth Century*. New York: Monthly Review Press.

Brewer, A. (1980) *Marxist Theories of Imperialism*. London: Routledge and Kegan Paul.

Brown, W. B. (1984) Firm like behaviour in markets. The administered channel. *International Journal of Industrial Organisation*, **2**(3), 263–73.

Bruno, M. (1982) World shocks, macroeconomic response and the productivity puzzle. In R. C. O. Matthews (ed.), *Slower Growth in Western World*. London: Heinemann.

Buci-Clucksmann, C. (1978) A propos the meaning and history of the crisis of the state. In N. Poulantzas (ed.), *The Crisis of the State*. Athens: Papazisis (in Greek).

Buckley, P. J. and Casson, M. (1976) *The Future of Multinational Enterprise*. London: Macmillan.

Cable, J. (1989) Organizational form and economic performance. In S. Thompson and M. Wright (eds), *Internal Organization Efficiency and Profit*. Oxford: Philip Allan.

Cantwell, J. (1988) The growing internationalisation of industry: a comparison of the changing structure of company activity in the major industrialised countries. Discussion Paper Series B, Vol. I (1988/89), No. 116, Department of Economics, University of Reading.

Cantwell, J. (1990) Theories of international production. In C. N.

Pitelis and R. Sugden (eds), *The Nature of the Transnational Firm*. London: Routledge.

Catephores, G. (1989) *An Introduction to Marxist Economics*. London: Macmillan Education.

Caves, R. E. (1971) International corporations: the industrial economics of foreign investment. *Economica*, **38**, 1–27.

Caves, R. E. (1982) *Multinational Enterprises and Economic Analysis*. Cambridge: Cambridge University Press.

Chamberlin, E. H. (1933) *The Theory of Monopolistic Competition*. Cambridge, MA: Harvard University Press.

Chandler, A. D. (1962) *Strategy and Structure*. Cambridge, MA: MIT Press.

Chandler, A. D. (1977) *The Visible Hand: the Managerial Revolution in American Business*. Cambridge, MA: Harvard University Press.

Chandler, A. D. (1986) Technological and organisational underpinnings of modern industrial multinational enterprise: the dynamics of competitive advantage. In A. Teichova, M. Levy-Leboyer and H. Nussbaum (eds), *Multinational Enterprise in Historical Perspective*, pp. 30–54. Cambridge: Cambridge University Press.

Clark, J. M. (1940) Towards a concept of workable competition. *American Economic Review*, **30**, 241–56.

Clarke, R. (1985) *Industrial Economics*. Oxford: Basil Blackwell.

Clarke, R. (1987) Conglomerate firms. In R. Clarke and T. McGuinness. *The Economics of the Firm*, pp. 107–31. Oxford: Basil Blackwell.

Clarke, R. and Davies, S. (1982) Market structure and price cost margins. *Economica*, **49**, 277–88.

Clarke, R. and McGuinness, T. (eds) (1987) *The Economics of the Firm*. Oxford: Basil Blackwell.

Clawson, P. (1983) A comment on Van Parijs obituary. *Review of Radical Political Economics*, **18**(2), 107–10.

Clegg, S. (1990) *Modern Organizations*. London: Sage.

Clifton, J. (1977) Competition and the evolution of the capitalist mode of production. *Cambridge Journal of Economics* **1**(2), 137–52.

Clower, R. W. (1965) The Keynesian counterrevolution: a theoretical appraisal. In F. A. Hahn and F. P. R. Brechling (eds), *The Theory of Interest Rates*. London: Macmillan.

Coackley, J. and Harris, L. (1982) Evaluating the role of the financial system. *Socialist Economic Review*, 1982.

Coase, R. H. (1937) The nature of the firm. *Economica*, **4**, 386–405.

Coase, R. H. (1960) The problem of social cost. *Journal of Law and Economics*, **3**(1), 1–44.

Coase, R. H. (1972) Industrial organization: a proposal for research. In V. R. Fuchs (ed.), *Policy Issues and Research Opportunities in*

Industrial Organization. New York: National Bureau of Economic Research.

Coates, D. and Hillard, J. (1986) *The Economic Decline of Britain*. Brighton: Wheatsheaf.

Cohen, R. B., Felton, N., Van Liere, J. and Nkosi, M. (eds) (1979) *The Multinational Corporation: a Radical Approach. Papers by Stephen Herbert Hymer*. Cambridge: Cambridge University Press.

Connolly, W. (1969) *The Challenge to Pluralist Theory*. New York: Atherton Press.

Cooter, R. D. (1989) The Coase theorem. In J. Eatwell et al. (eds), *The New Palgrave. Allocation, Information and Markets*. London: Macmillan.

Cowling, K. (1976) On the theoretical specification of industrial structure performance relationships. *European Economic Review*, **8**, 1–14.

Cowling, K. (1982) *Monopoly Capitalism*. London: Macmillan.

Cowling, K. and Mueller, D. C. (1978) The social costs of monopoly power. *Economic Journal*, **88**, 727–48.

Cowling, K. and Sawyer, M. (1989) Merger and monopoly policy. In *Beyond the Review*. Edinburgh: Industrial Strategy Group.

Cowling, K. and Sugden, R. (1987) *Transnational Monopoly Capitalism*. Brighton: Wheatsheaf.

Cowling, K. and Waterson, M. (1976) Price cost margins and market structure. *Economica*, **43**, 267–74.

Cubbin, S. J. (1988) Market structure and market performance, the empirical research. London Business School, Working Paper Series, no. 40.

Cullis, J. and Jones, P. (1987) *Microeconomics and the Public Economy, a Defense of Leviathan*. Oxford: Basil Blackwell.

Curry, B. and George, K. (1983) Industrial concentration: a survey. *Journal of Industrial Economics*, **31**, 203–55.

Dahl, R. (1956) *A Preface to Democratic Theory*. New York: Atherton Press.

Dahlman, J. (1979) The problem of externality. *Journal of Law and Economics*, **1**, 141–62.

Dasgupta, P. (1986) Positive freedoms, markets and the welfare state. *Oxford Review of Economic Policy*, **2**(2), 25–36.

Dasgupta, P. and Stiglitz, J. E. (1988) Potential competition, actual competition and economic welfare. *European Economic Review*, **32**, 569–77.

Davies, S. (1987) Vertical integration. In R. Clarke and T. McGuinness (eds), *The Economics of the Firm*, pp. 88–106. Oxford: Basil Blackwell.

Davis, L. and North, D. (1971) *Institutional Change and American Economic Growth*. Cambridge: Cambridge University Press.

Delbeke, J. (1984) Recent long waves theories: a critical survey. In C. Freeman (ed.), *Long Waves in the World Economy*. London: Frances Pinter.

Demery, D., Duck, N., Sumner, N., Thomas, R. L. and Thompson, W. N. (1989) *Macroeconomics*. Harlow: Longman.

Demsetz, H. (1973) Industry structure, market rivalry and public policy. *Journal of Law and Economics*, **16**, 1–9.

Devine, J. N. (1986) Empirical studies in Marxist crisis theory: introduction. *Review of Radical Political Economics*, Spring and Summer, **18**(1, 2), 1–12.

Dewey, D. (1959) *Monopoly in Economics and Law*. Chicago: Rand McNally.

Dixit, A. (1980) The role of investment in entry deterrence. *Economic Journal*, **90**, 95–106.

Dixit, A. (1982) Recent developments in oligopoly theory. *American Economic Review*, **72**(2), 12–17.

Dobb, M. (1973) *Theories of Value and Distribution since Adam Smith*. Cambridge: Cambridge University Press.

Domhoff, W. (1986) State and ruling class in corporate America. In R. Edwards et al., (eds) *The Capitalist System*. Englewood Cliffs, NJ: Prentice-Hall.

Donaldson, L. (1990) A rational basis for criticism of organisational economics: a reply to Barney. *Academy of Management Review*, **15**(3), 1–8.

Dow, G. K. (1987) The function of authority in transaction cost economics. *Journal of Economic Behavior and Organization*, **8**, 13–38.

Downs, A. (1957) *An Economic Theory of Democracy*. New York: Harper and Row.

Drucker, P. (1976) *The Pension Funds Revolution: How Pension Funds Socialism Came to America*. New York: Harper and Row.

Dugger, W. (1983) The transaction cost analysis of Oliver E. Williamson: a new synthesis? *Journal of Economic Issues*, **17**, 95–114.

Dumenil, E., Glick, M. and Rangel, J. (1987) Theories of the Great Depression. *Review of Radical Political Economics*, **19**, 16–42.

Dunning, J. (1958) *American Investment in British Manufacturing Industry*. London: Allen and Unwin.

Dunning, J. (1981) *International Production and Multinational Enterprise*. London: Allen and Unwin.

Dunning, J. (1989) *Explaining International Production*. London: Unwin Hyman.

Dunning, J. (1990) The eclectic paradigm in international production: a personal perspective. In C. Pitelis and R. Sugden (eds), *The Nature of the Transnational Firm*. London: Routledge.

Dunning, J. and Rugman, A. (1985) The influence of Hymer's dissertation on theory of foreign direct investment. *American Economic Review Papers and Proceedings*, **75**, 228–39.

Eatwell, J. (1982) Competition. In I. Bradley and M. Howard (eds), *Classical and Marxian Political Economy*. London: Macmillan.

Eatwell, J., Milgate, M. and Neuman, P. (1989a) *The New Palgrave. Allocation, Information and Markets*. London: Macmillan.

Eatwell, J., Milgate, M. and Neuman, P. (1989b) *The New Palgrave. General Equilibrium*. London: Macmillan.

Edwards, R. (1979) *Contested Terrain: the Transformation of the Workplace in the Twentieth Century*. New York: Basic Books.

Edwards, R. C., Reich, M. and Weisskopf, T. E. (eds) (1986) *The Capitalist System*. Englewood Cliffs, NJ: Prentice-Hall.

Eichner, A. S. (1976) *The Megacorp and Oligopoly*. Cambridge: Cambridge University Press.

Eichner, A. S. and Kregel, J. A. (1976) An essay on post-Keynesian theory, a new paradigm in economics. *Journal of Economic Literature*, **13**, 1293–314.

Emmanuel, A. (1972) *Unequal Exchange*. London: New Left Books.

Engels, F. (1968) The origin of the family, private property and the state. In K. Marx and F. Engels, *Selected Works*. London: Lawrence and Wishart.

Fama, E. F. (1980) Agency problems and the theory of the firm. *Journal of Political Economy*, **88**, 288–307.

Feiwell, G. (1974) Reflection on Kalecki's theory of political business cycle. *Kyklos*, **27**, 21–47.

Feldstein, M. (1973) Tax incentives, corporate saving and capital accumulation in the United States. *Journal of Public Economists*, **2**, 159–71.

Feldstein, M. (1974) Social security, induced retirement and aggregate capital accumulation. *Journal of Political Economy*, **82**, 905–26.

Feldstein, M. (1978) Do private pensions increase national saving? *Journal of Public Economics*, **10**, 277–93.

Ferguson, R. P. (1988) *Industrial Economics: Issues and Perspectives*. London: Macmillan Educational.

Fine, B. and Harris, L. (1976) State expenditure in advanced capitalism: a critique. *New Left Review*, **98**, 97–112.

Fine, B. and Harris, L. (1979) *Rereading Capital*. London: Macmillan.

Fine, B. and Murfin, A. (1984a) *Macroeconomics and Monopoly Capitalism*. Brighton: Wheatsheaf.

Fine, B. and Murfin, A. (1984b) The political economy of monopoly and competition. *International Journal of Industrial Organisation*, **2**, 133–46.

Flatow, S. V. and Huinsken F. (1978) In J. Holloway and S. Picciotto (eds), *State and Capital: a Marxist Debate*. London: Edward Arnold.

Fourie, F. C. V. N. (1989) The nature of firms and markets: do transaction approaches help? *South African Journal of Economics*, **157**(2), 142–60.

Francis, A. (1983) Markets and hierarchies: efficiency or domination? In A. Francis et al. (eds), *Power, Efficiency and Institutions*. London: Heinemann.

Francis, A., Turk, J. and Willman, P. (eds) (1983) *Power, Efficiency and Institutions*. London: Heinemann.

Frank, A. G. (1972) *Lumpenbourgeoisie: Lumpendevelopment*. New York: Monthly Review Press.

Freeman, C. (ed.) (1984) *Long Waves in the World Economy*. London: Frances Pinter.

Friedman, M. (1962) *Capitalism and Freedom*. Chicago: University of Chicago Press.

Friedman, M. and Friedman, R. (1980) *Free to Choose*. London: Secker and Warburg.

Friedman, M. and Schwartz, A. J. (1963) *A Monetary History of the United States, 1867–1960*. Princeton, NJ: Princeton University Press.

Fudenberg, D. and Tirole, J. (1986) *Dynamic Models of Oligopoly*. London: Harwood Academic Publishers.

Funke, M. (1986) Influences on the profitability of the manufacturing sector in the UK: an empirical study. *Oxford Bulletin of Economics and Statistics*, **48**(2).

Galbraith, J. K. (1987) *A History of Economics: the Past as the Present*. London: Penguin.

Galbraith, C. S. and Kay, N. (1986) Towards a theory of multinational enterprise. *Journal of Economic Behavior and Organization*, **7**, 3–19.

Gamble, A. and Walton, P. (1976) *Capitalism in Crisis*. London: Macmillan.

Gaskins, D. W. (1971) Dynamic limit pricing. *Journal of Economic Theory*, **3**, 306–22.

Geroski, P. A. (1988) In pursuit of monopoly power: recent quantitative work in industrial economics. Working Paper Series 41, London Business School.

Geroski, P. and Jacquemin, A. (1989) European industrial policy. In A. Jacquemin and A. Sapir (eds), *The European Internal Market, Trade and Competition*. Oxford: Oxford University Press.

Gerstenberger, H. (1985) Theory of the state: special features of the discussion in the FRG. *German Political Studies*, **2**, 69–92.

Gilbert, R. J. (1988) The role of potential competition in industrial organisation. *Journal of Economic Perspectives*, **3**(3), 107–27.

Glyn, A. and Sutcliffe, B. (1972) *British Capitalism, Workers and the Profits Squeeze*. Harmondsworth: Penguin.

Goldstein, P. J. (1985) The cyclical profit squeeze: a Marxian micro-foundation. *Review of Radical Political Economics*, **17**(1/2), 103–28.

Gouph, I. (1975) State expenditure in capitalism. *New Left Review*, **92**.

Gouph, I. (1979) *The Political Economy of the Welfare State*. London: Macmillan Educational.

Graham, E. M. (1978) Transatlantic investment by multinational firms. A rivalistic phenomenon? *Journal of Post Keynesian economics*, **1**(1), 82–9.

Gramsci, A. (1971) *Selections from the Prison Notebooks*. London: Lawrence and Wishart.

Green, C. (1987) Industrial organization paradigms, empirical evidence and the economic case for competition policy. *Canadian Journal of Economics*, **20**, 482–505.

Green, D. G. (1987) *The New Right*. Brighton: Wheatsheaf.

Green, F. (1982) Occupational pension schemes and British capitalism. *Cambridge Journal of Economics*, **6**, 267–83

Habermas, J. (1976) *Legitimization Crisis*. London: Heinemann.

Hadjimathcou, G. (1976) Economic theory and expanding state activity. *Thames Papers in Political Economy*. London: Thames Polytechnic.

Harberger, A. (1954) Monopoly and resource allocation. *American Economic Review Papers and Proceedings*, **44**, 77–87.

Harris, L. (1986) Working class strength: a counter view. In D. Coates and J. Hillard (eds), *The Decline of Modern Britain*. Brighton: Wheatsheaf.

Harrison, J. (1980) State expenditure and capital. *Cambridge Journal of Economics*, **4**, 379–92.

Hayek, F. A. (1976) *The Road to Serfdom*. London: Routledge and Kegan Paul.

Hayek, F. A. (1978) *New Studies in Philosophy, Politics and the History of Ideas*. London: Routledge and Kegan Paul.

Heald, D. (1983) *Public Expenditure: Its Defence and Reform*. Oxford: Martin Robertson.

Henley, A. (1987) Labour's shares and profitability crisis. *Cambridge Journal of Economics*, **11**.

Hennart, J. F. (1982) *A Theory of Multinational Enterprise*. Ann Arbor: University of Michigan Press.

Herman, E. S. (1979) *Corporate Control, Corporate Power*. Cambridge: Cambridge University Press.

Hilferding, R. (1981) *Finance Capital*. London: Routledge and Kegan Paul.

Himmelweit, S. (1974) The continuing saga of the falling rate of profit – a reply to Mario Cogoy. *Conference of the Socialist Economists Bulletin*, **9**, 1–6.

Hirch, I. (1978) The state apparatus and social reproduction: elements of a bourgeois state. In J. Holloway and S. Picciotto (eds), *State and Capital: a Marxist Debate*. London: Edward Arnold.

Hirschman, A. (1970) *Exit, Voice and Loyalty*. Cambridge, MA: Harvard University Press.

Hobbes, T. (1651) *Leviathan*. 1967 edition, London: Collins.

Hobsbawm, E. (1968) *Industry and Empire*. London: Weidenfeld and Nicholson.

Hodgson, G. (1974) The theory of the falling rate of profit. *New Left Review*, **84**,

Hodgson, G. (1988) *Economics and Institutions: a Manifesto for a Modern Institutional Economics*. Oxford: Polity Press.

Hodgson, G. (1989) Institutional economic theory: the old versus the new. *Review of Political Economy*, **1**(3), 249–69.

Holloway, J. and Picciotto, S. (1977) Capital – crisis and the state. *Capital and Class*, **2**, 76–101.

Holloway, J. and Picciotto, S. (1978) *State and Capital: a Marxist Debate*. London: Edward Arnold.

Hood, N. and Young, S. (1979) *The Economics of the Multinational Enterprise*. Harlow: Longman.

Howard, M. C. (1987) *Profits in Economic Theory*. London: Macmillan.

Howard, M. C. and King, J. E. (1985) *The Political Economy of Marx*. Harlow: Longman.

Hymer, S. H. (1970) The efficiency (contradictions) of multinational corporations. *American Economic Review Papers and Proceedings*, **60**, 441–8.

Hymer, S. H. (1976) *The International Operations of National Firms: a Study of Foreign Direct Investment*. Cambridge, MA: MIT Press.

Hymer, S. and Resnick, S. A. (1979) International trade and uneven development. In R. B. Cohen et al. (eds), *The Multinational Corporation: a Radical Approach. Papers by Stephen Herbert Hymer*. Cambridge: Cambridge University Press.

Hymer, S. and Rowthorn, R. (1979) Multinational corporation and international oligopoly. In R. B. Cohen et al. (eds), *The Multinational Corporation: A Radical Approach. Papers by Stephen Herbert Hymer*. Cambridge: Cambridge University Press.

Imai, K. and Itami, H. (1984) Interpenetration of organisation and market: Japan's firm and market in comparison with the US. *Inter-*

national Journal of Industrial Organisation, **2**, 285–310.

Itoh, M. (1975) The formulation of Marx's theory of crisis. *Conference of the Socialist Economists Bulletin*, **10**, 1–19.

Itoh, M. (1988) *The Basic Theory of Capitalism: the Forms and Substance of the Capitalist Economy*. London: Macmillan.

Jenkins, R. (1987) *Transnational Corporations and Uneven Development*. London: Methuen.

Jensen, M. C. and Meckling, W. (1976) Theory of the firm: managerial behaviour, agency costs and ownership structure. *Journal of Financial Economics*, **3**, 304–60.

Jessop, B. (1977) Recent theories of the capitalist state. *Cambridge Journal of Economics*, **1**, 353–73.

Kalecki, M. (1943) Political aspects of full employment. *Political Quarterly*, **14**(4), 322–31.

Kalecki, M. (1971) *Dynamics of the Capitalist Economy*. Cambridge: Cambridge University Press.

Karageorgas, D. (1977) *The Economic Role of the State*. Athens: Papazisis (in Greek).

Kay, N. (1984) *The Emergent Firm: Knowledge, Ignorance and Surprise in Economic Organisation*. London: Macmillan.

Kay, N. (1990) Markets, false hierarchies and the evolution of the modern corporation. *Journal of Economic Behavior and Organisation*,

Keller, R. R. (1975) Monopoly capital and the great depression: testing Baran and Sweezy's hypothesis. *Review of Radical Political Economics*, **7**(4), 65–75.

Kessler, D., Masson, A. and Strauss-Kühn, D. (1981) Social security and saving. *Geneva Papers on Risk and Insurance*, **18**, 3–50.

Keynes, J. M. (1936) *The General Theory of Employment, Interest and Money*. London: Macmillan.

Kilpatrick, A. and Lawson, T. (1980) On the nature of industrial decline in the UK. *Cambridge Journal of Economics*, **4**, 1.

Kindleberger, C. P. (1969) *International Business Abroad*. New Haven, CT: Yale University Press.

Kindleberger, C. P. (1973) *International Economics*, 5th edn. Homewood, IL: Richard D. Urwin.

Kindleberger, C. P. (1984) *Multinational Excursions*. Cambridge, MA: MIT Press.

Kindleberger, C. P. (1986) International public goods without international government. *American Economic Review*, **76**(1), 1–13.

King, M. (1975) The United Kingdom profit crisis: myth or reality. *Economic Journal*, March, 33–54.

Kirzner, Z. (1973) *Competition and Entrepreneurship*. Chicago: University of Chicago Press.

Klein, B. (1983) Contracting costs and residual claims: the separation of ownership and control. *Journal of Law and Economics*, **26**, 367–74.

Knickerbrocker, F. T. (1973) *Oligopolistic Reaction and Multinational Enterprise*. Cambridge, MA: Harvard University Press.

Kotz, D. M. (1982) Monopoly, inflation and economic crisis. *Review of Radical Political Economics*, **14**(4), 1–17.

Lall, S. (1980) *The Multinational Corporation: Nine Essays*. London: Macmillan.

Landes, D. S. (1966) *The Rise of Capitalism*. New York: Macmillan.

Langlois, N. R. (1987) *Economics as a Process, Essays in the New Institutional Economics*. Cambridge: Cambridge University Press.

Latsis, S. (1976) *Method and Appraisal in Economics*. Cambridge: Cambridge University Press.

Leijonhufvud, A. (1968) *On Keynesian Economics and the Economics of Keynes*. Oxford: Oxford University Press.

Lenin, V. I. (1971) *Imperialism: the Highest Stage of Capitalism*. Moscow.

Liebenstein, H. (1966) Allocative efficiency vs X-efficiency. *American Economic Review*, **56**, 392–415.

Lieberman, M. B. (1987) Excess capacity as a barrier to entry: an empirical appraisal. *Journal of Industrial Economics*, **35**(4), 607–27.

Lindbeck, A. (1988) Individual freedom and welfare state policy. *European Economic Review*, **32**, 295–312.

Lipietz, A. (1982) Credit money: a condition permitting inflationary crisis. *Review of Radical Political Economics*, **4**(2).

Lipietz, A. (1986) Behind the crisis: the exhaustion of a regime of accumulation. A 'regulation school' perspective on some French empirical work. *Review of Radical Political Economics*, **18**(1, 2), 13–32.

Lipsey, R. and Lancaster, K. (1956) The general theory of the second best. *Review of Economic Studies*, **24**, 11–32.

Littlechild, S. C. (1981) Misleading calculations of the social costs of monopoly power. *Economic Journal*, **91**, 348–63.

Littlechild, S. C. (1988) Three types of market process. In R. N. Langlois (ed.), *Economics as a Process*. Cambridge: Cambridge University Press.

Lively, C. (1978) Pluralism and consensus. In P. Birnbaum et al. (eds), *Democracy, Consensus and Social Contract*. London: Sage Publications.

Loasby, J. B. (1990) The firm. In J. Gosby (ed.), *Foundations of Economic Thought*. Oxford: Basil Blackwell.

Lucas, R. (1975) An equilibrium model of the business cycle. *Journal of Political Economy*, **83**.

Luxemburg, R. (1963) *The Accumulation of Capital*. London: Routledge and Kegan Paul.

Lyons, B. (1979) Price-costs margins, market structure and international trade. In D. Currie et al. (eds), *Microeconomic Analysis*. London: Croom Helm.

Lyons, B. (1987) Strategic behaviour by firms. In R. Clarke and T. McGuinness (eds), *The Economics of the Firm*. Oxford: Basil Blackwell.

McGuinness, T. (1987) Markets and managerial hierarchies. In R. Clarke and T. McGuinness (eds), *The Economics of the Firm*. Oxford: Basil Blackwell.

Machiavelli, N. (1958) *The Prince*. London: Everyman.

McKenzie, L. W. (1989) General equilibrium. In J. Eatwell et al. (eds), *The New Palgrave. General Equilibrium*. London: Macmillan.

McManus, J. C. (1972) The theory of the multinational firm. In G. Paquet (ed.), *The Multinational Firm and National State*. London: Collier-Macmillan.

McMicheal, P., Petras, J. and Rhodes, R. (1974) Imperialism and the contradictions of development. *New Left Review*, **85**, 83–104.

Maddison, A. (1980) Western economic performance in the 1970s: a perspective and assessment. *Banca Nazionale del Lavoro Quarterly Review*, **33**, 247–90.

Magdoff, H. (1969) *The Age of Imperialism: the Economics of US Foreign Policy*. New York: Modern Reader.

Magee, S. P. (1977) Information and the multinational corporation: appropriability theory of direct investment. In I.N. Bhagwati (ed.), *The New International Economic Order*. Cambridge, MA: MIT Press.

Malcolmson, J. M. (1982) Trade unions and economic efficiency. *Economic Journal Conference Papers Supplement*.

Malcolmson, J. (1984) Efficient labour organisation: incentives, power and the transaction costs approach. In F. Stephen (ed.), *Firm Organizations and Labour*. London: Macmillan.

Manne, H. G. (1965) Mergers and the market for corporate control. *Journal of Political Economy*, **75**, 110–20.

Mandel, E. (1967) The labour theory of value and monopoly capitalism. *International Socialist Review*, July/August, 22–42.

Mandel, E. (1975a) *Late Capitalism*. London: Verso.

Mandel, E. (1975b) International capitalism and supranationality. In H. Radice (ed.), *International Firms and Modern Imperialism*. Harmondsworth: Penguin.

Marginson, P. (1985) The multinational firm and control over the work process. *International Journal of Industrial Organisation*, **3**, 37–56.

Marglin, S. (1974) What do bosses do? The origins and functions of hierarchy in capitalist production. *Review of Radical Political Economics*, **6**, 60–112.

Marglin, S. A. (1983) Knowledge and power. In F. H. Stephen (ed.), *Firms Organisations and Labour: Approaches to the Economics of Work Organisation*. London: Macmillan.

Marglin, S. A. (1984) *Growth Distribution and Prices*. Harvard Economic Studies Vol. 155. Cambridge, MA: Harvard University Press.

Marris, R. (1967) *The Economic Theory of Managerial Capitalism*. London: Macmillan.

Marris, R. and Mueller, D. C. (1980) The corporation, competition and the invisible hand. *Journal of Economic Literature*, **18**, 32–63.

Martin, R. and Rowthorn, B. (1986) *The Geography of Deindustrialisation*. London: Macmillan.

Marx, K. (1954) *Capital*, Vol. I. London: Lawrence and Wishart.

Marx, K. (1959) *Capital*, Vol. III. London: Lawrence and Wishart.

Marx, K. (1973) *Grundrisse*. Harmondsworth: Penguin.

Marx, K. and Engels, F. (1968) The Communist Manifesto. In K. Marx and F. Engels, *Selected Works*. London: Lawrence and Wishart.

Mattick, P. (1969) *Marx and Keynes*. Boston, MA: Porter Sargent.

Means, G. C. (1935) Price inflexibility and requirements of a stabilising monetary policy. *Journal of the American Statistical Association*, **30**.

Milgrom, P. and Roberts, J. (1982) Limit pricing and entry under incomplete information: an equilibrium analysis. *Econometrica*, **50**, 443–60.

Miliband, R. (1969) *The State in Capitalist Society*. London: Quarter Books.

Miller, J. A. (1986) The fiscal crisis of the state reconsidered: two views of the state and accumulation of capital in the post-war economy. *Review of Radical Political Economics*, Spring and Summer, **18**(1, 2), 236–46.

Mills, C. W. (1963) *The Power Elite*. Oxford: Oxford University Press.

Minns, R. (1981a) *Pension Funds and British Capitalism: the Ownership and Control of Shareholding*. London: Macmillan.

Minns, R. (1981b) A comment on 'finance capital and the crisis in Britain'. *Capital and Class*, **14**.

Minsky, H. P. (1978) The financial instability hypothesis: a restatement. *Thames Papers in Political Economy*. London: Thames Polytechnic.

Modigliani, F. (1958) New developments on the oligopoly front. *Journal of Political Economy*, **66**, 215–32.

Moseley, H. (1978) Is there a fiscal crisis of the state? *Monthly Review*, **30**, 34–45.

Moseley, H. (1982) Capital and the state: West German neo-orthodox state theory. *Review of Radical Political Economics*, **14**, 24–32.

Moseley, H. (1985) The rate of surplus value in the post war US economy: a critique of Weisskopf's estimates. *Cambridge Journal of Economics*, March.

Moseley, H. (1987) The profit share and the rate of surplus value in the US economy, 1975–85. *Cambridge Journal of Economics*, **11**.

Mueller, D. C. (1976) Public choice: a survey. *Journal of Economic Literature*, 395–433.

Mueller, D. C. (1989) *Public Choice II. A Revised Edition of Public Choice*. Cambridge: Cambridge University Press.

Munnell, A. (1976) Private pensions and saving: new evidence. *Journal of Political Economy*, **84**, 1013–32.

Murray, R. (1971) The internationalisation of capital and the nation state. In H. Radice (ed.), *International Firms and Modern Imperialism*. Harmondsworth: Penguin.

Niskanen, W. A. (1973) *Bureaucracy: Servant or Master?* London: IEA.

Nordhaus, W. (1975) The political business cycle. *Review of Economic Studies*, **42**, 1969–90.

North, D. C. (1981) *Structure and Change in Economic History*. New York: Norton.

Nozick, R. (1974) *Anarchy, State and Utopia*. Oxford: Basil Blackwell.

Nye, J. S. (1988) The multinational corporation in the 1980s. In C. Kindleberger and P. Audretsch (eds), *The Multinational Corporation in the 1980s*. Cambridge, MA: MIT Press.

O'Connor, J. (1973) *The Fiscal Crisis of the State*. New York: St Martin's Press.

O'Connor, J. (1978) More on the fiscal crisis of the state. *Monthly Review*, **30**, 54–7.

O'Connor, J. (1980) Some reflective criticisms on Mosley's critical reflections on the fiscal crisis of the state. *Review of Radical Political Economics*, **11**, 60–5.

O'Connor, J. (1982) The fiscal crisis of the state revisited: a look at economic crisis and Reagan's budget policy. *Kapitalistate*, **9**, 41–61.

O'Connor, J. (1987) *The Meaning of a Crisis: a Theoretical Introduction*. Oxford: Basil Blackwell.

Offe, C. (1972) Political authority and class structure: an analysis of late capitalist societies. *International Journal of Sociology*, **2**(7),

Olson, M. (1965) *The Logic of Collective Action*. Cambridge, MA: Harvard University Press.

Ouchi, W. (1981) *Theory Z*. Reading, MA: Addison-Wesley.

Palma, G. (1978) Underdevelopment and Marxism: from Marx to the theories of imperialism and dependency. *Thames Papers in Political Economy*. London: Thames Polytechnic.

Palloix, C. (1976) *L'internationalisation du Capital-Elements Critiques*.

Paris: François Maspero.

Paraskevopoulos, D. and Pitelis, C. (1990) Capacity expansion, preemption and strategy signalling. Presented at the Royal Economic Society Conference, Nottingham, April.

Penrose, T. E. (1959) *The Theory of the Growth of the Firm*. Oxford: Basil Blackwell.

Philips, A. (1971) *Technology and Market Structure: a Study of the Aircraft Industry*. Lexington, MA: D. C. Heath.

Picot, A. and Wegner, F. (1988) The employment relation from the transaction cost perspective. In G. Dlugos et al. (eds), *Management under Differing Labour Markets and Employment Systems*. Berlin, New York: Walter de Gruyter.

Pitelis, C. N. (1985a) The tendency towards the socialisation of the ownership of the means of production and the realisation of profits in the post war UK economy. Presented at the Conference of Socialist Economists, Manchester.

Pitelis, C. N. (1985b) The effects of life assurance and pension funds on other savings: the post war UK experience. *Bulletin of Economic Research*, **37**(3), 213–29.

Pitelis, C. N. (1987a) *Corporate Capital: Control Ownership, Saving and Crisis*. Cambridge: Cambridge University Press.

Pitelis, C. N. (1987b) Internalisation and the transnational corporation: a critique. Discussion Papers in Industrial Economics. Nottingham: University of Nottingham.

Pitelis, C. N. (1987c) On the existence of the state. Discussion Papers in Industrial Economics. Nottingham: University of Nottingham.

Pitelis, C. N. (1990a) Stephen Herbert Hymer. In P. Arestis and M. Sawyer (eds), *A Dictionary of Dissenting Economics*. Cheltenham: Edward Elgar.

Pitelis, C. N. (1990b) Review of R. Jenkins' '*Transnational Corporations and Uneven Development*'. *International Review of Applied Economics*.

Pitelis, C. N. (1990c) Neoclassical models of industrial organisation. In B. Dankbaar et al. (eds) *Perspectives in Industrial Organization*. Dordrecht: Kluwer.

Pitelis, C. N. (1991a) The effects of advertising (and) investment on aggregate profits. *Scottish Journal of Political Economy*, **38**(1), 32–40.

Pitelis, C. N. (1991b) The transnational corporation: a synthesis. *Review of Radical Political Economics*, **21**, 4.

Pitelis, C. (1991c) The (transnational) firm and the (nation) state. *Review of Radical Political Economics/Capital and Class*, joint special issue.

Pitelis, C. N. (1991d) Competition theory and competition policy: a strategy for Europe. In *Costs and Benefits of Europe*. London: Pinter, forthcoming.

Pitelis, C. N. and Pitelis, I. (1987) States, corporations and pluralism. Discussion Papers in Industrial Economics. Nottingham: University of Nottingham.

Pitelis, C. and Pitelis, I. (1991) On the possibility of state neutrality. *Review of Political Economy*, **3**(1), 15–24.

Pitelis, C. N. and Sugden, R. (1986) The separation of ownership from control in the theory of the firm: a reappraisal. *International Journal of Industrial Organization*, **4**, 69–86.

Pitelis, C. N. and Sugden, R. (eds) (1990) *The Nature of the Transnational Firm*. London: Routledge.

Pollin, R. (1986) Alternative perspectives on the rise of corporate debt dependency: the US post-war experience. *Review of Radical Political Economics*, Spring and Summer, **18**(1, 2), 205–35.

Poulantzas, N. (1969) *Political Power and Social Class*. London: New Left Books.

Poulantzas, N. (1975) *Classes in Contemporary Capitalism*. London: New Left Books.

Poulantzas, N. (1978) *The Crisis of the State*. Athens: Popazisis (in Greek).

Putterman, L. (1988) The firm as association or commodity: efficiency, rights and ownership. *Economics and Philosophy*, **4**, 243–66.

Putterman, L. (1986) *The Economic Nature of the Firm: a Reader*. Cambridge: Cambridge University Press.

Radice, H. (1975) *International Firms and Modern Imperialism*. Harmondsworth: Penguin.

Rawls, J. (1972) *A Theory of Justice*. Oxford: Clarendon Press.

Reekie, D. W. (1979) *Industry, Prices and Markets*. Oxford: Philip Allan.

Reid, G. (1987) *Theories of Industrial Organization*. Oxford: Basil Blackwell.

Reynolds, P. T. (1987) *Political Economy: a Synthesis of Kaleckian and Post-Keynesian Economics*. Brighton: Wheatsheaf.

Reynolds, P. J. (1989) Kaleckian and post-Keynesian theories of pricing: some extensions and implications. *Thames Papers in Political Economy*. London: Thames Polytechnic.

Ricardo, D. (1817) *The Principles of Political Economy and Taxation*. 1973 edition, London: Dent Dutton.

Ricketts, M. (1987) *The Economics of Business Enterprise: New Approaches to the Firm*. Brighton: Wheatsheaf.

Robinson, J. (1933) *The Economics of Imperfect Competition*. London: Macmillan.

Robinson, J. (1978) The organic composition of capital. *Kyklos*, **31**,

5–20.

Roemer, J. F. (1981) *Analytical Foundations of Marxian Economic Theory*. Cambridge: Cambridge University Press.

Rowthorn, B. (1971) Imperialism in the seventies – unity or rivalry? *New Left Review*, **69**.

Rowthorn, B. (1976) Late capitalism. *New Left Review*.

Rowthorn B. (1977) Inflation and crisis. *Marxism Today*, November.

Rowthorn, B. (1980) *Capitalism, Conflict and Inflation*. London: Lawrence and Wishart.

Rowthorn, B. (1981) Demand real wages and economic growth. *Thames Papers in Political Economy*. London: Thames Polytechnic.

Rugman, A. M. (1986) New theories of the multinational enterprise: an assessment of internalisation theory. *Bulletin of Economic Research*, **38**, 101–18.

Rugman, A. M. (1987) Multinationals and trade in services: a transaction costs approach. *Weltwirtschaftliches Archiv*, **123–4**, 651–67.

Rutherford, M. (1989) What is wrong with the new institutional economics (and what is still wrong with the old)? *Review of Political Economy*, **1**(3), 299–318.

Sawyer, M. C. (1982a) *Macroeconomics in Question*. Brighton: Wheatsheaf.

Sawyer, M. (1982b) On the specification of structure performance relationships. *European Economic Review*, **18**, 295–306.

Sawyer, M. (1985) *The Economics of Michal Kalecki*. London: Macmillan.

Sawyer, M. (1986) *The Economics of Industries and Firms*, 2nd edn. London: Croom Helm.

Scherer, F. M. (1980) *Industrial Market Structure and Economic Performance*, 2nd edn. Chicago: Rand McNally.

Schott, K. (1982) Marxist economic theories of the state. Discussion Papers in Economics, no. 26. London: Department of Political Economy, University College.

Schotter, A. (1981) *The Economic Theory of Social Institutions*. Cambridge: Cambridge University Press.

Schmalensee, R. (1988) Industrial economics: an overview. *Economic Journal*, **98**, 643–81.

Schreiber-Servan, J. (1968) *The American Challenge*. London: Hamish Hamilton.

Schumpeter, J. (1942) *Capitalism, Socialism and Democracy* (5th edn, 1987). London: Unwin Hyman.

Scott, J. (1985) *Corporations, Classes and Capitalism*. London: Hutchinson.

Scott, J. (1986) *Capitalist Property and Financial Power*. Brighton:

Wheatsheaf.

Sen, A. (1988) Freedom of choice. *European Economic Review*, **32**, 269–94.

Shaikh, A. (1977) Crisis theory in economic thought. *Thames Papers in Political Economy*. London: Thames Polytechnic.

Shaikh, A. (1978) An introduction to the history of crisis theories. In *US Capitalism in Crisis*. New York: Union of Radical Political Economics.

Shackle, G. L. S. (1969) *Decision Order and Time in Human Affairs*. Cambridge: Cambridge University Press.

Shepherd, W. G. (1984) Contestability vs competition. *American Economic Review*, **74**(4), 572–9.

Shepherd, W. G. (1985) *The Economics of Industrial Organization*. Englewood Cliffs, NJ: Prentice-Hall.

Sherman, H. (1977) Monopoly power and stagflation. *Journal of Economic Issues*, **11**(2), 269–84.

Sherman, H. (1979) A Marxist theory of the business cycle. *Review of Radical Political Economics*, **11**(1), 1–23.

Smith, A. (1776) *The Wealth of Nations*. 1977 edition. London: Dent.

Spence, A. M. (1977) Entry, capacity, investment and oligopolistic pricing. *Bell Journal of Economics*, **8**(2), 534–44.

Spence, M. (1983) Contestable markets and the theory of industry structure: a review article. *Journal of Economic Literature*, **21**, 981–90.

Stafford, B. (1986) Theories of decline. In D. Coates and J. Hillard (eds), *The Economic Decline of Modern Britain*. Brighton: Wheatsheaf.

Stafford, B. (1989) De-industrialisation in advanced economies (a review of R. E. Rowthorn and J. R. Wells, 'De-industrialisation and Foreign Trade'). *Cambridge Journal of Economics*, **13**, 541–54.

Steedman, I. (1977) *Marx After Sraffa*. London: New Left Books.

Steindl, J. (1952) *Maturity and Stagnation of American Capitalism*. Oxford: Oxford University Press.

Steindl, J. (1979) Stagnation theory and stagnation policy. *Cambridge Journal of Economics*, **3**, 1–14.

Stigler, G. (1963) A theory of oligopoly. *Journal of Political Economy*, **72**, 44–61.

Stigler, G. (1988) The effect of government on economic efficiency. *Business Economics*, **23**, 7–13.

Stiglitz, J. E. (1986) *Economics of the Public Sector*. New York: Norton.

Stone, K. (1974) The origins of job structures in the steel industry. *Review of Radical Political Economics*, **6**, 61–97.

Stopford, J. M. and Dunning, J. (1983) *Multinational Company Performance and Global Trends*. London: Macmillan.

Sugden, R. (1983a) Why transnational corporations? University of Warwick Economics Research Paper no. 222.

Sugden, R. (1983b) The degree of monopoly, international trade and transnational corporations. *International Journal of Industrial Organisation*, 1, 165–87.

Sugden, R. (1990) The importance of distributional considerations. In C. Pitelis and R. Sugden (eds), *The Nature of the Transnational Firm*. London: Routledge.

Swann, D. (1988) *The Economics of the Common Market*, 6th edn. Harmondsworth: Penguin.

Sweezy, P. M. (1942) *The Theory of Capitalist Development*. Oxford: Basil Blackwell.

Sweezy, P. M. (1978) Corporations – the state and imperialism. *Monthly Review*, November, 1–10.

Sweezy, P. (1981) Marxist value theory and crisis. In I. Steedman (ed.), *The Value Controversy*. London: Verso.

Sylos-Labini, P. (1962) *Oligopoly and Technical Progress*. Cambridge, MA: Harvard University Press.

Teece, D. J. (1980) Economics of scope and the scope of the enterprise. *Journal of Economic Behavior and Organization*, 1, 223–47.

Teece, D. J. (1981) The multinational enterprise: market failure and market power considerations. *Sloan Management Review*, 22, 3–17.

Teece, D. J. (1986) Transaction cost economics and the multinational enterprise: an assessment. *Journal of Economic Behavior and Organization*, 7, 21–45.

Tirole, J. (1988) *The Theory of Industrial Organization*. Cambridge, MA: MIT Press.

Tobin, J. (1980) *Asset Accumulation and Economic Activity*. Oxford: Basil Blackwell.

Trajtenberg, R. and Vigorito, R. (1983) Economics and politics of the transnational phase of capitalism: introductory concepts. *Research in Political Economy*, 6, 157–223.

Tugendhat, T. (1971) *The Multinationals*. Harmondsworth: Penguin.

Tullock, G. (1976) *The Vote Motive*. London: IEA.

Utton, M. A. (1982) *The Political Economy of Big Business*. Oxford: Martin Robertson.

Van Parijs, P. (1980) The falling rate of profit theory of crisis: a rational reconstruction by way of obituary. *Review of Radical Political Economics*, 12(1), 1–16.

Van Parijs, P. (1983) Why Marxist economics need microfoundations: postscript to an obituary. *Review of Radical Political Economics*,

References   245

15(2), 111–24.

Vernon, R. (1971) *Sovereignty at Bay*. Harlow: Longman.

Vernon, R. (1981) Sovereignty at bay ten years after. *International Organisation*, **35**(3), 517–29.

Vincent, A. (1987) *Theories of the State*. Oxford: Basil Blackwell.

Wagner, A. (1958) Three extracts in public finance. In R. A. Musgrave and A. T. Peacock (eds), *Classics in the Theory of Public Finance*. London: Macmillan.

Wallerstein, I. (1980) The future of the world economy. In T. K. Hopkins and I. Wallerstein (eds), *Processes of the World System*. London: Sage.

Warren, B. (1971) The internationalisation of capital and the nation state: a comment. *New Left Review*, **68**,

Warren, B. (1973) Imperialism and capitalist development. *New Left Review*, **81**, 3–44.

Waterson, M. (1984) *Economic Theory of the Industry*. Cambridge: Cambridge University Press.

Weeks, J. (1979) The process of accumulation and the profit squeeze hypothesis. *Science and Society*, 259–80.

Weeks, J. (1981) *Capital and Exploitation*. Princeton, NJ: Princeton University Press.

Weisskopf, T. E. (1979) Marxian crisis theory and the rate of profit in the post-war US economy. *Cambridge Journal of Economics*, **3**(4), 341–78.

Weisskopf, T. E., Bowles, S. and Gordon, D. (1983) Hearts and minds: a social model of US productivity growth. *Brooking Papers in Economic Activity*, **2**, 381–441.

Weisskopf, T. E., (1985) Sources of profitability declines in advanced capitalist economies. Mimeo, University of Michigan.

Williamson, O. E. (1963) Managerial discretion and business behaviour. *American Economic Review*, **53**, 1032–57.

Williamson, O. E. (1967) Hierarchical control and optimum firm size. *Journal of Political Economy*, **75**(2), 123–38.

Williamson, O. E. (1968) Economics as an antitrust defence: the welfare trade-offs. *American Economic Review*, **58**, 18–36.

Williamson, O. E. (1975) *Markets and Hierarchies*. New York: Free Press.

Williamson, O. E. (1981) The modern corporation: origins, evolution, attributes. *Journal of Economic Literature*, **19**(4), 1537–68.

Williamson, O. E. (1985) *The Economic Institutions of Capitalism*. New York: Free Press.

Williamson, O. E. (1986) *Economic Organisation: Firms, Markets and Policy Control*. Brighton: Wheatsheaf.

Williamson, O. E. (1987) *Antitrust Economics*. Oxford: Basil Blackwell.

Williamson, O. E. (1990) The firm as a nexus of treaties: an introduction. In M. Aoki, B. Gustafsson and O. E. Williamson (eds), *The Firm as a Nexus of Treaties*. London: Sage.

Williamson, O. E. and Ouchi, W. G. (1983) The markets and hierarchies programme of research, origins, implications, prospects. In A. Francis et al. (eds), *Power Efficiency and Institutions*. London: Heinemann.

Wolf, C. (1979) A theory of non-market behaviour: framework for implementation analysis. *Journal of Law and Economics*, **22**(1), 107–40.

Wright, E. D. (1977) Alternative perspectives in Marxist theory of accumulation and crisis. In J. Schwartz (ed.), *The Subtle Anatomy of Capitalism*. Santa Monica, CA: Goodyear.

Yaffe, D. (1973) The Marxist theory of crisis, capital, and the state. *Economy and Society*, **2**, 186–232.

Yamin, M. and Nixson, F. I. (1984) Transnational corporations and the control of restrictive practices: theoretical issues and empirical evidence. Mimeo, Trent Polytechnic.

Index